REWIRING THE SOUL

Finding the Possible Self

How Your Connection to Yourself
Can Make All the Difference

Gabriella Kortsch, Ph.D.

Advance Praise for *Rewiring the Soul*

"*Rewiring the Soul* is a revelation of insight into the foundations of human suffering and transcendence. It not only lays out the essential steps for inner freedom and joy but it also illuminates the way to true human potential: the stunning and dynamic "Possible Self." Written with clarity, compassion and wisdom, this chronicle is not one of mere speculation, but arises from the depths of hard won personal experience. Gabriella Kortsch is a spiritual master for our time."

- PAUL RADEMACHER, Executive Director, The Monroe Institute; author of *A Spiritual Hitchhiker's Guide to the Universe*

"Gabriella Kortsch uses her talent and experience to write the instruction manual on rewiring the soul. An in-depth guide on life, love, spiritual evolution and our integration within the universe."

- MICHAEL HABERNIG & APRIL HANNAH; Producers of *The Path: The Afterlife* and The Path 11 Documentaries

"This meticulously researched and crafted book is clearly the masterwork of a profoundly gifted healer of the soul, one who thinks deeply, feels deeply, and cares deeply about the well-being of the world and its humankind. Reading it will change your life; beginning to live actively any of its ideas, principles, and suggestions will *transform* your life. And bring you safely and joyfully home to your true self, your soul. I found it dazzling, challenging, and wondrously useful."

- PEGGY RUBIN, Director, Center for Sacred Theatre, Ashland, Oregon; author of *To Be and How To Be, Transforming Your Life Through Sacred Theatre*

"*Rewiring the Soul* is one the best introductions to the spiritual life I've ever read. Not esoteric but real-world and practical. Read it and Soul is no longer just a dogma, nor hypothesis, it is made real and as much a part of your being as your toes. We usually shut off our inner voice, yet by recognizing this aspect of ourselves we begin to discover our essential nature, our intuitive truth, and that becomes our loving guide. The author illustrates the limitations of living only as the mind's Ego, and demonstrates in practical terms how we can transcend this by awakening a conscious viewpoint, following the path of our intuition and feelings, no longer separated from our body and the reality around us, and integrating at last our Soul's inner guidance and wellspring of love. The implications are profound."

- PETER SHEPHERD; Founder, Trans4mind: http://www.trans4mind.com; author of *Daring To Be Yourself*

"I thought I could pick just one chapter to write a review, but I couldn't …. I was glued to the chair as I read *Rewiring the Soul* … a literary, in-depth masterpiece to the human psyche, behavior and ultimate transformation. Exquisitely written, beautifully executed."

- ALI R. RODRIGUEZ, Business Coach, co-author of *Mastering the Art of Success* with Jack Canfield and Mark Victor Hansen (Aug. 2011)

"A glance at the contents of *Rewiring the Soul* will tell you much about the values promoted: *awareness, freedom, peace and love.* I fully agree with the author that it is all about re-connecting with our authentic 'loving self': it is only then that we can deeply transform our life while also inspiring a transformation in the lives of others! Through this powerful book, Gabriella Kortsch *honestly* shares her love of serving the inner potential and the spiritual growth of human beings with passion, joy and commitment."

- ELISABETTA FRANZOSO; International Speaker, Coach, author of *Stella's Mum Gets Her Groove Back: A True Story*

Also by Gabriella Kortsch, Ph.D.

Rewiring the Soul
E-book for Kindle
Available globally July 10, 2011

Relationships:
Collected Articles

Relationships:
Priceless Tools for Self-Understanding, Growth, and Inner
Freedom (4-Hour Audio CD Workshop)

Fatherless Women and Motherless Men:
The Influence of Absent Parents on Adult Relationships
(4-Hour Audio CD Workshop)

Awakenings
Collected Poems 1968 – 1998
Available December 2011

Background Music:
Living Life To A Different Beat
Available 2012

The Master Call a Butterfly
A Novel
Available 2012

REWIRING THE SOUL

Finding the Possible Self

How Your Connection to Yourself
Can Make All the Difference

Gabriella Kortsch, Ph.D.

Pages 180-82: Excerpts from *Selfishness and Self Love* by Erich Fromm. Copyright © 1939 by Erich Fromm. Reprinted by permission of Dr. Rainer Funk, Literary Executor of Erich Fromm.

Cover Design by Ignacio Martel

Library of Congress Cataloging-in-Publication Data

Kortsch, Gabriella
Rewiring the soul: finding the possible self – how your connection to yourself can make all the difference / Gabriella Kortsch.
Includes biographical references and index.

ISBN-13: 978 – 1460988473
ISBN-10: 1460988477

1. Spiritual life 2. Self-realization 3. Happiness 3. Love 4. Wisdom 5. Mental Healing I. Kortsch, Gabriella II. Title

2011907705

To Ignacio and Erik and Fernando

Without you,
none of it would have been possible

And to Ina and Michael Kortsch

With you it began

CONTENTS

Introduction

A Marriage of Psyche and Soul

*Have patience with all things, but chiefly have patience
with yourself. Do not lose courage in considering your own
imperfections, but instantly set about remedying
them – every day begin the task anew.*
St. Francis de Sales

*T*his book was written for you.* It's no accident that you
picked it up or decided to buy it. There are no
coincidences and the fact that you are holding this
book in your hands simply means that you have now come to a
place where you can begin, should you so decide, to apply its
information. Lest you are put off by its deceptive simplicity, each
chapter contains, in distilled and synthesized form, teachings that
will allow you to live a life filled with well-being and satisfaction that
in most cases can only be understood after many years of
searching. Often the ways by which I came to understand the
information were very roundabout, and included not only experiential
living where I took my share of emotional risks, but also a pursuit of
knowledge and understanding that took me down many intellectual,

academic and professional paths. Much joy but also heartache, pain and many tears went into what I've extracted into the essence of this book and I offer it from the bottom of my heart and with much love so that you, the reader, may apply it in order to make your own life rich, abundant, and filled with love, joy, peace, harmony, and inner freedom.

An extensive appendix and bibliography have been included with information about books, authors, films, videos, documentaries, and websites that have played an important role in bringing me to the place of understanding at which I currently find myself, for the reader interested in pursuing some of those paths, or even just for the curious reader who wants to compare my wandering with his or her own path. Whether what meant much to me coincides with your own steps towards growth and understanding is less important than the recognition that ultimately *all roads truly do lead to Rome*.

Each chapter can stand on its own, and can be read as such, and therefore it is not necessary to go through the book in chronological order. Many of the most important and key pieces of information that this book contains are repeated over and over again in different words and in different chapters, with slightly different twists, because they are all so interlocked. What affects one part of this soul we are trying to rewire in order to get closer to the place we *intended ourselves to arrive at when we decided to come here*, affects all others, and the method by which you achieve this merging with one part of your soul, automatically affects the other parts. This is the way I know how to do it. It is – by no means – the only way.

Throughout this book the path to resolving everyday life and its problems while simultaneously converging with the inner quest for connection with the soul is signposted. This process allows life to take on a revolutionary new meaning: resolving personal and interpersonal issues while keeping the inner connection to the soul in mind leads to *unprecedented growth* that is simply not possible if psycho-emotional matters and spiritual concerns are not combined. *Only to* grow psychologically and emotionally is not enough. And *only* to grow spiritually is not enough either. All three dimensions need to be developed in order to realize your full potential. If you are willing to assume total responsibility for the self and to start what is an on-going journey, you will quickly begin to glimpse the first fruits of the ultimate goal: inner well-being, freedom, peace, harmony and joy. This book sets out the pathway to self-mastery and self-discovery and walking that pathway will be the most exciting adventure of your life.

The main principle upon which this entire book is based, is the fact that if we do not begin our way back to our soul – our true core - within ourselves, from the smallest corners of our selves outward, in order to bring ourselves and our lives to a place where we are truly well, where we can love ourselves and then emanate this love outward, then we will not reach the goal, because we will have started the process from the outside in. If you want to play pro basketball, you are going to have to start by learning how to dribble. If you want to be a cordon bleu chef, you'll have to learn how to separate eggs. And if you want to find your way back to your soul, you'll have to learn how to love yourself, recognizing that this "self" that you are learning how to love is your inner essence, your soul, and learning how to love yourself is the foundation of each of the chapters of this book. Learning how to love yourself is a fundamentally underlying principle of all that follows, and conversely, all that follows is built on loving yourself. By loving yourself, all the other issues this book addresses can be resolved, and by loving yourself, your life will flow in ways you can now only imagine.

If you resonate with the talk about soul in this book, then you are in the right place. But if you find the talk about soul distressing, off-putting, ludicrous, or nonsensical, you may nevertheless find that there is so much other, more psycho-emotional material you resonate with, that the talk about soul is peripheral enough that you can allow it to rest on the sidelines and nurture yourself with all the other parts. It is understandable if you feel uncomfortable with talk about the soul because our society does not often take us there – although for those who are observant, it is happening more and more in books, films, documentaries – even in some weekly television series. But if you are uneasy with such talk, and yet feel pulled to continue with the book, think of the soul as your intuition, as the voice that sometimes speaks to you, and that you – probably – most often do not listen to. Think of it as a part of yourself that you have not yet discovered: that you have not yet become acquainted with.

Thomas Moore, author of *Care of the Soul*, writes:

> *The ordinary acts we practice every day at home are of more importance to the soul than their simplicity might suggest.*

Our soul often gets forsaken very early on. That doesn't mean we can't find our way back to it. We live our lives with stumbling blocks or pain and wonder why it appears that it doesn't get all that much easier as time goes on. Or we see that we keep repeating patterns but we either still don't learn, or else we think that we keep falling into the hands of people who make things difficult for us (*I always fall in love with people who are not loyal to me; my friends always use me; my co-workers always steal my ideas; my children / spouse / parents / friends always disappoint me*). Either way, things just aren't working out for us on the outside and definitely not on the inside. So to begin to find our way back to our forsaken soul it helps to have a road map. Think of it as a treasure map where each clue leads you on to the next clue that will eventually lead you to the treasure you are so fervently seeking, and that treasure is you, your love for yourself, and ultimately, your soul, your inner connection – and rewiring - to your true self.

For that to work, you actually have to set out on the path towards the first clue. It's not enough that you read about clues and how to best find clues, if you don't, in fact, take that first step in the direction of the place where the first clue presumably will be found. And that's precisely where many people – even highly educated people – fail. Because they don't take that first step.

I call it the *'I've been to all the seminars, and I've read all the books, I even had a therapist, but still nothing in my life has changed'* syndrome. People attend workshops and seminars, lectures and classes, they read all the right books, and they get very excited, even momentarily highly motivated, and yet, after the workshop is over, or after they finish reading the last page of the book, they feel a let-down, an anti-climax. And so, in order to feel the excitement again, to get the next fix, to find the next adrenaline rush, they book another weekend seminar, or buy yet another book, and the cycle is repeated over and over again. *But nothing changes.*

So what's different about this book? Won't it just happen again, as it has so many times before?

It might. You see, there really is no magic formula. No silver bullet. It's a bit like the alcoholic who wants to stop drinking, but thinks it can be achieved by putting the addiction into the hands of a third party – like a clinic – where it will all be taken care of, or the cigarette smoker who wants to stop smoking, and also thinks it can be achieved by putting the addiction into the hands of a third party – like a hypnotherapist – who will take care of it. The clinic or the hypnotherapist can really only then be effective, when the addict *has also taken the internal decision to put an end to whatever the addiction is.* And in that case, the clinic or the hypnotherapist is in many instances, in fact, superfluous and no longer truly necessary.

In other words, for this book to work for you, you must take the internal decision to start walking your talk. It's not enough to read. It's not enough to attend the workshops, seminars, classes, and lectures; *you have to start actually doing something.*

I was already in my early 30's when I realized this. I had gone down the road I've described above, and was sitting on my terrace in southern Spain reading yet another book that had raised my energetic frequency as I purchased it and began to read it, but as I got about halfway through, a sinking feeling started settling in my solar plexus. *I knew I had not yet done anything the author suggested, nor had I taken any kind of steps suggested by a lot of the other information I had been receiving.* Yes, numerous insights had come my way, and I now understood so much more than before, but understanding and actually applying this understanding to one's life is not the same thing.

Among thousands of men perhaps one strives for perfection; and among thousands who strive perhaps one knows me in truth.
The Bhagavad Gita

So the sinking feeling at the pit of my stomach had to do with the fact that I knew I was going to have to find another book or seminar to fill the void, once I finished this one. I needed the adrenaline rush of yet more information that could change my life so that I could get through my days. It had to do with the fact that I knew *nothing had really changed*, despite all the reading, despite this latest great book, despite all the workshops, retreats, and seminars.

And so I knew I had to do something different. And the something different had nothing to do with reading another book or attending another weekend retreat. *It had to do with me.* And suddenly I knew – as I sat there on my sun-drenched terrace with the open book in my lap – *I simply had to decide to choose one of the dozens of techniques, philosophies, or methods I had been reading and learning about, and begin following its precepts.* I knew as surely as I knew my name that it really did not matter which method I chose, as *long as I began*. The rest would fall into place.

And so I began.

Do you know why it's not so terribly important that you choose *the right method* or *the right technique that you learned somewhere*? It's because once you start moving, the very motion you create, the momentum of your own growth and self-discovery, will then move you to the next step and the one after that and the one after that.

As you walk though the dark forest that myth so compellingly tells us about, that Joseph Campbell (and T.S. Eliot) wrote about – the journey of the hero - the dark forest where you think you are lost and where you are, in fact, rather fearful, *helpers* appear along your path. Myth, folk lore, and fairy tales across all cultures and epochs speak of a seeker or a hero of some kind finding a magical potion that allows him to see in the dark, or he may be given a gift of a cloak that makes him invisible, he may find a staff that points him in the right direction if he doesn't know which path to take. In real life our unexpected helpers come clothed in slightly different guises, but they come to our aid in similarly eye-opening ways. However, *none* of this will happen if you don't begin.

And so the most important thing is that you begin. That you have the courage *and the faith in yourself and your purpose* to begin. Amazing things may then begin to happen and events and people will appear in your life to guide you to the next step. Finding a measure of inner joy, peace, and freedom – *rewiring your soul* – is a journey. It's a process, and it can only happen if you take the first step. And you aren't taking any steps by reading more books or going to more seminars *if you don't begin the inner process*. Just make the decision to choose one of the ones you already have under your belt, and go with it. At least for that all-important first step. Somewhere down the road you may wish to correct course, get a better map, stop for a break at that lovely camping ground (or that five star hotel at the luxury resort on the Balinese beach), and so you may stop to read another book, or get more ideas at another workshop. But basically your main purpose is to continue the process, to follow the path you have embarked upon, *in order to reach that goal*.

Inner joy, peace, harmony, and freedom are not small matters. We may be plagued all our lives without them, desperately knowing that something is not right, but not really knowing what to do about it, how to fix it, how to feel better. And so we go down the substitute byways to make ourselves feel better, that many know so well: professional prestige, social standing, academic recognition, financial power, external appearance, youth, creating "busy-ness", whether in work or social life, alcohol, sex, shopping, gambling, drugs, and so on. And for a time they help us. Or we delude ourselves into believing that they make life livable. Until we realize that it really is a delusion. For some people the delusion may even be the belief that by attending many spiritual workshops and learning many new spiritual techniques, they are, in fact, changing – and although in some ways they do change because of their new understanding - on the immediate day-to-day level nothing really shifts, *because they still often don't apply it to their daily lives* and therefore *their own house* continues to be in disorder.

So we can talk about how *spiritual* we are, with all our trips to India, Egypt, Africa, or Peru, all our weekend yoga retreats, all the energy work we have done on ourselves, how often we meditate, but when it comes right down to it, we do it while we are there in those countries, or in those retreats or workshops, or lying on that massage table, or sitting in a lotus position, but the carry-over into our daily lives has simply not taken place. Our relationships are in tatters, our self-esteem is buried deep within subterranean soil, we fear spending time alone with ourselves, our thoughts and emotions have the power to throw us into continual turmoil and hence *we continue to be blind to ourselves ... our soul is still an unknown quantity.* And so we come back to our search for inner joy, peace, harmony, and freedom. Perhaps after long frustration and unhappiness. Or after heartfelt emptiness. Or heartache and pain, inner chaos and desperation. Whatever the reason, when we re-orient ourselves to the search for inner freedom, often without even knowing that that is what we are searching for, what we know with certainty is that the way we have lived up to that moment has not been what we really wanted for our lives.

Why Rewire the Soul?

At first glance it may sound strange to talk about rewiring the soul, when it appears that what has run amuck is our psyche, our emotions, our reactions, our grip on life. Nevertheless, what lies beyond all of this *is* the soul, and it *is* the soul that requires rewiring, if all the rest of it is to function well. Think of it as the engine of a car; if all other elements of the car are in pristine order, but the engine is not, there will be problems. You may still get the car to start, but it will not work well. No matter how much you tinker with the brakes, and the oil filters, or replace the tires, if the engine is not in top shape, the car will simply not render what it is capable of.

Or put into different terms: imagine that the problem with the smooth running of your car is that you are not even aware of the fact that you have an engine, or what to do with it, or what its purpose is. Under such circumstances, clearly all of your maneuverings with the car would not be very fruitful, would frustrate you, and could possibly even harm the car. But once you became aware of the engine and its potential purpose, you could begin to learn about it, and thus comprehend how all the rest of the car's pieces interact in order to create a magnificent machine.

The soul only then has a chance to shine through, to support us in our daily endeavors, and to bring us to those places inside of us where we are truly capable of great joy, when it has been rewired, or − to put it into other terminology − when it has been *saved*. Lest you think I'm going religious on you, fear not, it is not that kind of *saving* that this refers to, although the use of the expression *saving the soul* by organized religion, has always seemed very appropriate to me to describe a magnificent process that nevertheless would perhaps come about more easily without the benefit of official intermediaries between the individual and the divine.

What does rewiring, or saving the soul mean? Simply put: letting your soul be all that it may, all that you meant it to be *before you came*, all that you are, that you have been − as that *eternal* being that you are. But when you are born, so much of that is forgotten and forsaken – perhaps quite intentionally, as many authors and thinkers indicate. Our parents, our families, our home environment, our neighborhoods, our churches, our schools, our partners, the very way we are taught to think, all of this can create great forsaking, and can, indeed, cause near total disconnection and can destroy. How else do you explain the rampant heartache, addiction, pain and misery that populate our world?

In my private practice I have had innumerable occasions to look at the broken and forsaken souls of so many people, so many wonderful and magnificent people, who simply no longer know where to go or what to do in order to gain – regain - an iota of that wonderful state of inner being filled with joy, harmony, peace, and freedom that is our heritage. And of course the worst part is that most people don't know this; don't know that we *deserve* this state of being, that we have a right to it, that it is our challenge, goal and mission, and that it does form part of our soul heritage.

Why are we here? I mean, why are we here on earth? To be born, grow up, dedicate ourselves to a family and a profession, and then die? Is it to accumulate honor, wealth, prestige, to keep our bodies looking good, preferably young, and to live well? To honor our parents, help our neighbors, and generally be good people and try to live a good life? All of that is, of course, part of it. By going through such a process in our life, we have a chance to rewire our soul, or to reconnect with that which we forget when we are born. In the end, everything serves our purpose, even in the forgetting, or perhaps *precisely* because of the forgetting.

But the truth clearly is that while most of us go through some or all of the above-described situations, very few of us reconnect with our souls, or even know what reconnecting means. A part of our being is finite: the body, all that we do and accomplish in the external sense here during our lifetime, but another part of our being is infinite and eternal.

It follows that if something is infinite and eternal it existed before the finite part – the body – did. And if it existed before, there was consciousness before. Perhaps not the kind of consciousness you are currently aware of, as you live your life, but consciousness nevertheless, that allowed you to make choices about *what you were going to learn next* - and where you were going to be next. So exactly about what were these choices being made?

Most authors that venture down this arguably slippery path agree that the choices have to do with the challenges and goals you "sign up" for, in other words, the challenges and goals *you decide* you will have in a lifetime. Evidently *these* goals do not generally coincide with the goals you seek to fulfill as you go through your life, *simply because you aren't aware of them* until you do rewire your soul, or reconnect with your soul. And the challenges you sign up for coincide even less with those external goals you seek, because they are generally growth-inducing challenges of a type that you would not voluntarily – in the guise of your finite self - choose: they involve frustration, pain, fear, deprivation, and a host of other difficult feelings and situations, *although they often serve - but not always - to wake us up*. That is why we choose them.

What do they wake us up to? Ultimately they wake us up to our eternal self, although initially we may merely wake up to the fact that we have poor boundaries, a bad temper, or that we don't love ourselves. They wake us up to the fact that we are *more* than the body we inhabit, the profession we have, the state of our bank account, our position in society, and so on. And so these challenges serve a great purpose, if we can only see them from that point of view. Here is where some of our idiomatic expressions such as *every cloud has a silver lining* can be better understood.

In this process of waking up to our eternal self, learning to love the self, and rewiring the soul, we have our work cut out for us in order to unlearn so much and take new ways of being and understanding on board. These new ways have to do with how we deal with our relationships, our emotions, our thoughts, negativity and pain. Learning new ways comes from a greater psychological understanding of ourselves, but totally interconnected with the knowledge that this psychological and emotional understanding forms the underpinnings of the goal we ultimately seek on a totally different – both higher and deeper - level.

When we wake up to our eternal self, when we become *conscious* in the way described in so many mystic paths, because we wake up out of our deep sleep, we can begin to rewire the soul. We can begin to walk our way towards that part of ourselves that, by connecting with it, will cause our life to change to a degree that if we were without that connection (as we are when we are still asleep) we can only barely discern.　.

The changes will not necessarily be totally visible to others, but you will feel them in your innermost self, because you will be – once they (the changes) commence – a person who begins to be filled with light, with joy, with peace and inner freedom, with a degree of contentment and satisfaction that you would rarely, if ever, have experienced before.

Waking up to your eternal self – showing you, the reader, one of the many roads that works - is the purpose of this book. I said earlier that when you decide to follow a system, a path, a method – whatever – that you have read about or learned about in a workshop, I meant exactly that. This book is no more than one of many ways to get to the same place.

When I was 15 I read what I then considered to be an amazing novel by John Fowles called *The Magus*. It was also made into a movie with a very young Candice Bergen, Anthony Quinn, and Michael Caine. In that book I read an excerpt of *Little Giddings* by T.S. Eliot for the first time. It was:

> *We shall not cease from exploration*
> *And the end of all our exploring*
> *Will be to arrive where we started*
> *And know the place for the first time*

Reading that, I knew exactly what it meant to me. I knew instantly that I would spend much of my life searching, seeking, and exploring, and that I would return to where I already was at that time (at age 15) and recognize – or know – the place for the first time. I already knew so many things, but there seemed to be a haze spread over it all, a bit like a distant memory that is simply not clear enough to grasp and relate to, but all the same, you know that you have it there within yourself. Sometimes I felt like the student who wants to answer a question the teacher has posed, is certain that he knows the answer, but hesitates, just in case he is wrong, and yet, when another answers, he mentally kicks himself, because *he did know; his answer was indeed the correct one*, but he was not yet confident enough to bring it out openly. From that point forward my life went through enormous changes, some joyful, and some so painful and frightening that at times I simply had no idea how to continue, but I did know I had to continue. In so doing, I learned much.

Another reason I refer to rewiring the soul is because the more you look *inside* in your quest to conquer worldly, or psycho-emotional problems and difficulties, and not simply from the perspective of improving your life and your relationships, the more you realize that in so doing you are walking closer to your true self, to all that you can be in all senses of the word, and the more you find yourself living your life – *no matter what the outer circumstance* – in a way that gives you inner peace and freedom, the more you *rewire your soul*, the more you move closer to your soul.

Final Notes

I'd like to reiterate that as you go through this book you may find that information in some chapters repeats parts of what you already read in a previous chapter. That is deliberately so for a number of reasons. First, everything is holistically inter-connected. Therefore frequently what is helpful in one sector of your life, can also have a beneficial influence on other sectors and in very similar ways. Secondly, marketing techniques have proven that in order for an individual to decide to purchase a given product, he needs to hear about that product, or see it represented in photographs or commercials, at least nine times. Our psyche is similar, and the more some of this information that is being presented here is repeated, the more you will begin to assimilate it and make successful use of it.

Some of the chapters have some very specific guidelines to implement the suggestions of that chapter. The guidelines, more than exercises of any kind, may be questions that you can ask yourself when you find yourself in a place where life is not as good as you would like it to be. The answer to that inner dialogue will then lead you to view what is currently happening with slightly different eyes, potentially to undertake some type of – generally brief and simple - activity in order to shift your inner energetic frequency.

But please understand that while the suggestions I make are not difficult to begin to implement, they are, nevertheless, suggestions that in one fashion or another will need to begin to form the fabric of your life. Not exactly my suggestions, but what they imply. They imply that you are *making a priority of yourself and your inner state of well-being* in order to move closer to your soul. That isn't something that you will accomplish merely by reading this book, or even merely by beginning to internalize some of its suggestions. You will only accomplish this monumental task – the most important task of your life – if you are willing to make it a vital part of each and every day of your life. Not because you will be spending hours each day doing something complicated and time-consuming, but because as the ideas discussed here permeate your consciousness and your life, you will either live in a new way by living with your love for yourself (or your desire to *know* what it is to love yourself) and your soul in mind each and every day, or you will not. And if you do, the promise is that the rewards will be immeasurable.

Before enlightenment; chop wood, carry water.
After enlightenment; chop wood, carry water.
Zen Proverb

SECTION ONE

SETTING THE STAGE FOR AWARENESS

Chapter One

Thoughts:
Portal to Awareness

We are what we think. All that we are arises with our thoughts.
With our thoughts, we make the world.
Buddha

The concept that our thoughts make us as we are is one that many people all across the globe are now familiar with, thanks in part to popular books and movies, and thanks as well to more and more conversations about these topics even at some very sophisticated dinner tables. Neuroscientific studies as well are pointing us in the direction of this concept from the position of work carried out in the field of mindfulness, which is another way of dealing with thoughts, of choosing which ones to have, or not to have, with a very specific goal in mind, even if the goal is totally inner-oriented, such as inner peace. Only a few years ago to say something like *thoughts become things* would have caused consternation, or ridicule, and yet now many consider that using our thoughts to make us as we are, or that our thoughts create our reality, forms part of their *Weltanschauung* and is in fact something they think they already believe they are familiar with. For some this means repeating affirmations, for others it means repeating a favorite mantra, for yet others, it means immediately replacing any negative thought with a positive thought, and still others believe that by distracting themselves with all manner of positive actions, they will essentially hold the thoughts that are not conducive to a good life at bay.

With all due respect, I beg to differ. All of the above contains much truth, and while there is no doubt that following some of those precepts puts you on a better path towards an integration of thought, feeling and action, an essential ingredient nevertheless, is missing.

But let me backtrack for a moment. What is it about our thoughts that causes our life to be one thing or another? What do our thoughts contain that is so powerful, that they literally make our lives go down a specific path?

> *Thoughts become things. Be careful what you think*
> Michael Dooley

There are scientific explanations that emanate from neuroscience, cellular biology and molecular biology, and the field of epigenetics (a section within biology that studies changes to the DNA that come about due to aspects that are not genetic), to name only a few. There are energetic explanations that emanate from disciplines as diverse as Chinese acupuncture and Western energy psychology (EFT, or emotional freedom techniques is arguably the best known of these energy meridian techniques). And there are more esoteric or mystical explanations that take us into the arena of spirituality, life as lived by the sacred yogis, the initiatic mystery schools and traditions that have been revived by some magnificent teachers over the past decades, as well as many others. Illuminating works have been written about these subjects and in this book I will not be repeating them, although you can find some of them (mainly the ones that were important for my own development and understanding) referenced in the Bibliography.

The aim of this book is not so much to repeat what other thinkers have said and written, but to find a synergy between that and the concept of rewiring the soul by focusing on inner well-being generated by loving the self that is the thread that ties each of the chapters of this book together.

By examining the lack of awareness of our thoughts and beginning to understand how we can change this, we will automatically be taking one of the most fundamental steps towards reconnecting with, or rewiring the soul. Awareness of our thoughts, awareness of the constant mind chatter that so many authors over the centuries and even millennia have written about, is an underlying principle in this process, without which nothing will change in the direction this book is focusing on. Without awareness of our thoughts we would find it difficult to get anywhere at all in this quest to come closer to the soul. Although thought *appears* to speak of a more rational world and the soul belongs to that more ephemeral or evanescent realm of the spirit that so frequently eludes us, nevertheless, as stated, it is with awareness of our thoughts that we need to begin our journey toward our soul. Encapsulated within our thoughts we have the best chance of *catching the ego*, as you will read about in a later chapter, and by catching the ego, we will have progressed enormously in the quest for inner peace.

So let's return to our main topic: *doing something with our thoughts so that our lives improve.* Not only can our lives improve, but we can bring about changes in all manner of ways that have to do with our inner well-being, and precisely because of that, this also touches on loving the self and that all-important rewiring of our soul that I keep touting.

First Things First

You know that you have thousands of thoughts every day. Most of them come into your mind in ways you can't even explain. You're taking out the garbage and suddenly you're thinking about how you didn't quite make the impression you would have liked to at the executive meeting at work. Or you've just made love, and it truly was great, but the next thing you know you're thinking about the play you want to write – and you've wanted to write it for decades – but you just know that it'll never happen. Or you're having lunch with your brother, discussing something about your childhood friends, and suddenly it crosses your mind that although he is a success, you most certainly are not, and you simply can't imagine that you will ever get there. And in the middle of it all you remember that you need to pick up milk and eggs at the store. You get the idea.

Thoughts arise unbidden out of the morass of your mind and begin to plague you. It is speculated that we have anywhere between 5,000 and 70,000 thoughts per day. Seemingly you have no control over them. They flit about willy-nilly and just as suddenly as they appear, they leave you stranded, and another stray thought (or a dozen) makes its way into your mind. If you ever decide to examine this, take the thread of your thoughts back as far as you can at any given moment, and you will see how much of it resembles random channel surfing with a remote.

Occasionally pleasurable thoughts or positive thoughts find their way into your head as well, but they tend to appear just as haphazardly, and generally, a good deal less frequently. One very simple reason for this is that we have acquired a lifelong habit of thinking one way as opposed to another. This is not about any specific thoughts. This is about an inner tendency that we pay little attention to - an inner tendency that we could call our self-talk, or that we could call the way we - blindly - manage our thoughts. *We just let them come as they will and tend to believe we can do nothing about it.* And so it is that the proportion of our positive or pleasurable thoughts is much lower than the more negative and less agreeable thoughts that far out-number the good ones. We don't seem to realize that this is in fact something that lies in our hands ... something we can definitively do something about, so that these proportions change. We can be in charge of how much of our thinking and feeling time is spent in one or the other arena. But much more importantly, we can also choose *what* we think. Not just whether the general tenor of our thoughts is slanted to the positive as opposed to the negative, but *exactly what we think about all day long.*

Many of my clients tell me when I first propose this concept, that they simply cannot help thinking this way or that way. That is how they are, they inform me. Some are highly intelligent, sophisticated and cosmopolitan individuals from numerous different countries around the globe, including a few whose names are internationally recognized, and yet most adhere to this token, blind belief the majority of us have been socialized into - in mass herd mentality style - that we cannot do anything about our thoughts. *Nothing could be further from the truth.*

These thoughts that come about in such an unbidden fashion, originate in our subconscious mind: we have become habituated to them in such a way that they come about automatically. When something is automatic, there is not much about it that is conscious. When you drive your car home every evening after work, unless something unexpected happens on the road, you are generally so *not* conscious of the actual way home, that when you reach home, you realize that you didn't even see that enormous financial center the city is planning on tearing down, or the park two blocks from your house with the flowering shrubs at the south end, or the ivy-covered home with the three little boys on tricycles you always pass on your daily jog at the corner of SW 54th Terrace and Boheme Drive, and so on. You didn't see any of it because you were driving your car in automatic mode.

That's ok when you are driving the car and when you know your reflexes will kick in to bring you back to conscious mode in the case of danger. But it's not ok when we're talking about your *automatic* thoughts, or your *automatic* reactions because of those thoughts, or your *automatic* feelings because of those thoughts. If most of everything you think, feel and do is *automatic*, then how much of what you are thinking, feeling, doing, and how you react to events can truly be conscious and aware? And it follows that if we have to ask that, we then have to ask *how much of your life is conscious and aware.*

Perhaps you've approached your supervisor for a raise. Perhaps you even had some positive self-talk as you prepared yourself for that meeting with him. But you soon realize during the course of the conversation that the raise won't happen any time soon. Oh, it was couched in kind language, but it won't happen. Now your automatic mode takes over. Under their own steam your thoughts run into areas such as: *this is the way it always is; I can never advance; other people have so much more luck than I do*, etc. As you have those thoughts, you begin to feel worse, by rapidly descending degrees of negative inner emotions. And because you are in automatic mode, it will not only take you longer to recuperate, but it will also strengthen the already strong neural pathways that you have been building since you were very young that essentially feed a self-image that is more negative than positive. We all had so many negative messages when we were young, at home, at school, in church: don't ride your bike so fast, you'll fall; don't hold your pencil that way, it's wrong; don't think about sex, it's bad.

Furthermore, the way you are feeling will also fuel your blind reactions to other events that day. Perhaps your teenage son comes in telling you he dented the car. You might jump at him verbally for his carelessness – or maybe you will simply go several levels deeper still in your inner emotional state – just like that – with no conscious choice about it on your part. After all, it's been one hell of a bad day.

In order to change these neural pathways, in order to create new and different ones, it will be necessary to become aware of what you are doing. Some authors contend that this – changing core beliefs - is only possible with very sophisticated techniques that you can only learn at very sophisticated seminars and workshops for very sophisticated amounts of money. My contention – and that of some very respected leaders in the fields of psychiatry, neuroscience and biology – is that you can become aware – and hence change deeply rooted beliefs and habits - by yourself. Or in a group. Or with a partner or a friend, but it does not require sophisticated techniques nor outrageous sums of money.

Becoming aware of what you are doing can begin in many different ways. Obviously you need to become aware of your thoughts, just as you need to become aware of your feelings and your reactions. This process of becoming aware will allow you to begin to change those heretofore subconscious thoughts.

Paying attention to your feelings is a very important part of it. Your emotions give you so much information about your thoughts.

And your emotions, as you begin walking down this path of increased awareness, are infinitely easier to observe than each and every one of your thoughts. However, when you do begin to observe your emotions, using them, as it were, as a sort of energy barometer for the inner state of your well-being, then you can begin to query what you have just been thinking about (that brought you to that inner state) in order that you may truly become conscious of those thoughts so that you will be able to change them consciously - *but not by merely masking them with somewhat more positive thoughts.* When you change your thoughts consciously, you are doing so with choice. You are doing so by realizing that the other thoughts – the ones that led you to feel the way you are currently feeling - are not taking you to a place you really want to be visiting because they're bringing you to a place where you are angry, or sad, or annoyed, or impatient, or worried, or jealous, and so on. And so, by recognizing the thoughts that led you to that feeling place, you can look at them dispassionately, ask yourself if you want to remain in that particular place, and if not, *choose* to move elsewhere with your conscious thoughts.

There is a very important aspect to this process and that is realizing that you are not – and I repeat – *not* pretending that the way you were feeling a moment ago is not valid. You're not going to cover it up with a blanket or roll the rug over it, so to speak, in order to then pretend all is well, or *pretend* that you are feeling better. What you are doing is recognizing that you have these feelings, that they are not serving you at this moment, furthermore that they came from a set of thoughts that came unbidden, and that therefore you are now going to choose to focus on another set of thoughts *of your own conscious choice.* Additionally, you are not pretending that whatever the problem may be that is connected to those thoughts, i.e., not having received a raise at work, has been resolved. All you are doing is deciding to focus elsewhere – just for now – to shift how you feel.

Shifting the inner state can make a huge difference to future results on both the inner and outer level. Recognize the colossal difference between thinking thoughts that come unbidden and carry you emotionally wherever they will, or thinking thoughts that are consciously chosen by you in order to enhance your inner emotional state, or to help bring about a given, desired inner emotional state. It's like being in prison, and being served whatever is on the menu, like it or not, or being able to not only choose the restaurant at which you reserve a table, but to also be able to choose any number of succulent dishes from a varied menu.

Imagine you are shown a photograph of something that does not please you, perhaps a violent scene, or a video of the destruction of the rain forest. Close by you, there is a glorious painting, and just by shifting your eyes from one of the scenes I just described, you can feast them on the striking painting. Perhaps it's a copy of an Impressionist work, perhaps it's something much more modern. The point is, as you shift your eyes to the more pleasing scene, you are also shifting your inner energetic frequency. By doing so are you denying the veracity of violence in the world as depicted in one of the scenes you did not like? Or are you denying the ever-growing destruction of the rain forest? You are not. Or are you perhaps trying to forget about the existence of violence or rain forest destruction? You are not. What you are doing is deliberately moving yourself to an inner place where you are able to access a higher, more positive energy, in order to – should that be part of your agenda – be able to do something about the problem of violence or rain forest destruction from that better place and from within your particular parameters. And if it's not your agenda, you have achieved something very important for yourself at that particular moment in your life – you have created an inner state that consists of a much higher frequency simply by choosing where you focus your attention. And you can do exactly the same with thoughts of inner pain, anxiety, anger, and turmoil. Think: do you consciously choose a healthy salad over junk food? Do you consciously choose to exercise instead of being a couch potato? *This is exactly the same.* Begin to consciously choose healthy thoughts by following the process I am describing, over those other thoughts that harm you.

As a single footstep will not make a path on the earth, so a single thought will not make a pathway in the mind. To make a deep physical path, we walk again and again. To make a deep mental path, we must think over and over the kind of thoughts we wish to dominate our lives.
Henry David Thoreau

Recently friends and I were hiking in the Sierra Blanca, a range of mountains close to my home and a member of the group made the comment that she did not like to go up a certain trail because it entailed passing a garbage-strewn area which "upset her". I suggested that it was a question of choice and focus. Does she need to look at the garbage deliberately? Are there not many breath-taking sights (I live in a coastal area in southern Spain on the Mediterranean with impressive views down to the coastline directly below, as well as to the straits of Gibraltar and Africa) that she can *choose* to focus on, as opposed to focusing on the garbage. Finally, even if her eyes focus on the garbage for a moment – before she makes the choice to focus elsewhere – is it not feasible for her to recognize that allowing the sight of irresponsibly strewn garbage in nature to affect her negatively, on an inner energetic level, *is also a choice about which she has a choice*?

Translating this to the arena of one's personal emotional life, if the emotion you have become aware of is the pain of abandonment, because just prior to becoming aware of it, you were listening to a sad love song on the radio that reminded you of the fact that you are still suffering because your partner left you, or your father abandoned the family when you were four, then by deliberately choosing to shift to another "scene", whether that is inside your head, or outside, by gazing at something in the environment that is pleasing to the eye, or concentrating for a few moments on an inner scene that creates pleasure in you – perhaps you enjoy the thought of traveling around the world in a sailboat, and whether you will ever do so, or not, is immaterial – you will be able to shift your inner energy, and from that place of higher energetic frequency, you will be able to view or think about the "problem" in another way.

Not only that – and this aspect may be even more crucial to the process - you will have lessened the strength of the neural pathway associated with that memory because you will have consciously pulled back from it and will have replaced it with that other series of thoughts. Or you may perhaps even find that you are no longer in a place where you need to think about the problem … at least not right now.

Continuing to think about something – whatever it is – that takes you to or leaves you in a bad place, strengthens those neural connections and will make it more and more "normal" or habitual for your thoughts to go there frequently, and once there, to insist on staying there, mulling over the situation, wallowing in it, so to speak. But by refusing to continually go there, or by – as illustrated above – choosing to focus on something else once you become aware that your thoughts have taken you there again – will work to lessen those neural connections that decrease the quality of your life, while simultaneously working to grow new ones that enhance your life. Not only that, fomenting your well-being in this way, brings you closer to rewiring your soul … because it is your soul's desire and challenge to be in a place of joy.

So what you've accomplished now, in a relatively simple way, is to have changed your thoughts and to have changed how you feel inside, by taking stock of your feelings, *by becoming aware of your feelings*, and by recognizing that you can do something to shift them. Shifting what you focus on, and shifting what you think about as you focus on the new thing, changes your inner well-being, changes your inner state of energy, and hence changes how you feel. And guess what? You did it. Not some pill, not alcohol, not a session with a therapist, not some retail therapy, not sex, not food - just you and your conscious focus. *This is the beginning of a totally different way of living your life!*

But bear something very important in mind. What you have just accomplished may only last a few moments. That inner state of well-being is not now *ipso facto* a permanent fixture in your life. You will need to continue renewing your connection to it over and over again until it begins to become more automatic. And that means that the process described above will have to be repeated frequently over the course of your day – every day – until the new neural pathway is stronger. This reminds us of Zig Ziglar's famous quotation:

> *People complain about motivation not lasting. Neither*
> *does bathing. That's why we recommend you do it every day.*

So what that means is that your inner state of well-being via your decision to exercise conscious awareness over your thoughts is in your hands only as long as you actually continue to do this. If you stop doing it, it will obviously no longer work. If it works once or twice and you stop doing it because you now expect it to be there forever, it will obviously no longer work. This – like so much else in life – requires intention, attention, awareness and practice.

You Can Choose to Be in Charge of Your Thoughts

Let's understand a fundamental factor. You can't cheat your thoughts, or better said, you can't cheat yourself with your thoughts. If you are thinking you are a loser, or if you are thinking you will never be able to achieve whatever it is that lies closest to your heart, just by pretending you are not thinking that, and covering it up with other thoughts, such as affirmations, or a positive thought about something, will not get you far because underneath it all you will still have the other thoughts. Those other thoughts can be dealt with in a multitude of ways, and there are many methods out there for you to explore. But the one I recommend, and the one I use is awareness and mindfulness. Paying *attention* by remaining aware and having the *intention* to continue doing so every day is one of the ways how it is done.

If you will work on the state of your inner sense of well-being, as you spend more and more time in that place of well-being, by the conscious choice of your thoughts, by having made the decision to take charge of the mind chatter, you will gradually see that the perception you have of yourself also begins to change. One major reason for this is because you are consistently showing yourself how valuable you consider yourself to be and how much you love yourself, by continually and deliberately bringing yourself to this inner state of well-being. And while there are simple exercises you can do to support the move in this direction, understand that the better you feel, i.e., the more you are in charge of your thoughts, and hence how you are feeling because of the nature of those thoughts, the more difficult it becomes for you to entertain thoughts about your lack of value or worth or capability.

Some Simple Steps to Take:

1.   Place some post-it notes throughout different areas of your home (refrigerator, bathroom mirror, computer screen, etc.) and office (inside a drawer that you open frequently, and on your computer screen there as well, etc.) with the following words written on them: *How am I feeling right now?* And: *What am I thinking now?* Note: if you feel awkward having these words visible for others to see, choose any phrase you wish, or a quotation such as: *What we think, we become* (from the Buddha) or: *A man is what he thinks about all day long* (from Emerson), or any other quote that means something to you, but remember, that every time you see the post-its with whatever you have chosen to write on them, what you are really meant to do, is to become aware of what you are feeling and/or thinking at that very moment. This (or any other kind of reminder you care to use) is a very important first step, and only as you begin to implement it, will you become aware of how truly central it is to all that follows.

2.   Now you are going to be aware of how you are feeling or the thoughts that you are thinking at least several times a day because the post-its have caused you to stand back a moment to reflect on that.

3.   So now you can ask yourself if you wish to continue feeling that way or wish to continue thinking those thoughts that are creating those feelings in you. Typically, you will answer no to that question. *You do not wish to continue feeling that way or continue having those thoughts.*

4.   Tell yourself you have a choice about the thoughts and a choice about the feelings (for more information on the feelings, please go to the chapter on emotions).

5. If you have a choice about the thoughts, ask yourself what other thoughts you might like to have just now, in order to focus on them, as opposed to the ones that are currently running about amok in your mind.

6. Perhaps you had been thinking about how to pay the bills at the end of the month. Or perhaps you had been thinking about the fact that your firm has been downsizing people in your department and that you might be next. Or perhaps you had been thinking about how awful you looked in those clothes and that you don't seem to be able to lose the weight, or that you thought you had seen your wife flirt with the neighbor yesterday, or that the garage needs a good cleaning and you simply don't know how to find the time. Your thoughts may have been plaguing you about your husband's health diagnosis: he has become diabetic and that entails a number of changes in your lives. Perhaps you were worrying about a quarrel you had with your best friend, or steeped in remorse about not having been more helpful with your ailing mother before she died. Does any of it sound familiar?

7. So you look at those thoughts – if any of them have to do with a real problem that you might be able to solve, decide then and there that you will take a set time period every day from now on – perhaps 15, 30 or 60 minutes, or even several hours) to work on solving that problem, to brainstorm, research the internet, confer with an expert, and in general, to do everything you can think of to proactively resolve it, *but only for that amount of time each day*. So when the time is up, you move on to think about something else. This means, that if you think about the problem during the rest of your day, in that fashion so familiar to most of us, that starts with an inner nagging, a dull feeling at the pit of the gut, and that continues with ominous thoughts of doom, well then as soon as you become aware of the fact that it's not your "problem-solving" time, you begin to focus on something else (unless you had a brilliant idea about it, in which case just jot it down for the next day's "problem-solving" period).

8. But let's imagine the thoughts were not about some problem, that they were simply negative ones, drag-you-down-into-the-mud thoughts. Again, as soon as you become aware of the fact that you are once again there, ask the question *"Do I want to be here in my thoughts?"*, and since

we assume that your answer is going to be no (if it's "yes", you may wish to consider that you are wasting your time reading this book), then with the conscious awareness that you are currently focusing on something that you do not wish in your life, or that you do not care to continue focusing on, you deliberately and consciously decide to focus on something else. But remember, it's NOT by pretending the problem or the negative feeling does not exist, it's by *choosing* – just for now – to focus elsewhere in order to shift your inner state.

9.   What else? There are many options. Here are several ideas:

    a.   Have a "prepared" scenario ready to think about, one that gives you pleasure, perhaps the thought of backpacking on Marco Polo's Silk Road gives you pleasure, so think of that for a few moments – all we're hoping to do is to cut your focus from the negative thoughts to something of another type of energy. Your scenario might be taking a cruise down the Nile like Poirot and his companions in the Agatha Christie novel, your scenario might be imagining that you are a cordon bleu chef in a Michelin star-rated restaurant in Paris, it might be thinking about your new car, or the instrument you are learning how to play. It might be thinking about the wild profusion of blooms in your grandmother's garden when you were a child, perhaps it's about your ideal life partner, the business you want to build, or anything at all, as long as it serves to help you focus on something that creates a sense of well-being or pleasure in you.

    b.   Perhaps you prefer – and this is my recommendation - rather than focusing on some scenario, to focus on something here and now, something in front of you, something you can see, feel, hear, smell, or even taste. You may see an evergreen from your window, or hear a child's contagious laughter, or smell jasmine, or feel the sun, or wind, or rain on your cheeks. You may hear the rough caw of a seagull as it swoops overhead, or the soft soughing of the wind through the trees. As you deliberately and consciously choose to focus on that, you are not only pulling yourself away from the negative thoughts, but you are also bringing yourself into the present moment, which, as you will see in the chapter on gratitude and the now, is one of the absolutely best and most effective and proven ways to remove yourself from pain and negativity.

10. OK. So far so good. You have managed to become aware of a negative train of thoughts and you have consciously chosen to focus on something that brings you to an inner place of well-being. *What now?*

11. Now you continue doing that. Again. And again. And again. And yet again. In other words, you go on with whatever you need to be doing at that moment (work, wash the dishes, drive your children home from school, let down the hem of your son's trousers, practice conjugating French verbs, finish playing the tennis match, negotiate a trade treaty, continue your research into finding a cure for cancer, play your role in the daily matinee on Broadway), and each and every time you catch yourself in the negative thought place again, you repeat what we did above. You do it over and over and over again, until one day you will realize that negative thoughts hardly ever find space in your mind anymore. It's not that they no longer appear, but that you immediately undertake to focus elsewhere, and therefore give them precious little time to bring you into that difficult place. You will have become so aware of yourself and your thoughts, and you will have become so connected to your inner self, that you hardly need to refocus any more: you will have rewired your soul.

Changing yourself helps to change the world. Trying to change the world before changing yourself is a useless exercise.

Chapter Two

Emotions: Keeping Your Energy High

Man is lost and is wandering in a jungle where real values
have no meaning. Real values can have meaning to man
only when he steps on to the spiritual path, a path
where negative emotions have no use.
Sai Baba

The fact that emotions affect our well-being is as obvious as the fact that the sun rises every morning, and you certainly did not need to buy a book to hear this ... at least, until you begin to look at it from the point of view that you can do something about your emotions. In the chapter about thoughts we already began to have a look at the effect of emotions on our state of well-being. We *also* have choices about what we feel, as counter-intuitive as that may sound to you just now.

In the same way that people will generally say that they can't do anything about their thoughts, they will also say that they can't do anything about their emotions. They will tell you that they are easy to anger, very impatient, highly sensitive, and so on, and have implicit belief in this being something about which they cannot do anything. This is the way they are. Perhaps it's due to genetics: *my mother was exactly the same*, perhaps it's due to *my character*, but whatever it is due to – or so they believe – it is out of their hands. *That's just the way I am*, they say. And by so saying (and believing), *of course* it is out of their hands, and they truly can't do anything about it!

Whether you believe you can do it, or you can't, you're right.
Henry Ford.

But that is only because that is how they think. And that is how they believe. It is *not so* because it truly is out of their hands. In other words, they *can* change their emotions!

Before continuing, I'd like to comment briefly on a subject well-covered in the past years by a growing number of excellent books, but both in order to put it on the table for those readers who have not run across this idea before, as well as to refresh the memory of those who have, it's important to say a few words about the fallacy of genetic determinism.

When something is genetically determined, it means that your genes determine that you will get cancer, or multiple sclerosis. Or that you will have congenital heart disease. Or that you will be an A-type personality, just like your father. Or that you will be overly sensitive, just like your mother, or explosively angry, etc.

And because it is genetically determined, it means that you are not able to change any of it. It was believed when the human genome project began to approach completion that scientists would be able to determine exactly which genes were responsible for each of our known diseases, character traits, and so on, but it was quickly realized that this was not the case. Scientists were stymied for many reasons, not the least of which was that the number of genes in any given human being was not an exponential multiple of those in the common slug, but a very similar amount (insultingly, some felt) as those found in the slug.

Around the time that many geneticists were being stymied, some cellular biologists were coming to realize that what the entire science of biology had been built upon: genetic determinism, heritability, and so on, was in fact, not quite what it was made out to be. The study of epigenetics, "a second genetic code that controls the activity and programming of an organism's DNA, reveals how behavior and gene activity are controlled" *by the way in which someone perceives the environment*. So the former idea of genetic programming or determinism has been usurped by the *new biology*, as it is called, that states that "our perceptions of the environment, including our consciousness, actively control our genes. Through epigenetic mechanisms, applied consciousness can be used to shape our biology and make us "masters" of our own lives."

As you can imagine, this is big. It's essentially as big a paradigm shift as it was when Copernicus stated that the sun did not revolve around the earth. And in similar fashion, just as there were detractors then, so there are detractors now (mainly proponents of a Newtonian or mechanistic worldview). But there are more and more scientists – in diverse disciplines – that attest to this new biology.

And it follows, if we take this new biology on board, that we now know we can become, as stated above, total masters of our own lives. If you wish to read more detailed material about this subject, please see the Appendix.

And that takes us right back to the topic of this chapter: emotions. There you are, in pain from a rejection. Or there you are, filled with fear about going on stage in a few moments, to give a speech. Or there you are, so angry that you can barely think straight, because you have just seen that your business partner has embezzled money from the joint account. Examples abound.

Let's not forget that the little emotions are the great captains of our lives and we obey them without realizing it.
Vincent Van Gogh

If we now determine that we are going to make use of the research, we know that if we consciously decide to change our perceptions about a given event, we can change how it will affect us, not only emotionally and psychologically, *but also on a cellular level* (and that is where the fallacy of genetic determinism comes into play). By consciously deciding to change our perception of it, we come closer to the state I am referring to as *rewiring the soul*. The reason for this is very simple: it is an individual's given right to feel good, to be in a state of joy, to experience, what Chris Griscom refers to when she states that *ecstasy is a new frequency* (this is in fact the title of one of her books). The closer a person is able to come to this state by his or her own conscious volition, the closer he/she connects to the vibratory state from which he came prior to arriving here. And that is a soul state. *Which is precisely what joy and happiness are all about!*

The basic premise of this book is that rewiring that soul is necessary in order to live a life of inner freedom and peace *here on earth*. In order to rewire the soul it simply is not enough to be spiritual or meditate, although those options are wonderful and may take you a long way. An excellent article by Mariana Caplan, Ph.D. refers to *spiritually transmitted diseases.* Some of these are Fast-

Food Spirituality, Faux Spirituality, Identifying with Spiritual Experiences, The Spiritualized Ego and Spiritual Pride and of course the reason they even come into existence is because well-meaning people who walk down a spiritual path without having done some of the actual work on *themselves*, such as that which this book discusses, fall into the trap of these spiritually transmitted diseases. They simply are not clear enough about themselves, aware enough about themselves, in order to be able to avoid that trap.

So clearly, it is also necessary to heal the self. Some would argue that healing the self can take place with meditation and spirituality and although I agree in principle, in practice, that is often not the case. I am thinking of a motivational, inspirational guru, known world-wide for his spiritual focus on life, who nevertheless announced publicly in recent years that he is only now - after decades of presenting the public with ever more books and CD's - truly working on some of the most fundamental aspects of what we might call his own psychological personality. And I don't say that in a disparaging way. Quite the contrary, I admire his open admission of this inner work and many of his books have stood me in good stead over the last 30 years of my own life. Clearly, we will all have to continue work on ourselves until the day we leave this world, but what is also obvious, is that living a spiritual life, or meditating, or even *knowing* much of what I am presenting here in this book *is not enough*. Just as I wrote in the introduction, it has to actually be incorporated into your daily life. It has to be incorporated into how you deal with problems in your life, into how you deal with your relationships, into how you deal with your inner demons, and so on. If you don't do that, and simply meditate, practice yoga, and chant, not much will change, at least not quickly.

There are several analogies here: how long does it take you to build strong biceps? And isn't it also true that the exercise needs to be done consistently? Then, after some time of seeing few tangible results, you begin to see the strengthening and toning of the muscle. And what about learning how to drive? When you begin, there is so much to remember, that some people almost panic, and others wonder how they will ever be able to do this. Yet once it's properly learned, it becomes automatic. You get in the car, fasten your seatbelt, put the key in the ignition, and it's possible you will have no more conscious memories of the drive you took until you park the car. *Because you've learned how to do it so well, that you no longer need to think about it, unless there is an emergency.*

Both analogies fit what we're trying to accomplish in this book. The muscle building that is taking place – if you do the required work at the gym – will not be visible for some time. The work you do on your state of awareness about your choices, about taking responsibility for your inner well-being, is hard at first, simply because you are not used to doing these things, and because you have no muscle to speak of in that particular department, and furthermore, you will frequently forget to do what you have set out to do. Then you'll have to deal with your anger, annoyance, or despondence at yourself for forgetting as well as doing all you are trying to learn. And so it's not only challenging, but at first you may only see barely discernible results, or perhaps none at all.

> *The finest emotion of which we are capable is the mystic emotion.*
> Albert Einstein

You may say, after a few days of trying, that everything is still the same. *But it's not.* Just like with muscle building, in this case you are building and strengthening new neural pathways in your brain, in your pre-fontal cortex, that area of the brain behind your forehead. And by being consistent about this work for some time, you *will* see the results. The car analogy fits as well, because just like with the car, where at the beginning you feel that there is so much to remember, you do everything awkwardly, and get the impression that no progress is being made, but then, one day, you realize it has become second nature, so too it occurs with becoming more and more aware at every moment of your life.

At the beginning, if you don't make a supreme effort to remember to do it all the time, and give yourself reminders about doing it, you simply forget. Hence the post-it's I suggested you use in the last chapter. But after that early effort, it begins to become more and more familiar, and you are more and more aware more and more of the time, until one day you realize that it has become part of who you are … you have formed a strong new neural pathway. And by the way, this is a neural pathway – the one formed by conscious awareness – that has been demonstrated to be instrumental in helping us reach higher levels of inner well-being on a consistent basis. I imagine that you will fully agree with me that it sounds as though that might be a rather desirable goal.

Our brains are so flexible, so malleable, that once neuroscientists finally realized, several decades ago, that the brain is capable of neuroplasticity (born of geriatric research), i.e. that the brain can change – at any age, as opposed to being fixed and static, and that in this process of change, new connections between existing neurons are established, new neural pathways come into being, those same scientists also began to realize that neurogenesis (growing new brain cells) was taking place, radically opposing the age-old belief that we only get the neural cells we were born with, and once a brain neuron died, that was it. No further chances of getting another to replace it. And that simply was not true! Generations – my own included – were raised on this erroneous belief.

This made an enormous difference to the way we view ourselves and the capacity of our brains to make lasting changes. Until the early 1950's it was believed that it was impossible to run a four-minute mile because no one, in all recorded history of measuring time in races had done so, and yet one day a man called Roger Bannister (who later – interestingly, enough - became a neurologist) did run the four-minute mile. Immediately something was set in motion in the brains of all those who heard of this, especially in the brains of runners, because very rapidly, not only was this heretofore unheard of feat replicated, but surpassed! All because now people viewed the *possibility* of such speed differently and hence a portion of their cerebral real estate changed.

So getting back to our topic of emotions, if someone is in pain because of a rejection (personal or professional), they will probably need some time to recuperate. Depending on the state of their self-love, or self-confidence, or self-approval, this may take more or less time. Some people never fully recuperate from an important rejection. Some shut down, or close themselves off from others in order to not experience such a feeling again. But much of this depends on the *perception* the individual has of the event. To some degree the perception is based on the individual's childhood, as well as on any prior experiences he may have had in the arena of rejection, as well as how those experiences were reacted to. Most people don't necessarily even think about these things. They simply *react*. I've been rejected, so now I feel awful, so now I am very low. This is all very understandable. *But certainly not optimal.* Nor necessary! A more healthy reaction to (and therefore perception of) the rejecting event might be an immediate inner dialogue:

- Why is my well-being so tied up in *not* being rejected?
- Was I rejected for a job, raise or promotion?
- Does someone not want to date me / love me / marry me?
- Does this mean I am worth less (worth a lesser amount) – as a human being (man or woman) than what I was worth just *before* I was rejected?
- If my worth or value is *not* less than it was a few moments ago, then the *only* thing that has changed is *my perception* of myself and the event.
- Is it possible for me – just for the moment – to focus on something different than my pain or negative feelings about what just transpired?
- Something pleasurable such as a thought about a situation that brings good feelings to me, or a brisk (even if brief) walk that

causes oxygen to flow to my brain, increasing the levels of serotonin and endorphins in my brain, allowing me to feel – even if only marginally – better and above all, allowing me to recognize that I can be instrumental in changing how I feel.

- Or let me become consciously mindful of something in front of me that I can focus on, either because it is beautiful, or because it creates a sense of gratitude in me, or simply because it is there (much as a small child is capable of completely focusing on a blade of grass, or an ant carrying a bread crumb three times its size), and by focusing on it mindfully, I come into the now, the present moment, as opposed to focusing on the feelings that the rejection just evoked in me. (See also the chapter on gratitude and the now). In the now where I am *not* focusing on past or future thoughts or feelings about rejection *there is peace*. This is balsam – even if only momentary, at this point in my development – for the heart and ultimately for the soul!
- If I can consciously choose to focus on something different, not a distraction as much as something that will, even if just for a few moments, elevate my mood, albeit slightly, or change the state of my energetic frequency, my inner vibration, I´m putting myself in a position to change my state of inner well-being.
- That will enhance my efforts to begin to perceive this event with new eyes.
- It will also begin to show me how to take responsibility for my inner well-being (my happiness – see the chapter on happiness in this book), as opposed to expecting that my happiness depends on outer circumstances (as in this example it depends on not being rejected).
- Furthermore, it will begin to show me how I can find that road to inner freedom and inner growth. The more I enhance my sense of well-being, the closer I come to walking on that road at all times. And the more I walk on that road, the more I have rewired my soul, connecting to my true inner self, the self that Joseph Campbell, the world-renowned mythologist, stated was our divine self, our inner divinity, the god within.
- Finally, by viewing this event (rejection) with new eyes, I can also, from the better inner place, make new choices and better decisions about potentially more optimal ways to behave in a similar situation in future.

Keeping Your Energy High

One of my sons lives in Dubai, and when I have been there, as well as in Abu Dhabi and the Musandam Peninsula of Oman along the Persian Gulf, I notice how energized I feel there, in ways that are externally-motivated due to the extremely fast-paced life style that is common, particularly in Dubai, but also due to finding myself in cultures foreign to me, that I have enormous curiosity about, and that cause my blood to race in the best sense of the word.

Feeling energized due to something external is great, but there is so much that we can do not only to feel energized, but also to keep our energy, our inner energy, in a high place, in a place where we consistently feel good. This means that we need to watch how we feed our brains, heart and spirit.

Feed the brain?

Of course! Just as we feed our bodies, hopefully with a greater percentage of healthy rather than junk food, so it is also very important how we feed our brain, heart, and spirit. What we read, or what we watch on TV, or discuss with our friends, even the *kind* of friends we spend our time with, the objects we surround ourselves with in our homes, the things we choose (if we are aware) to focus on (or simply focus on willy-nilly, because we are *not* aware), all has a huge impact on our emotional state - the state of our inner energy.

So watching horror movies that give us an adrenaline rush as we wait with bated breath for someone to be sawed into several pieces, or attacked, *Jack-the-Ripper* or *Freddy*-style may make us *feel* energized, may even make us go back for more of the same in order to get that same feeling of the high that the adrenaline surge gave us, but none of that energy is left the next day when we wake up.

What happens when you eat empty sugar products? You get a quick rush, but soon after you are either craving more, or simply feel bloated. No real physical energy. So it is with much of what is available on TV and radio, in the press, cinema, and so on. Even - I am sorry to say - with many of our conversations.

When you are initiating the process of change I am recommending in this book, it is so very important to continually be vigilant about all those things with which you nourish all parts of yourself! But there is so much to choose from, just as there is an abundant choice in the supermarket. You can find fantastic foods there that truly nourish your body and cells, and then there is all the artificial, pre-packaged stuff with empty calories. You get to choose.
So when you make choices about what goes into your brain, heart, and spirit, try to consider how you will nourish these, as opposed to giving them empty calories. Think carefully about the programs you watch, the books you read, the content of the conversations in which you participate. *All of this shapes you*, and what you do day in and day out, will become your life, so choose wisely.

A friend was monitoring the quality of her food intake due to gastric complications that could lead to a potential diagnosis of stomach cancer. One day as we sat together in a restaurant, I observed how carefully she chose her food, and what attention, therefore, she paid to the health of her body. I applaud this very much, because of course, if we are not in charge of what we feed ourselves, we soon lose sight of that all important element of our well-being: our physical health.

A few days earlier she had gone through a very difficult time emotionally due to the physical pain this whole situation was causing, and had reached out to me to ask for some help, some support, and some encouragement. Again, I also applaud this very much, because our social support network, our family and friends can make all the difference when we find ourselves in a difficult place with our physical health.

In the course of our conversation during the lunch, I heard in an aside from her husband that she had had an equally difficult emotional bout a few days before the lunch due to rampant fear involving the evolution of the gastric complication: would it be a cancer diagnosis or not? During the general conversation some books were mentioned. My friend was reading a number of potentially interesting ones, but indicated that one in particular was very depressing. She told us as well that news on TV was discouraging. None of the books she was reading were ones that I would put into the category of *raising her energy*.

Later, over coffee at her home, I saw many magazines and books about. There was much of interest, politically, economically, some good literature, and so on, but again, there was little that I would put into the category of *raising her energy*.

As we stood alone for a moment, I told her how much I admired her fortitude in choosing her food, and in not being swayed by a momentary palate-driven desire to forego the medical advice she had been given. *But*, I said, *in an ideal world you would pay just as much attention to the food you put into your mind, your spirit and soul, as you do to the food you put into your body*.

This goes to energy. *Please realize that how you nourish your mind is what gives you weakness or strength when you most need strength in times of fear, worry and stress.* So feed yourself well. Look at the menu and choose wisely.

Think of the radio: when you drive to work every day are you listening to endless variations of *"can't live without your love"* or *"I am nothing without you"*, that merely keep you in a state of false belief about love? Or are you listening to an irate political, religious, or sports commentator whose goal it is to incite you into arguing about whatever happens to be the subject of the day? Or inane social babble that fills you about as much as two tablespoons of sugar? Don't misunderstand: all of the above is ok if not done in excess. A bit of sugar is ok too. I make a mean black chocolate mousse with freshly whipped cream, and I just might check out the gossip magazines along with the other clients at the hair salon. But it's the typical excess that most of us resort to that results in a loss of energy to our spirit. Maybe we say there's nothing else to listen to in the car, or when we get home at night we're too tired to watch something "educational".

Fair enough. But how about preparing for the daily car ride by always having a selection of CD's (or podcasts on your iPod, iPad, or iPhone) that actually stimulate you towards totally different directions? How about listening to some interviews available on the internet (and freely - and legally - downloadable) with some of the big names in fields of cutting-edge science, spirituality, business, leadership, motivation, etc.? There are many topics, speakers and authors. The point really is that this type of material will drive your inner energy up a number of notches, and the more you *feed* yourself with this genre, the more you will notice that it gets harder and harder to remain on a lower level within.

And isn't that part of the quest we are on? Getting to a place of inner freedom and joy with a strong energetic frequency?

It is the content and the energy of what you read, watch, do, and listen to, as well as the topics about which you converse in your daily life, that determine where your own energetic frequency lies.

So it's a good idea to make a habit of listening to CD's in your car as you drive to and from work, a drive many of us do alone, and at best we tend to listen to music or the news, or perhaps an audio book, and at worst we basically just waste that precious time, impatiently wishing we had already arrived at our destination or fretting about what we have to do when we get there. Another great moment in our day for listening to this type of material may be as you shave or put on your make-up.

I realize however, that it is not always easy to get good CD's to listen to, especially for people who live in countries outside of the USA, UK, Australia, and Canada. That's why in the Appendix you can find some magnificent websites I frequently use to get the latest information available about a great many subjects on the edge of discovery, enlightenment, and understanding. Most are free, although not all, and I recommend them highly if you want to begin to shift your inner energy.

Using your emotions as a barometer for your state of well-being is a magnificent way to remain aware, because it helps you to train yourself to observe your emotions as opposed to merely enduring them. And by recognizing where your emotions are, you can then choose to take them to a better place in order to positively impact your state of inner well-being.

The more you spend your days in a good place on an inner level, the more you will come to understand that you are in charge of your well-being. The direction in which your emotions move need not be outside of your own conscious control. Even when very bad things happen, you can still choose to react in ways that are not blind. (See the section in the chapter on pain and forgiving that refers to some well-known global figures that have chosen to be in charge of their own emotions and reactions despite extreme life events).

You can choose how you look at the event, you can choose the actual thoughts you have about the event, you can choose to take charge of what may be mounting hysteria or panic inside of you, and you can choose to live through a process of deep grief due to loss or death from a position of observation by constantly being aware of your feelings and standing slightly apart from them.

By this I neither mean that you will *control* difficult feelings by repressing them, nor do I mean that you will not feel the full gamut of emotions. But I do mean that the process of becoming aware of yourself as you observe yourself being angry, bitter, jealous, or sad, will eventually allow you to stand at a small distance from the part of you that is experiencing the emotion and observe yourself undergoing that process. (We will be discussing much more about the subject of awareness in Chapter Four). From that place of awareness and observation, you can calm yourself, you can help yourself feel less bereft, less out of your depth, and take yourself to a place where you know that you will be able to deal with this, and come closer to yourself in the process. You will be rewiring your soul.

Do you imagine the universe is agitated? Go into the desert at night and look at the stars. This practice should answer the question.
Lao Tzu

Chapter Three

The Ego:
Who Is In Charge?

Ego is to the true self what a flashlight is to a spotlight.
John Bradshaw

M ost of us are under the firm control of our ego. At least we are until we become aware of the difference between the ego and the awakened, or aware and conscious mind. As long as the ego is in control, you generally have no idea what it means to be an observer of yourself.

The multitude of existing definitions for the ego – especially in the world of psychoanalysis - gives us an idea how much this concept has raised interest and created concern over time, but the way I am using the term *ego* here, in tune with the way it has been used in *A Course in Miracles,* as well as by Eckhart Tolle, Joel

Goldsmith, Chris Griscom, Deepak Chopra, Wayne Dyer and others, refers to that part of the self that needs to control, judge, and criticize. It compares, it diminishes, it divides, it separates. It gives undue value to external things and situations, and above all, the ego manipulates – not only others – but especially you, when it causes you to believe that it (the ego), above all else – and especially more than you - knows what is good and right for you.

Here's what generally happens when your ego is in control of you:

- You need to prove you are right (i.e., you are not capable of letting go of the need to be right)
- You need to show that you are more powerful than others, whether this be financially, physically (your strength, your youth, your beauty, your sports ability, etc.), sexually, socially, psychologically, intellectually, morally or professionally (i.e., you are not capable of letting go of the need to show the world your power or importance)
- You need to feel you are in control (i.e., you are not capable of letting go of the need to be in control)
- You need to judge (others, or a situation), or rather, you judge, because that is what you do (i.e., you are not capable of letting go of the judgmental thoughts that accompany you day in, day out). If you doubt this statement, try going through just one morning without judging anyone or anything or any situation!
- You need to feel yourself being approved of by others (i.e., you are not capable of feeling good without a measure of such approval, or at the very least, it is very hard for you to do so)
- You feel your importance due to the state of your bank account or stock portfolio, due to what is parked in your driveway or what is moored at the berth in the marina, due to your professional accomplishments and academic credentials, due to the size of your home and the neighborhood in which it stands, due to the status or beauty of your spouse or partner, due to your own physical beauty, thinness, or youth, due to the friends you have and the events you attend, the places at which you vacation, and the labels on the clothes you wear (i.e., you are not capable of feeling important without taking such things into consideration, or you would feel diminished without such outer aspects to enhance your importance)
- You identify with your ethnicity, religion, politics, family background, etc., (i.e., you are not capable of imagining your identity without those elements)
- You identify with the incessant mind chatter – or, in the words of Deepak Chopra – the internal dialogue, that is so much a part of you, that you consider it to be you. You do not imagine that you

could exist without it, because *that's how I am; that's how I think* (i.e., you are not capable of living your life without this chatter)
- You believe in your total separateness from all other human beings. You are even – as you see it – separate from those you love the most. (i.e., you are not capable of understanding – and believing – that we are all intermingled molecules: that we are all one, that we are all connected by a field of energy that binds us all together because we have all sprung from one and the same source energy. For more about this topic, see Chapter 17.)

Interestingly, many people equate the ego and self-esteem. Or, conversely, equate the ego and being selfish or self-centered. Neither is true. Your ego may make you very pious and self-righteous, for example, uprightly moral and respectable, and that clearly has nothing to do with being selfish, at least not in the conventional understanding of the word. But you develop those qualities (piety, morality, respectability), if they are coming from the ego, mainly because you believe others will see you as a "good" person, and not so much motivated by a deep-rooted desire to be good or ethical.

The most common ego identifications have to do with possessions, the work you do, social status and recognition, knowledge and education, physical appearance, special abilities, relationships, personal and family history, belief systems, and often political, nationalistic, racial, religious, and other collective identifications.
None of these is you.
Eckhart Tolle

On the other hand, if you have a healthy sense of self-esteem, and as long as it is not a case of having self-esteem that makes you arrogant (in which case it would not be a healthy sense of self-esteem anyway), then you probably are beginning to get a handle on your ego as it is described in the above list and are diminishing its importance in your life. In this case I would prefer to call that healthy self esteem a sense of healthy self-love.

Your Love of Self (or Lack of it) is the Power that Manages the Ego

Consider this: When the ego takes over, when we need to *win*, or when we need to *prove* that we are right, or when we need to show *how much more we know*, or when we need to demonstrate, by virtue of our toys, *how much more we are worth* in financial terms, or when we need to make others aware, by dropping the names of those we know or rub shoulders with, *how much more important we are* in social or professional terms ... when we do all of this in order to satisfy the ego, our lack of love of the self is showing us *how little we truly value ourselves.*

If your ego needs the type of satisfaction I've just painted, you clearly suffer from a lack of love for the self, else you would not need any of this. If you love yourself fully, this love (and feeling good about yourself) does not depend – in any way – on what you *have* or what you *are* in the external world. The more conscious you are, the more you will become aware of the pull of your ego and the less you will wish to follow it. And the places into which it wants to pull you, assuming you have begun to differentiate between your conscious and your not conscious self, are always places where you don't feel - in the long run - as good as you feel when the ego is not running the show.

If you want to reach a state of bliss, then go beyond your ego.
Deepak Chopra

When your love of self is healthy, *you have no need to satisfy the ego's empty needs because those needs are no longer your needs.* And that is why your love of self - or the level (and health) of your love of self is the power that manages the ego. *The less you love yourself, the more you need outer trappings of any kind to feel good. And the less you love yourself, the more you will listen to the ego's insistence that those outer trappings will make you happy.*

Love Yourself First

This almost seems old hat. Overdone. Been there, done that. The topic, I mean. *Love yourself first.* But it isn't. You know why? *Because people are still not doing it.* Most of us have still not learned that old adage that if we don't love ourselves first, we can't really love anyone else. Do you know why? Because you'll be loving them for all the wrong reasons. Oh, you might believe that you love them, and in some fashion you do, *but for all the wrong reasons.* (we'll go into this topic in greater detail in the chapters on self-love and relationships, but here are a few points that are germane to our current topic of the ego).

These are some of those wrong reasons for which we love others:

- I'm so happy when I'm with him/her
- He/she makes me feel so good
- I feel so secure when I'm with him/her
- I need him/her so much! (in this instance, the person actually *believes* that *needing* someone is proof that they *love* them. Whew!)
- I've never felt like this before … only he/she can *give* me this feeling
- When we're not together, I feel so lost
- When we're not together, I feel like a part of me is missing
- When we're not together, I just don't really enjoy doing things

Are you beginning to get my drift? *All of the above* indicate someone who is in love due to something he/she is getting from the beloved. *That is the reason they are in love.* Obviously this is not a conscious process. It could almost be described as being related to being mercenary and calculating in some fashion … except for the fact that this goes on subconsciously.

It happens.

We realize we feel better around the beloved. We begin to define why we feel better around that person. Hence statements such as the above. And then – presto – we believe we are in love.

The degree to which you can let go and embrace death, whether that be your own death, the death of a loved one or the death of your ego, relationships and belief systems, is the degree to which you can experience Samadhi (enlightenment).
Chris Griscom

All is not lost, however. In other words, if you are still with me, this doesn't mean you now should give up your relationship in order to find yourself and discover how to love yourself first. But it *does* mean, that now you should begin to realize that these reasons that make you believe you are in love are in fact pointing to the bits of you that you have not yet *filled for yourself*. So you go looking to fulfill them though another.

And it is your ego that drives you there. (This recognition of unfulfilled bits of yourself, by the way, through your new understanding of your relationship, is precisely one of the reasons why relationships can be so conducive to growth, as you will read about in Chapter 15.)

By beginning to fill your needs yourself, as opposed to needing others to do this for you, you begin the process of self-love, self-respect, self-esteem and self-acknowledgement. This is not selfishness or egotistical behavior. Doing this, waking up about yourself, will lead you to a place where – when you then love – you *will love as you were never able to as long as you needed the other for the fulfillment of your own needs.* And doing this; loving yourself in this healthy way, will mean that your ego will begin to lose its grip on you and your life.

Coming Out From Under the Ego's Yoke

How can you come out from under the yoke of the ego? How can you change your life so that you, instead of the ego, are in charge? How can you begin to see and hear when the ego is attempting to be in charge of your life so that you can, indeed, rid yourself of its hold over you? Can you imagine how different life would be, if you were able to do this?

I find one of the easiest ways to begin to observe the ego is in our need to be right. What happens when you give up the need to be right? Here's the deal: when you give up the need to be right, many things change:

- It's impossible to argue with you
- You can keep your cool no matter what
- Others come to realize that you know that *your* opinion – even though you may stick to it through thick and thin - is not more important than *theirs*. That goes a long way to improving communication
- Your ego is no longer invested in proving anything to the other person
- You feel great no matter what the other person decides to believe
- You don't need to convince anyone of anything, *no matter how much you believe in it*
- You can keep your belief about whatever it is *you are right about*, but you don't need to be bothered about proving it to the other person
- No more power struggles
- You give up the need to control others' behavior, thoughts, actions and reactions
- You *know* it is preferable for *both* to win, not just you
- In a nutshell, your life becomes a lot easier – just like that!

Obviously I'm not talking about facts that are easily checked, such as the capital of a country, or the metric equivalent of one yard. I'm talking about opinions, ideas, ideologies, religions, philosophies, ways of living one's life, in other words, all those ephemeral, evanescent things that populate our lives, our thinking and feeling, and yet that have no *true* right or wrong.

So what's the point of it?

Imagine you are the parent of a teenager who is pushing your buttons. Clearly, you have to show your child how wrong he/she is and how right you are; clearly you have to show your child – if necessary by anger – that he/she *must* change because he is wrong and you are right … or do you?

Intolerance itself is a form of egoism, and to condemn egoism intolerantly is to share it.
George Santayana

What would happen if you let go of the need to be right, and you kept your eyes instead on the love between the two of you? Keeping your eyes on the love instead of on the need to be right will promote the health of the relationship much more than proving you are right would, but even more importantly than that, by keeping your eyes on the love (even if it's the partially buried love, or the forgotten love, or hidden love), you will be showing your child so many things:

- That love is more important than being right
- That when love is given priority, other things simply become less important
- If you show your child at each and every step of the way that you will choose love over the need to prove how right you are, your relationship *will improve* (and as an added benefit, of course, you will be starting to get accustomed to how it feels *to not let the ego manage your life*)
- At the beginning of such a process, you might say to your teen: *I know you think what you are saying is right, and I know that normally I react like this* (whatever 'this' is), *but I've decided that I love you too much to continue doing this, and so I just want you to know that I love you, and that I am determined not to fight with you anymore. Our relationship is too important to me.* Such words will not cure your relationship like magic, but they will certainly begin the process of change.
- What is also of supreme importance here is that you begin to look at your relationship with your child (even an adult child) as an indicator about you, rather than an indicator about him or her. So instead of thinking *it's all their fault, and if only they would change, all would be well*, think instead, *what can I do to change my way of dealing with this situation?* Ask yourself how you can

look at the difficulty from the point of view of *your attitude* in each problematic situation. So I am not saying that your child should be allowed to be rude, take drugs, or attempt to take over the household with his whims, but I am saying that when any of the things happen that tend to happen, and that make life so miserable, you could stand back, assess the situation instead of reacting to your buttons having been pushed, and begin to *choose how to react*, from a position of love and compassion, and from a place where you have decided *in advance* that you will not fight over who is right or wrong, but that you will do your utmost to promote understanding, trust, and love.

And if you're the teen, battling with a parent over who is right, take the same message to heart ... if your parent is not reacting as I have indicated above (and you can imagine that most *do not react that way*, because they never learned about this – they might never even have learned about the idea of standing back and looking at the self), then you can be the one to do so, as long as you are willing to give up the need to be right, and if you are willing to let love be more important than proving you are right.

On another note, we might imagine you are the husband or wife, or life partner embroiled in a bitter battle with your partner about some issue or many issues. Apply the same principles as indicated above. Remember that keeping love (as opposed to the idea of winning a war) front and center may help you re-orient your position in the battle. *That reorientation* on *your* part may bring both sides to a place where win-win becomes a real possibility.

The problem is that we have allowed our egos, the part of us which believes that we are separate from God and separate from each other, to dominate our lives.
Wayne Dyer

And in all instances, please do remember that healthy boundaries are important, and that putting love first *never means you should let anyone walk all over you, or mistreat* you, and to understand that more clearly, you may wish to go to the chapter on boundaries.

However, giving up the need to be right *does not mean* - by any stretch of the imagination - *that you have to accept what the other person takes to be right as yours*. In other words, just because you are ok with not proving to others that you are right, or with not bending them to your will, you continue to *know that you are right for yourself.* And you allow others to continue in their own belief. And whatever is right for you, is something that you adhere to. So I am *not* advocating that you go over to another's belief.

Let's take another example: you vote liberal and the other person votes conservative (or whatever opposing parties your country has). If you decide you need to convince the other person of how wrong he is and how right you are, you will probably never see eye to eye and you may even need to end the relationship. If, however, you can allow him his belief in the rightness of his convictions and how he votes, and you maintain your own belief, all can be well. But let's say you decide on that path and the other person wants to prove to you how wrong you are ... do you understand how impossible it will be for him to argue with you if you refuse to engage?

Refusing to engage in arguments is such a wonderful tool to teach yourself about the ego. At the beginning you will probably feel like you want to regurgitate in your *need* to engage. But if you can agree with yourself from the outset – before the potential argument even comes into your life – that you will refuse to engage, then, when the moment of the potential argument arises, and you feel like you will choke if you don't insist on your own opinion being the right one, you will be able to stand back and look at this need of yours, *you'll be able to understand that the need comes from the ego and not from the part of you that you are trying to enhance – the self, the soul – and hence, you will not engage.* Or if you do (and don't kick yourself for it, give yourself some kudos for trying, and at least you will have gone through this whole process in your head, you may not have "won" this round (with yourself), but you will have acknowledged that this is the road you wish to take and in a future occasion you can try again.

Not engaging doesn't mean never stating your opinion and it certainly doesn't mean avoiding difficult or potentially confrontational situations. It simply means not arguing about who is right and stating that it is your conscious intention not to argue about it.

Ask yourself this: *exactly why is it so important to convince the other person that you are right*? What will change? Because you do realize that if they feel just as you do, and believe that it is crucial to convince you of how right *they* are, you are at an impossible impasse, unless one of you is stronger than the other. If you are the parent, or the boss, or the one with the money, or the one who manipulates better, or the one who *needs* the other one less emotionally, then of course you will probably win.

But here's what will happen next: you will have a lot of resentment on your hands which will, eventually, explode. That's how revolutions and coup d'états come about, not to mention acrimonious divorces and bad relationships between parents and children. *Resentment from having to give in to a stronger party can be poisonous.* And the stronger party (as well as the one who gave in) is typically ruled by the needs of the ego to be right.

What can you do if you are married to someone who wants to do things a given way and you do not? Do you get divorced? Do you give in? Or do you find a win-win solution where each party may need to give up part of what they believed in, in exchange for a solution that works for both? This is only possible if *both* parties are willing to give up the need to be right about *their* way of doing it, and agree that there could be a third way, one that gives *each* of the partners a degree of satisfaction.

And by the way, *this is never 'not' possible.* So it means that both parties will begin the process of standing back from their own ego's needs in order to be able to climb to this newer, more aware level of the relationship. Read that last sentence again, please. If you don't do that, you will not be able to escape the rut of eternal argument and need to prove the other wrong.

Here's another thing: once you give up the need to be right, you start listening to what others have to say … really listening, instead of impatiently waiting for them to stop talking, so that you can have your turn (to talk about all the things you are thinking about while they are talking). And not only do you start listening, you start to become interested in what they are saying *even if you don't think it's right*, because by giving up the need to be right, you begin to see others in a new light, a light of generosity, compassion, non-judgment and non-criticism.

> *Avoid having your ego so close to your position that when your position falls, your ego goes with it.*
> Colin Powell

That space, where you can accept them as they are as opposed to wanting them to be *your* way, is a sacred space because it's one of the steps that leads you towards the understanding that *we are all one* and therein lies another kind of freedom, not only on the individual level, but also on the global one. And that new light in which you are now capable of seeing others, a light of generosity, non-judgment and non-criticism is the light that shines when the ego is not running the show. It's really not so hard to understand.

This example I have written about so extensively here, about giving up the need to be right, is merely one way you can come to *recognize* your ego, and by recognizing it, you can stop letting it control you and your life and your thoughts and your feelings and your opinions and your choices and your actions and your reactions so that the *real* you, instead of the ego is in charge. Do you see exactly *how much* the ego tends to control us while we remain unaware?

Therefore in order to replace your own inner control over the self as opposed to the ego's control over you, it requires, above all else, as explained above, vigilant awareness of yourself. Prior to this point you could be likened to someone who was asleep and now you are awakening from that sleep and slowly coming to consciousness. You may still be groggy, you may still fall back on the pillow and catnap, but basically you are awake, and in the state of being awake, it is much harder for you to ignore what is truly happening inside of you. Once awake, falling asleep is not something that happens again so easily. Stay awake, pay attention to all the byways your ego wants to take you on, and observe yourself as you start going there. Are you able to stop? How strong is your ego? Are you able at least to pause, if not stop? If you are able to pause, can you have an inner dialogue about what you think is going on inside of you? Who wins?

The Observer

If you are able to think of this process in terms of *who wins*, you are well on the road to understanding the ego's influence over you, and getting to a place where it will be easier and easier for you to leave it behind. *It is in the observing of yourself that you begin to see that you are not the ego. You begin to see there is someone else there altogether, else how do you explain the observer?*

The observer is a term that has largely arisen from eastern philosophies, religions, and from meditative states. Even if you don't meditate (where the observer would be the part that is sitting still and in silence but would nevertheless be observing as thoughts appear – at the beginning with great frequency, later, in the case of more seasoned meditators, less and less - in an *egoic* attempt to tear you away from the silence), you can nevertheless understand the concept of the observer with an example.

Try to remember an occasion where you became very angry, and where you blurted out, with considerable vehemence, words that you knew you would regret. In the blurting out of those words, a part of you was *already* acknowledging that you would regret them, a part of you was thinking *why do I do this?* And so, the part that blurted and the part that acknowledged the future regret and was thinking, were two separate parts of you. The one that blurted was the ego. It reacted blindly to a stimulus. And the other part was the observer.

The ego is not you, but when it does things or thinks things or feels things, you feel as though it were you. You are so used to allowing the ego to take over, that you have little knowledge or experience of what you could or would be if you – instead of your ego – were in charge.

The trick (if you can call it that) is to let the observer become stronger and stronger in order to weaken the ego. The more you are aware of this observer (you) and of the ego (also you, but as John Bradshaw so aptly puts it in one of the quotes at the beginning of this chapter: *Ego is to the true self what a flashlight is to a spotlight*), the more you will be able to take decisions that favor the observer, that favor the aware part of the self, the part of the self that is rewiring your soul in this process you have undertaken to find true inner peace, freedom, harmony and joy.

You are not your ego.

Chapter Four

Awareness: Becoming Conscious

You cannot find your soul with your mind; you must use your heart.
You must know what you are feeling. If you don't know what
you are feeling, you will create unconsciously. If you are
unconscious of an aspect of yourself; if it operates
outside your field of awareness, that aspect
has power over you.
Gary Zukav

Coming to awareness or becoming conscious is one of the most elementary things you can do for your own process of growth. And yet, there is nothing elementary about it, because if it were elementary, we would all be doing it with no need to read books about it.

The initial process of coming to consciousness has a lot less to do with spirituality, which is something that many associate the term consciousness with, than simply with the fact of coming to awareness about yourself. That awareness takes you on the road to spirituality and eventually to the rewiring of your soul that is at the heart of this book, and that is deeply concerned with our spirituality. However, first you need to start in a place you can handle; a place you can deal with, a place that makes sense in your daily life. All journeys start with a single step, as Lao Tzu said, but that single and first step – in the case of coming to consciousness – has so much more to do with you and how you perceive your very personal world, than with becoming spiritual, in the commonly-accepted connotation of such an undertaking.

How you perceive your world when you are a child is what may make you, for example, feel that you are not loved enough, even in the case of parents who are loving. Or, again, as a child, it may make you feel rejected, or disapproved of, in some fashion when you attempt to approach someone close to you – perhaps a parent or an older sibling. This *perception* of the event is what shapes you and may cause you to say, decades later, that because of what happened - perhaps you are calling the event traumatic - you are unable to live a good or happy life, since when someone goes through those experiences – you believe - it is not possible to live a good life. Furthermore, whenever you recall your childhood, perhaps you choke with emotion, or conversely, perhaps you have no emotion about it at all, and you tell yourself it has no importance.

But this perception of yours is not necessarily correct. In other words, perhaps you *were* being loved, or you *weren't* being rejected or disapproved of, but because this was the way you *perceived* it, there were psycho-emotional consequences that have affected you in your life to this day. Take the example of Pierre (not his real name), a Belgian in his sixties with numerous failed relationships – in part due to the fact that he never was able to trust women. This was caused by a number of unfortunate circumstances in his childhood. When he was not yet a year old he had to be hospitalized and due to WWII ravaging Europe, his father was off at the front, and his mother had to return to her village to work. The hospital was in Bruges and too far and costly for her to visit more than once every few weeks. It broke her heart, because she loved her baby fiercely, but she simply found herself in a position where she was unable to arrange matters differently. The very young child that he was, perceived - on some subconscious level - that he had been abandoned and betrayed by his mother, as evidenced by his adult relationship choices with women who eventually cheated on him.

So you can see that *what really happened is not at times, in fact, as important as how it was perceived*. Additionally, it is not typically possible to talk to a child about becoming conscious, and furthermore, it's fully possible that no one is even aware of the child's erroneous perception of those events anyway (even in the case of an older child).

Nevertheless, that early perception – subconscious though it may be – has the power to taint a life in painful ways until the individual becomes aware of the connection between the past and the present and then – from that position of awareness, chooses to develop another way of reacting *now* – hence beginning the process of developing another neural pathway – that allows him to live a richer, fuller, more satisfying life *because it has a measure of inner peace.*

Another child who may have truly experienced – objectively speaking - a lack of care from neglectful parents, may nevertheless have perceived that he was loved, and therefore would have less of a trauma connected to that early time in his life than Pierre, in the example above. Again, it is the child's perception of the events that is the deciding factor, and the perception of any event – at any point in an individual's lifetime - will color it for him throughout his life ... until he comes to consciousness.

Coming to consciousness, however, is not enough to clear up past erroneous perceptions or trauma. And frequently, of course, the trauma was caused by a perception of events that was not erroneous in the least, that was totally correct, and that left its indelible mark on the psyche. Coming to consciousness is the process by which the clearing up can begin to take place. Coming to consciousness means, in many different ways, that you begin to look at an event less as something external that happens to you with the power to hurt you or negatively impact you, than as something that while it does often take place externally, can give rise to an internal consciously aware decision about the manner in which you choose to react to it.

In the jargon of my profession, we might say that by becoming conscious of yourself and the events of your life, the narrative of your life changes. This means that the way in which you tell the story of your life (even if only to yourself) changes, because now you have another kind of awareness about those events, their impact on you, and most importantly, how you have now decided to understand and deal with the impact of those events, in such a way that your current life allows you to choose to create new reactions, as said, new habits, new neural pathways that will eventually lead you to inner well-being, and to a sense of peace and security.

All historical experience demonstrates the following: Our earth cannot be changed unless in the not too distant future an alteration in the consciousness of individuals is achieved.
Hans Kung

Doing such a thing clearly implies first being aware of the self and being fully conscious of the manners in which it habitually reacts (the habitual reactions belong to the "blind" self, the unaware self, or the "reactive" self, i.e., the self that reacts without thinking, without awareness, and hence blindly) in order to even be able to see, realize and understand that another way of reaction is possible.

In my own life, after a rather tumultuous and difficult childhood, I had found some measure of awareness through early reading I had been introduced to when I was about 15 in books by Henry Miller, Simone de Beauvoir, Hermann Hesse and Anäis Nin, and again in my early twenties through some of the collected works by Carl Gustav Jung, as well as Liz Greene, a Jungian analyst *and* humanistic astrologer, Viktor Frankl, and the mythologist Joseph Campbell.

My mid-teens when I was living in Canada, but spending time in Europe many summers to visit my father, were confusing and difficult for multiple reasons. I looked like a woman, and yet I was still a child in so many ways. Further, I was giving thought to subjects that did not appear to interest my high school friends, and I found it extremely difficult to find anyone with whom I could communicate about some of my inner perceptions and pain.

Later, when tragedy hit my life – having just barely turned 20 – with the unexpected and sudden death of my mother from cancer as I was traveling in Spain, I looked at the black hole her death had ripped into the fabric of my life and told myself I had to find a meaning in it and because of that belief and what I did with it during the next few years, I grew enormously in self-understanding.

However, I did not find my own *real* initial introduction to that new, conscious way of viewing myself and my early circumstances until I was already in my early thirties due to several rather small, and at first glance, relatively unimportant events.

The first happened during a weekend trip to Arcos de la Frontera, a small white-washed village in southern Spain. I was traveling with friends and had chosen to sit in the back seat of the car over a stretch that took us up into the country, over the Sierra Bermeja mountain range to the west of the Iberian Peninsula I had become so very fond of. As we drove, I turned my thoughts to a difficult personal situation and tuned out the conversation the others were having, occasionally glorying in the spectacular beauty of our surroundings. As I did so, and as we carried on up the hairpin turns, I realized I could now see – from a distance - one of the small villages we had left behind in a valley. A while later, I saw it again, but this time the distance was even greater, as we had climbed higher still, and so the village now appeared even smaller than the first time. This happened once more and on each occasion, I marveled at how much smaller, less important it seemed from that new perspective, and especially how much more than just the village I was able to see from so high up.

Suddenly something clicked in my brain. *This is how I need to look at my problem*, I told myself. *If I can only stand away from it and see it from a new and more distant, less immediate perspective, then just as the village appeared smaller and less important, so will my problem, and I will be able to see the bigger picture,* perhaps even learning something new in the process. I was entranced by this sudden realization – not at all original, I know – but for me it was monumental, and simply because of it, many things began to change in the manner in which I lived my life.

The second event – also in my 30's - occurred when I first read a series of books by Chris Griscom that address higher consciousness. She had became very popular in the 80's, first in Europe, and then in the US, having garnered some fame though one of Shirley MacLaine's books, given to me by my father, in which Shirley describes her own experiences with Chris' silver needles – her "windows to the soul" - and past life regression experiences. I later visited Chris Griscom's Light Institute on several occasions in magnificent New Mexico (that so poignantly reminds me in some ways of Spain, and in others of South Africa), in a town called Galisteo, and underwent a series of intensive past life regressions lasting three days each, spanning a period of two years. I was looking for a way to resolve a personal conflict – with regards to my own feelings about it - that had engendered much anger, bitterness, and pain both on my side, as well as on the part of the other individual involved.

When one realizes one is asleep, at that moment
one is already half-awake.
P.D. Ouspensky

Those of you who have read any of Dr. Brian Weiss's books, the Miami Mount Sinai psychiatrist who wrote, among several others *Many Lives, Many Masters*, will understand what happens during past life regression. Essentially one relives – in a very relaxed state - other lives that one has lived that are not *this* life. The purpose of this type of work is to better understand current challenges and tensions inasmuch as they were paralleled in some of those other lives, as well as connections both with difficult relationships as well as loving ones that have appeared and re-appeared across lifetimes, and with that understanding therefore potentially be more capable of resolving them in the current life in a growth-producing way.

The second time in that two-year period during which I went to New Mexico, I was surrounded by tenderness in my personal life, living in a beautiful home that overlooked the glorious turquoise waters of Cancun, Mexico, in the Yucatan Peninsula, and that respite of six years in my life was what allowed me, perhaps, to reach greater levels of understanding in the past life sessions because I felt *safer* in my daily life.

Those three-hour daily sessions at the Light Institute were grueling, mainly because of the kind of past life my subconscious insisted on regaling me with: past lives filled with murder and destruction and death by fire, torture, rape, brutality, etc., and of course, I was always the victim and – no surprises here - the perpetrator was that ignominious individual in my present life with whom I had the rancorous conflict. (In past life regression, one frequently and spontaneously "recognizes" people that form part of the current life and these people are not necessarily the same gender – or race - in the past life as in the present one). In one spectacularly horrendous lifetime that even involved one of my then very young sons, I died a particularly sad death, and as I felt the tears rolling down my cheeks as I lay on that massage table under a luminous open skylight in Galisteo, New Mexico in the sun-drenched treatment room, listening to the sighing of the wind through the trees, thinking *how could he have done such terrible things to me over and over again*, I suddenly *knew*, just as surely as I know my name, that what had really happened had been the reverse! *I had been the perpetrator, and the individual in my present life with whom I had such a distressing conflict, had been the victim.*

A radical inner transformation and rise to a new level of consciousness might be the only real hope we have in the current global crisis brought on by the dominance of the Western mechanistic paradigm.
Stanislav Grof

In other words, our roles, in that particular lifetime, had been reversed, although as I was reliving that life, I had not seen it, and I had automatically assumed myself to be the victim once again! And as I realized that, I realized as well that in many of those dozens and dozens of torturous lifetimes that I had been reliving in those sessions, I had also been the perpetrator. If you had asked me, I might have ventured the guess that we had shared equally in our roles of victim and perpetrator *

What a realization! Only some time later did I find information in another book by Chris Griscom, about the concept of *living the unspeakable*, of realizing that we have all played *all* the roles. We have all been the bad one and the good one, the light one and the dark one. Understanding this brings us so much closer to recognizing that as long as we believe in the need for duality (right/wrong, black/white, yin/yang, etc.), we will not be capable of moving on to a place where the concept of *we are all one* is a distinct possibility. As long as I see you as the bad one and me as the innocent one, or your race as the oppressive one and mine as the victim, your religion as the wrong one and mine as the right one, equality for all and harmony will not be possible. *Nor will compassion.*

And in so realizing, something shifted in me, and I began to assume much greater consciousness of my ordinary, everyday, daily life because I understood, almost analogically, you might say, that there was more than just one way to look at an event when something difficult happened to me. One way is looking at it from the perspective that the outer event decides how you react, i.e., if something sad happens to me, I will be sad, if something bad happens to me, I will be angry, and justifiably so. And especially, *if you have done something terrible to me,* I have no choice but to be angry, sad, hysterical, revengeful, etc.

However, another very different and much more liberating way of looking at it is from the perspective that your internal – and aware and conscious - self determines how you will react in the face of an event – any event *because you choose the best reaction for your inner well-being.* But again, this latter option is only possible if you have truly become conscious.

I'm not suggesting you need to believe in past life regressions in order to follow me here. Nor am I suggesting – even to those of you who do believe in reincarnation - that it is something I recommend you do. Many of my private clients have chosen to go down that road with me in my practice as an adjunct to psychotherapy, but many others have never expressed any interest in going there whatsoever and have nevertheless found themselves making progress by leaps and bounds in their lives. It's a fascinating thing to do, but not necessary at all in order to get to the same place of awareness about yourself and your own life. Getting to that place can be done as a day-by-day practice by *wanting to get there* and then implementing some simple steps and some tenacious follow-through. Many roads lead to Rome, and my initial steps into consciousness as described above are only some of the ways of many possibilities, as are the suggestions I make throughout the course not only of this chapter, but the entire book, merely other examples of those myriad ways to do so.

* This individual and I now have a cordial relationship. We are not necessarily best friends, but the rancor, the bitterness, the resentment have all given way to a livable friendliness and a realization, once again, why we had initially been attracted to one another. For me, it has become very clear that the role this person played in my life was fundamental not only to my evolving development, but also to my growth into higher consciousness. It was not he, himself who played this role, as much as our interaction,

and my subsequent reaction to that. Does he feel the same way about me? Has he also grown in such a fashion? Only he could answer that question.

It's a Full-Time Job

At some point you have to realize and assimilate that becoming conscious and aware is not something you do on Sundays, or in a weekend workshop, or when you feel relaxed, or during a week-long (or even month-long) retreat. *This – becoming conscious and staying conscious, is a full-time job.* Once you are embarked on that path, and having undertaken the decision to dedicate yourself to it, every day, all day, or as often as you can manage to remember to do so, it will eventually become second nature in the sense that you will no longer have to think about doing it.

At the beginning if you are angered by someone, you will need to remember to remain conscious in order to be aware of the fact that you do, in fact, have choices about how you react to this situation. As you grow in becoming accustomed to living consciously, if another person angers you, there is no need to even think about it, because as the anger begins its first nano-second ascent into your being, you are already scanning for other choices that serve you better, choices that you prefer simply because they allow you to remain in a more balanced inner state.

Making Conscious Choices: When Do I Practice Being Conscious?

That means that especially at the beginning you will need to make the conscious choice of how much *intention* you will put into paying *attention* to what it is you are thinking, feeling, doing, and saying. If you don't make such a conscious choice, and begin to apply some discipline in order to bring about this process, not much will happen. As this becomes more ingrained, more of a habit, you will notice that it soon requires less of an effort. It begins to become automatic. Do you remember when you learned how to drive a car? Wasn't it confusing? Mind-boggling? The number of things you had to remember to be aware of? The rear-view mirror, the clutch, the brake, the *road*, the side mirror, traffic all around you, the dashboard indicators, and so on. It might have seemed almost like a nightmare at the beginning, and even if it didn't, it certainly *took all of your* attention. But only for a time. It is something you now do without constantly needing to think about it, or reminding yourself about it.

And so it is with becoming conscious. You need to continually remind yourself about paying attention to it. At *the beginning that is precisely what is required. You need to constantly remind yourself in order to remain conscious, or to pull yourself back into consciousness, into awareness.*

Even if you have to resort to tricks such as sticking post-it notes up on your bathroom mirror and in the kitchen on the fridge, or your laptop monitor, or putting paper clips in your pockets so that when you feel them, and ask yourself what they are doing there, you remember to remember to remain conscious or to return to consciousness. Some people put a small smooth pebble in their change purse, so that when they see it, they are reminded to remember to be aware, others set the alarm on their mobiles to vibrate once an hour, or set the kitchen timer in a similar fashion, simply to use any method that works to help you remain conscious, or if you've slipped back into blindness, to help you come back from there.

Our normal waking consciousness, rational consciousness as we call it, is but one special type of consciousness, whilst all about it, parted from it by the filmiest of screens, there lie potential forms of consciousness entirely different.
William James

However, at the beginning, as you make a conscious choice to follow this process, you will also begin to realize the absolute need for you to decide to become totally responsible for yourself, you may wish to read the chapter on responsibility. And in so doing, you will realize that:

- *It is not enough to go to a seminar and get all excited with an high-octane adrenaline rush brought on by a particularly inspirational speaker.*
- *It is not enough to read yet another book that makes you feel so wonderful while you read it because it addresses all those issues that you so much want to work on.*
- *It is not enough to participate in yet another interactive and experiential workshop that blows your mind because of how you feel when you are performing whatever it is that the workshop is about.*

None of this is enough *unless* you also decide to take all these wonderful things that you are hearing, reading, and participating in, *and make use of them throughout your day, every day, to the end of your life.*

The Road to Inner Freedom

Many, if not most of my clients would complain that when we discuss methods by which they can find greater inner freedom and inner peace, it sounds like *such hard work*. They tell me that it's all very well for me to talk about it, since I've been doing this for such a long time, but that for them it is just going to take so long and be so hard.

In some ways they are right. None of this work is possible without some dedication and discipline. As discussed in other parts of this book, I often liken it to developing biceps and triceps in a weak or flaccid arm. In order to see some change, you need to be lifting weights or going to the gym on a regular basis for perhaps three months. You have to be consistent, and you have to believe - during those early days and weeks - that even though it appears that nothing is changing, that *something is indeed changing, and that you will soon see the desired results.* How long will it take the mind to make this change (as opposed to the muscles in the example)? If you keep at it, it is possible to see important changes in your reactions in as little as 21 days. We talk about becoming aware of the self and its reactions, making conscious choices at each step of the way *that are good for you on an energetic level* and choosing responsibility for the self in all senses of the word. These choices may not be the easiest or most immediately pleasing ones, but they *are* the choices that will *ultimately* give you the greatest sense of satisfaction with yourself.

When we arrive at this point, some clients then protest, indicating that there is no *proof* that the end result will give them what they are seeking (inner freedom and peace in their lives and relationships). But the fact is that I and untold others (and this number has grown enormously on a global scale over the past decades) vouch for it due to the effect it has had in our own lives. There are many books about this subject, and more and more volumes and much empirical research in the burgeoning field of neuroscience and neuroplasticity that indicate exactly what a practice of mindfulness does to our brain and our sense of well-being.

> *The world is not a problem; the problem is your unawareness.*
> Bhagwan Shree Rajnesh

By being mindful, or *paying attention with intention* over a period of only a few minutes every day, focusing on your breath, on your body as it moves or sits, on what you are seeing and what you *could* – if you so decide - feel gratitude for, etc., you begin to become aware of your awareness, and in this process specific sections of the brain are activated. Studies show that this process, a *state* of mind that you work on *with effort*, becomes a *trait*, a long-term aspect of your way of being that then *happens without effort*, and whose benefits cause you to, as evidenced by UCLA professor of psychiatry Daniel Siegel:

- Develop a greater capacity to regulate your body (for example, blood pressure and immune system improve
- Develop compassion by attuning to yourself and others in deeper and more meaningful ways. This also goes to developing a sense of oneness, as discussed in the chapter *Intermingled Molecules: We Are All One*
- Develop a willingness to approach, as opposed to withdraw from things. In other words, you regulate your affective states better and are able to engage with others in healthy ways
- Develop the ability to lessen and eventually extinguish fear as it arises
- Develop the capacity to pause before you act or react; you think about your options and choose the most adaptive, so you are developing a flexibility in your responses
- Develop the ability to have greater insight into yourself
- Develop greater empathy
- Develop a higher sense of morality in your life
- You may even be able to develop greater access to your intuition, which is fundamentally your body's wisdom, especially if we remember that our *gut* intuition and our *heart* intuition stem from, as discussed in the chapter on life meaning with regards to our second and third brains, the fact that we have billions of neural cells all throughout our body, and not just in the brain that resides in our skull.

All of these benefits – brought about as studies have demonstrated – thanks to the practice of mindfulness, are similar benefits to those that may also potentially be achieved through other mechanisms as evidenced by Buddhist monks practicing deep meditation over a period of decades.

Implementing mindfulness is not very difficult at all. Start with small steps. Make a practice of spending 15-20 minutes a day walking mindfully. Become aware of your breath as it comes and goes, the movement of your chest as you breathe, the feeling of your feet inside your shoes, touching the pavement. Become aware of the muscles in your legs as you walk. Become aware of the sun on your face, the wind in your hair, the butterfly that alights on a leaf close by. Each time you forget this, and go off somewhere in your mind, thinking about something that is in the past or in the future, or that creates negative emotions in you, as soon as you realize you've done that, bring yourself back to being aware.

As you do this over and over for a few minutes every day, you will soon notice that the practice has flowed over into many other areas of your life during many other moments of your day. This means that you will have begun to notice elements of your "now" moments in awareness more and more frequently throughout the course of your day, as opposed to almost solely being caught up in the tyranny of your mindless thoughts. *That is the beginning of being truly aware.*

Choose to Internalize Becoming Aware

What happens when you begin to become conscious and aware of the self? These are the basic concepts we discussed in the chapter on thoughts.

Your thoughts may come of their own inner volition without your own proactive participation in their evolution. They may take you here and there, tossing and turning your emotions, depending on what these thoughts are about. You may find yourself laughing at remembering your niece walking for the first time, every so often plopping down on a padded diapered bottom when she lost her balance, and standing up again, or you may feel pain, or even cry, as you hear the bittersweet lyrics of a love song and remember the lover that abandoned you, and yet in the very next moment you may be frozen with fear as you wonder how you will pay for your bills at the end of the month, or how you will possibly be able to learn all you have to learn in order to pass the exams at the end of the semester. Just as quickly, you may recall you are due to leave on a tropical vacation in two days and that suffuses you with joy.

All of that has been mental activity. There has been little or no awareness, other than awareness of the fact that you felt like laughing, crying, or that you were afraid or happy. *But there was no awareness that you could have had a hand in all of this.* In other words, you could choose where your thoughts were going to take you. You could, therefore, choose whether you wanted to experience the above-described emotions or not. How's that for a good idea?

But in order for that to happen, you would need to begin to bolster this state of awareness, encourage and foster it as much as possible in your daily life in order to make it become second nature. Generally speaking, we are not *aware* in this sense, generally speaking we do allow our thoughts to come and go willy-nilly, and hence, generally speaking, our lives are lived as though we were leaves in the wind, where we are blown here and there by whatever thoughts we may be harboring, but that we have not chosen.

One of the elements of becoming aware is that you become capable of *choosing your thoughts*, of choosing what you decide to focus on, and therefore, of choosing - in a much greater way than you do with mere mental activity - the manner in which your life unfolds and *how you feel about everything that forms part of your life*. In other words, when you are aware, your feelings are no longer decided by your thoughts or by what happens, but by the attitude you choose to take – from a position of awareness - about what happens and by the blind or reactive thoughts you consciously choose to have.

Another one of the elements of becoming aware is that you become capable of *living in the now*, by being present when you do anything, whether it's walking on the beach, driving the car to work, picking up some groceries at the store, or hosting a tea party for dolls with your daughter. In other words, you are fully and consciously aware of what you are doing at every moment, including things like your body's sensations, as well as your thoughts and feelings. Being so aware brings you totally into the present moment.

How you do it is your business - even *whether* you do it, is your business - but *these are some of the best roads to inner freedom and peace.*

Consciousness is a full-time job. Until you realize this, until you internalize it, until you decide to make this realization a central and fundamental part of your life, *and then act upon it*, becoming conscious - and living a conscious life - will elude you and slip from your grasp over and over again, just as wisps of fog over the sea evanesce in the morning light.

When you do things from your soul,
you feel a river moving in you, a joy.
Jalal al-Din Muhammad Rumi

SECTION TWO

SETTING THE STAGE FOR FREEDOM

Chapter Five

Choice:
Portal to Freedom

The last of the human freedoms is to choose one's attitude
in any given set of circumstances.
Viktor Frankl

Whenever I tell someone who is beginning the process of self-understanding, growth, taking responsibility for the self and hence rewiring the soul and reconnecting to the inner self, that we always, always, always have a choice, I frequently get a look of pain, sometimes a look of doubt, and most of all, a look of stalwart denial. Each chapter of this book is so deeply intertwined with all the other chapters – if you have the patience to read through them all – that at the end you will come to the very clear understanding, that what you do to change one aspect of yourself, immediately impacts on all others. If you decide to become conscious in one area of your life, you will see the overlapping of that same awareness in most other areas of your life. If you decide to look at the pain in one sector of your life – perhaps the most important sector of pain, the one that is causing you the greatest difficulty, then quite shortly you will find that anything else in your life that causes you discomfort, even if it's not the same measure of pain as in that deep, black pit of primordial pain, can be dealt with in ways that you have now learned to use for that other, deeper pain. Because of that, and I've said it elsewhere in this book, and will continue to say it: once you recognize that you *always* have a choice, *you can no longer blame anything on something outside of you*. And that is why many people don't like – at least at first glance – the idea of always having a choice and they will give you the wildest excuses for not having such a choice in *their particular circumstances*.

Here are some typical excuses:

- If my daughter talks to me that way, I have no choice but to be angry with her
- If my wife flirts with the football jock at the firm's annual Christmas dinner, I have no choice but to take her back home before she makes a total fool out of both of us, or to retaliate the next day by not talking to her, or by flirting with my department's new red-headed assistant
- If my local team sales leader drops production, I have no choice but to give him a stiff warning
- If another driver cuts me off in traffic, I have no choice but to get very angry at him and at the situation
- If I have been waiting for over ten minutes for the phone company customer service representative to get back on the line with me, who then doesn't even apologize for making me wait so long, I have no choice but to let him know in no uncertain terms, what I think of him *and* the company he works for
- I have no choice about my emotions (see also the chapter on emotions) ... how could I, after what has been done to me?
- I have no choice about my religious attitudes ... it's absolutely clear to me that my church, my religion, is the only right one
- I have no choice about my political attitudes
- I have no choice about my financial attitudes

A great deal of this comes from – as does so much else – our socialization, the way we were raised, our parents' attitudes, the socio-economic strata from which they themselves came, the neighborhood, culture, and the particular society in which we were raised, not to mention the religion, the ethnicity, the language, the country, even the continent. We could furthermore talk about things like whether the language we spoke in our parents' home was the dominant language of the culture in which we were raised, or about our birth order in the family (as opposed to our siblings), what our parents had achieved professionally and financially and socially by the time we were born (as opposed to our siblings), and the kind of relationship they had with their own parents and extended family.

The *reasons* for our belief that we do not have a choice are myriad, but *none* of them is truly valid. We need only look at some prime examples of our fellow humans to understand the kind of choice we always have, *no matter what*. These are some of my favorites:

- Nelson Mandela – most of the world knows that he was imprisoned by the South African apartheid regime for 28 years, much of that time in Robben Island. Mandela was a lawyer condemned to hard labor due to his outspoken beliefs, and allowed only rare visitors. He could have become bitter, vengeful, angry and full of hatred. Instead, when he was released, he forgave. Instead of seeking war against those who had incarcerated him, he sought peace. And so the world has not only a modern democracy, but also a shining example of what it means to always have a choice! He said: *For to be free is not merely to cast off one's chains, but to live in a way that respects and enhances the freedom of others.*

- Alexsandr Solzhenitsyn – this Russian author, recipient of the 1970 Nobel Prize in Literature, spent ten years of his life doing hard labor in the Gulag, where the Russian labor camps were found. He was sent there due to his political ideas, and yet nevertheless he found it in his heart to forgive, once he was released, to continue to write, and to live a life that proves that he believed in always having a choice! Solzhenitsyn carried on writing extensively after his release, living first in the USA, and then returning to Russia, but always as an example of someone who decided not to take the obvious choice: bitterness, hatred, and a desire for revenge, and instead opted to realize that there are other choices! He said: *a man is happy so long as he chooses to be happy.*

- Viktor Frankl – a Viennese psychiatrist imprisoned in Auschwitz where he lost his wife and almost all other members of his immediate family to the gas chambers. While in Auschwitz, and unaware of those facts, his life was nevertheless horrendous (he describes some of the events during this time in his renowned *Man's Search For Meaning*), and he realized it was *up to him* to have an inner attitude that would allow him to survive, to get from where he was to the other side of the atrocity and the horror, in order to be able to tell the world about it. Indeed, he wrote: *"If a prisoner felt that he could no longer endure the realities of camp life, he found a way out in his mental life– an invaluable opportunity to dwell in the spiritual domain, the one that the SS were unable to destroy. Spiritual life strengthened the prisoner, helped him adapt, and thereby improved his chances of survival."* He gave his life a meaning by so doing, and gave himself a choice that went far beyond feeling bitter, hateful, and desiring revenge. He chose differently because he saw he had an inner choice despite the onerous external circumstances. He said: *The one thing you can't take away from me is the way I choose to respond to what you do to me. The last of one's freedoms is to choose one's attitude in any given circumstance.*

- Aimée Mullins – while this young woman, born in 1976, is from a totally different generation than the above-mentioned men, and furthermore, was never imprisoned as opposed to what happened to each of them – she nonetheless overcame tremendous odds by realizing she had a choice. In her case, her choice had more to do with *how she perceived herself* and less to do with not choosing bitterness or hatred and revenge. Aimée is a double amputee, having lost both of her legs just under the knee as a child, because of missing fibula bones at birth. Despite that, she not only competed in the 100-meter dash and long jump competitions at the 1996 summer Paralympics in Atlanta, but also has graced the cover of magazines, and presents frequently as a motivational speaker on www.ted.com as well as others. When she was still very young, she was able to see that she had a choice about the manner in which she viewed herself: she could choose to see herself as a victim, as a disabled person, with limited possibilities in life, or she could choose to see herself as strong, vital, and with much to give others through her example. And so she has! She has said: *Confidence is the sexiest thing a woman can have. It is much sexier than any body part.*

- Christopher Reeve – known by the world of the 80's as Superman, was cut down in his prime due to a fall from a horse. He became a quadriplegic from one second to the next. Quite some time after it had happened, I read that for the first six months after the accident, he did not want to live. But then something changed. He made new choices. And although I don't know this, I have often imagined that precisely because he had become such an international icon during his days of flying through the cinematic skies in his persona as Superman, he was able to speak to so many with the courage he *chose* to bring forth, about his dilemma, about stem cell research, and ultimately, simply about showing courage in the face of adversity. We might even say that the rewiring of his own soul played a role in the manner in which he made new choices to become the man we began to become accustomed to seeing in his wheelchair on some stage or another, speaking about some topic, inspiring us, all around the world. It was his choice to do this as opposed to choosing victimhood and bitterness. He said: *I refuse to allow a disability to determine how I live my life. I don't mean to be reckless, but setting a goal that seems a bit daunting actually is very helpful toward recovery.*

▪ Sabriye Tenberken – you would never believe that Sabriye is blind. She was born in Cologne, Germany and at age 13 became blind from a retinal disease. Nevertheless, if you were to visit her in Tibet, where she now lives, you would simply not know that she is blind because she rides horses, she describes whatever she is talking about by its color: a blue-tinted wall, or a purple flower, and she even runs down stairs in the school she has brought into being for visually impaired children in Lhasa, the capital of Tibet. Tenberken holds a master's degree in Tibetology at Bonn University and *created* Tibetan Braille. When she was unable to get a job with any of the NGO's she applied to in order to do fieldwork in Tibet due to her blindness, she decided to travel to Lhasa along with her partner. After reams of red tape, she finally obtained permission to open her school for the blind children of Tibet and raised some much-needed seed money by selling her autobiography. And thanks to all of this phenomenal - what most of us would consider super-human effort - she has changed the lives of dozens of children without vision in Tibet, who had been marginalized, locked into dark rooms, and forgotten by society – even *their* society.

At her school the children not only learn Tibetan, Chinese and English, as well as all manner of practical skills like learning how to use computers and even making beds, but these children are also given dignity by Sabriye and her staff. Tibetans often consider blindness to be a punishment for bad behavior in other lives, and further, due to the fact that because of the high-altitude exposure to the sun, there is a rather high rate of eye disease in the country, it means that this geological factor coupled with the religious belief, signifies that Tibetans had no idea what to do with their blind. As Tenberken tells it, sometimes children would be tied to a bed for years, some had never been taught to walk, and therefore the school that she founded, restored dignity to many of these children. She also teaches blind adults to plant vegetables and raise animals and clearly believes that there should be no limits for the blind. What an incredible way – by doing so much for so many others in such a proactive and creative fashion - of overcoming her own adversity! And what a way of recognizing that we *always have a choice*! She said: *A lot of people say I can't do it because I'm blind or because I have red hair or because my feet are too big. Get the right team around you, don't set boundaries and go for it.*

- One final example: Bethany Hamilton, born in 1990, a skilled Hawaiian surfer beginning to compete, when at age 13 her left arm was ripped off by a shark. The arm was gone. But one month later Bethany was back in the water, teaching herself how to surf with only one arm, and in 2005, she took 1st place in the NSSA National Championships, a goal she had been trying to achieve since *before* the shark attack. What did she choose? It's obvious! She said: *People can do whatever they want if they just set their heart to it, and just never give up, and just go out there and do it.*

Remember when you are trying to change something about yourself in order to come closer to that inner self, that soul self, that loving self, among the many helpful things you can do in this process is to look at others that you could emulate. You can look at others that you admire. You can look at others that have done something that you have not yet done, but would like to (not necessarily the same thing, but the *spirit* of the thing), and you can bring their particular situation to mind whenever you find yourself in a difficult spot, in order to give yourself not only some inspiration and motivation, but also to give yourself courage. *What you admire in another lies within you in its nascent state.* So bring it forth, by recognizing the possibility and by giving yourself new choices!

Having choices means that you have freedom. If you believe that the only way to react in a given situation is the one you have always chosen (never mind that it perhaps has never served you well), then you have no freedom. Once you begin to see that there *are* choices, no matter what, you see that your repertoire of reaction has just broadened, the recognition of your freedom to choose the one that serves you best can be electrifying. Choosing the one that serves you best doesn't mean that you choose one that is egotistical, or that causes you to win and others to lose. Rather, it is a choice that allows you to maintain a sense of inner balance, of inner well-being: it's a choice that is good for your inner self, your soul. And here's the clincher: if it's good for *your* inner self, by ripple effect, it will be good for *all* those whose lives you touch.

We choose our joys and sorrows long before we experience them.
Kahlil Gibran

Here are some examples of how to choose differently:

- Choosing to focus on having survived a bad situation when you are angry at a driver who nearly caused you to collide with a truck, instead of choosing anger, allows you to remain – despite the scare such a near-collision may have occasioned – in a state of inner balance and inner well-being. Under those circumstances you may also choose to continue enjoying your day as opposed to being furious at the other driver's carelessness, and as opposed to telling others about your near mishap over and over again during the remainder of the day, and in so doing, reliving it, and thus strengthening more of the choice for anger

- Choosing to focus on the love that you feel for your recalcitrant child when there is a terrible quarrel or outburst on his part, instead of choosing anger or your need to be right, will not only allow you to deal with the situation in a much more calm manner, but it will also allow you to remain in a state of inner balance and inner well-being. In fact, choosing to focus on love in any difficult situation, will always help you deal with it in a more balanced manner that promotes well-being on both sides. Just remember, choosing to focus on love does *not mean forgetting about healthy boundaries* (also see the chapter on boundaries).

- Choosing to focus on the possibility that the clerk who is inattentive and rude may be having a bad day, instead of choosing anger or a need to assert your importance vis-à-vis the person whose job it is to serve you, will not only allow you to deal with the situation in a more healthy fashion, while protecting your boundaries, but it will also allow you to remain in a state of inner balance and inner well-being, and will ensure that your day continues in a positive fashion.

- Choosing to focus on maintaining your inner sense of strength and desire for growth and understanding when you are given a cancer diagnosis, as well as choosing to focus on things such as getting a second opinion, surrounding yourself with friends who continue to treat you as a vibrant human being, as opposed to someone around whom they now must tiptoe with grave faces, instead of choosing fear and a need to talk about it so much that your entire life becomes about this cancer, will allow you to remain in – or move towards - a state of inner balance and inner well-being. And such a state will be much more conducive to helping your body heal itself from the cancer than fear or worry or obsession will!

- Choosing to focus on polishing your CV, or brainstorming with trusted friends, while simultaneously choosing to maintain a motivated and inspired inner state (perhaps by listening to some of the hundreds and thousands of videos and audios available freely on the internet by inspired speakers (see the appendix for suggestions) when you lose your job, or earn too little to make it to the end of the month, instead of choosing desperation and worry and fear, will allow you to remain in – or move towards - a state of inner balance and inner well-being, that will, in turn, potentially be more conducive to finding a solution to your problem.

- Choosing to focus on what being abandoned by your spouse or lover might mean in your life, as well as trying to understand exactly why you feel you cannot live without this person, as opposed to concentrating on the pain that his/her departure has caused you. Does it mean, for example, that you should examine the possibility that you might be better off filling your *own needs*, as opposed to getting them fulfilled by another? Or could it mean that you are leaving your well-being in the hands of the beloved, as opposed to taking responsibility for it yourself? Or does it mean that the only *real* meaning in your life was your relationship with this person? So instead of choosing to focus on the terrible need and emptiness you may feel inside, due to being abandoned, or the bitterness, or anger, or pain that might arise, and focusing instead on what this might signify in the larger picture of your life, will allow you (or help to bring you on the road to allowing yourself) to remain in a state of inner balance and inner well-being and eventually to another relationship that will likely transpire differently because of your new focus. Remember: choosing to focus on pain or blame takes you exactly nowhere of value.

Choose to ask yourself – in any situation at all – whether you have other choices of reaction (inner or outer) that might serve you better than the one you are heading for. Simply by doing this you place yourself in a position of being able to *observe* what is going on: not only the situation, but *yourself*. And this observing of yourself, is what takes you far enough away from the situation to be able to simply allow it. It is what it is. Accept it for what it is *in this moment*. (Also see the chapter on awareness in order to better understand this concept of observing yourself via the practice of mindfulness.)

> *Heaven on earth is a choice you must make,*
> *not a place we must find.*
> Wayne Dyer

Eckhart Tolle tells a magnificent story of Paramahansa Yogananda who was traveling around the country lecturing. He had many followers, some of whom came to listen to him over and over again. One day he said to the crowd that he would tell them the secret of his happiness because he felt they had not yet – despite hearing him speak so frequently – understood what that secret was. He told them that it consists in *not minding what happens*. Not minding what happens means you are capable of letting it be, observing it, riding the wave, so to speak. He also said *No matter what you are doing, keep the undercurrent of happiness. Learn to be secretly happy within your heart in spite of all circumstances.* So hard. So simple. So wonderful once you get it!

Allowing the situation to be doesn't necessarily mean that you find it acceptable or appropriate. Perhaps your business partner has absconded with all the money you had put into the company account. Perhaps your spouse was unfaithful. Perhaps your best friend just refused to offer you moral support in a difficult situation. Nevertheless, accepting that *this is what it is* will allow you to find a place within you where you can first – before you do anything else, find inner equanimity, inner balance, inner well-being because of how you choose to react, *before* you do anything else, such as call your lawyer, the police, or however it is that you decide you need to handle the specific situation. Simply because something potentially disastrous has happened does not necessarily mean that you now need to react in a way, both inside and out, that will compound the disaster. If you maintain your eyes on yourself, in as conscious a fashion as you can muster, you will have a much greater possibility of making good choices.

A lifetime is composed of choices. Each choice leads to a probable different possibility or reality. Not choosing is also a choice. The choices an individual makes literally set the scene for much of the joy and misery that subsequently take place in that life. But none of this is possible without consciousness and awareness. When bad things happen, by remaining blind, unconscious, asleep and unaware, you have no choice but to react the way you always do when bad things happen. And that is generally a choice that does not serve you.

How can you begin? It really is very simple. Begin now. Begin today. With whatever choices you have to make for the rest of this day. Perhaps they are only food choices. Be aware of what they are and what consequences they may occasion. Are they good choices? Or perhaps it would be a good idea to become aware of your television viewing choices. Become aware of whether the length of time you watch is good for you. Perhaps cutting down on that amount of time, and using part of it to exercise might be a better choice. Or to listen to something motivational or uplifting and inspiring for a portion of that time. Or perhaps the type of show you watch is not the best choice. Is it a horror movie? Become aware of what it is about the movie that attracts you. Surely you are not an evil sadist who would like to saw innocent *live* people in two as they scream for mercy. But perhaps you feel more alive with the adrenaline rush such a film gives you. Become aware of that. Recognize it. Ask yourself why that is so. Perhaps you need to put more life into your life. Or put more meaning into it (see the chapter on meaning). Or perhaps your only choice today is to merely *be aware* of the fact that you have these choices, and that you could, in fact, change something about your routine.

Another choice you might do well in becoming aware of today is whether you are bored. If so, why? What is it about your life that causes you to be bored? Could you be making different choices about your activities or about the people you spend time with in order to be less bored? Or perhaps you could become aware of the fact that you are addicted – in a sense – to books of this nature (addicted to books like this very book, that you are holding in your hands right now). You read them all, but you make no changes. You allow yourself to be carried along by the energy of the book, but then do not bother to implement any of the necessary changes. Why? Become aware of what is happening. Are you too lazy to do the work it implies? Or frightened because of what the changes such work on yourself might imply for your life? Perhaps you would lose a portion of your identity that is used to being a victim, or lonely, or socially phobic, or always angry about your circumstances. (Caroline Myss has written extensively – and brilliantly – about this topic and used the term "woundology"). There could be any number of reasons. Simply become aware of what is going on and then become aware of the fact that you have other choices.

As you do this on a daily basis, you will – if you don't stop going through this inner process as described in the last couple of paragraphs – in a relatively short amount of time begin to make some new choices. And as you do that, other things will also begin to change in your life. Others will notice some of these changes, and some of it will have a ripple effect on their own lives. What a gift to give those whose lives you touch!

Imagine a world in which parents taught their children about this kind of awareness. Imagine a world in which parents themselves were so aware that when they had any kind of difficulty or confrontation with their offspring, their reaction would come from a place of total awareness, and hence of total choice. Do you understand that strife would simply cease to exist? Imagine a world in which adolescents (or anyone else) would feel attracted to each other and have sex, but choosing to do so from a place of total awareness. Such a place of awareness would help them make choices of safe sex or no sex. Do you understand there would no longer be unwanted pregnancies, and hence no need for abortions (at least not due to unwanted pregnancies)? Nor would there be STD's occasioned by such adolescent sex. Imagine a world in which people would look at substances such as alcohol and drugs or other addictions such as gambling from a position of total awareness and hence of total choice. Do you understand that choices to abuse substances would no longer be made? Imagine a world in which people in that position of total awareness and total choice would find themselves in situations where up to now they might have lied. Do you understand there would no longer be any desire to choose to lie about anything? Imagine a world in which heads of state and other governmental leaders themselves were the offspring of parents who had taught them about awareness and choice and therefore would come to any type of discussion or global community intervention from a position of total awareness and hence of total choice. From such a position of total awareness and choice bankers, capitalists, and anyone directly or indirectly involved in the world of global (or regional) finance, would choose to make choices that serve all, rather than only a few to the detriment of others, heads of government would not choose to pass laws that serve only the few, and developers would not choose to rape the land in order to become wealthy. Do you understand that strife, warfare, bloodshed, genocide, rape, pillage, human trafficking, child labor and so on would simply cease to exist under circumstances of total awareness on the individual level?

Do you also understand that under such a situation of total awareness and choice on the individual level, affecting in turn the community, national, and global levels, choices to spend billions on the development of arms or chemical warfare instead of on eradicating hunger, poverty and lack of clean water and education would be made very differently than they are now? Is this an impossible ideal? Not at all. It merely requires that we all individually do our utmost to become fully aware, and in so doing, recognize our choices. The more that do so, the more others will be pulled in. The world can be changed one individual at a time! And the more each individual does, the more all of us will understand that *we are all one.*

When only one changes, others are affected. When many change, the geometric expansion of those that are affected grows immeasurably.

Choice – and the more we are willing to embrace our right to choose and see alternatives at every turn of the road – brings us closer and closer to the richness of ourselves, to the fullness of responsibility we have for ourselves, and hence brings us closer and closer to a manner of inner freedom that those who choose not to choose will never taste.

I believe that we are solely responsible for our choices, and we have to accept the consequences of every deed, word, and thought throughout our lifetime.
Elizabeth Kubler-Ross

Chapter Six

Boundaries:
Path to Empowerment

Please all and you will please none.
Aesop

When someone steps all over your boundaries, you have not yet learned how to love yourself. When someone steps all over your boundaries, it may be that you learned that to be treated like that was acceptable behavior and so when you accept it – even to this day in your adult (or teenage) life - you are unaware of the fact that it is not right. Generally, when someone steps all over your boundaries, the love you learned about as a child or young person was somehow dysfunctional. Mainly the dysfunctional part had to do with you, even though it came about through others. In other words, you learned how to love yourself poorly, or not at all, and most particularly, you learned that it was ok for others to trespass your boundaries and to show you unhealthy types of love, such as being neglected, or being shown uncaring, cold, rejecting, manipulative or abusive love. You might have understood such behavior as love, but it was not. You might have believed you had to accept such behavior, but you don't.

You might have believed that there was little you could do about it, but you can. Much of this depends on your ability and willingness to learn how to love yourself.

Another thing that happened was that you did not learn to pay attention to your body's signals. I call those signals emails from your body to you. In other words one part of your innate wisdom (your body) is trying to communicate with you, is trying to give you some important information about something that is going on, and because you are being taught (in a dysfunctional fashion) that what is going on is ok, you learn to ignore those signals. Frequently the signals come from the solar plexus, the area in the vicinity of your stomach, and what you get is a slightly uncomfortable, or on occasion, even painful twisting in that region *when something is happening that is not right for you*. (Frequently small children who complain of a stomach ache when they are meant to go to school, in actual fact are feeling this twisting inside, although as opposed to having unhealthy boundaries, they are probably feeling it due to anxiety or stress. We may take them to the doctor to check them out and then tell them that it's nothing, and so they too, albeit for other reasons, learn to ignore the signals their bodies are sending them, because no one addressed the anxiety that had occasioned the painful tummy ache).

In the case of poor boundaries, your body is calling attention to the fact that something is going on that is not good for you and it is trying to tell you that you need to – ideally – take some steps. If you were to take those steps, you would be setting up healthy boundaries and hence beginning to show yourself that you care about yourself. By not taking those steps, you feel the twisting or wrenching, you learn to ignore it, even though you recognize it easily when it is described to you, and you do nothing about it. Or you may self-medicate (see also the chapter on self-soothing) with any number of remedies: food, sex, alcohol, drugs, prescription medication, self-harming, gambling, risky sex, boundless shopping or socializing, etc. The feeling you get in that region of your body is similar to the twisting that comes when you are driving down the highway and suddenly you hear police sirens approaching behind you. Adrenaline surges and until the police car has passed you, speeding on to pull someone else over, you believe you have done something wrong and that you are about to get a ticket. The twisting in your gut comes from a combination of the adrenaline surge and the fear (or concern) about getting the ticket. It subsides rapidly once you realize it had nothing to do with you, but in the case of boundaries being trespassed in your life, the twisting does not subside so readily, because the problem has not been solved. Furthermore, typically you are not even properly and consciously aware of it.

One of the problems with having poor, or unhealthy boundaries, is the fact that even when you realize that something is not right, and that perhaps something should be said or done, there can be such paralyzing fear associated with the action, that it comes to nothing anyway. The fear connects to feelings of being unloved or being even less loved than already. In other words, and herein lie the shackles that bind you to poor boundaries, if you accept whatever is being dished out (and we are talking here about any kind of unacceptable behavior, but not necessarily violent abuse, although that may also form part of the equation), you believe you have a chance of continuing to be accepted or loved by the other party. Perhaps only a small chance, but a small chance is better than no chance which is what would happen, or so you believe, if you were to say something. At least you will get some crumbs.

And so paralysis sets in. And it may set in very early in life. And therefore, by the time you become aware of what has happened, either because you've read something and it rings a bell, or you've attended a workshop, or you've seen a therapist, by this time you are so welded to that behavior that accepts unacceptable things, so welded to the fear of being rejected or cast out, that it becomes a very hard task to begin the process of unraveling this. But here's the good news: it starts and ends with self love. The more you give yourself the chance to love yourself, the more readily you will discard the unhealthy boundaries, no matter where you encounter them in your life.

Loving the self, accepting the self, respecting the self, admiring the self, all of these subjects are discussed in the chapter on self love, and I specifically suggest that if you have recognized yourself in this chapter on boundaries, that you make a particular point to pay special attention to the chapter about self love and take a very close look at it indeed.

Also consider this: imagine you had a six-year-old child of your own gender. Someone is harming your child in some way that is causing discomfort, anxiety, stress, pain (psychological, emotional, or physical). Don't you think you would immediately take measures to protect your child and make it feel *loved*, safe and secure? Don't you think you would immediately reassure your child and let it know how much you love it? This behavior of yours, so natural and obvious, is *precisely the behavior you need to adopt with yourself*.

Each time you feel the twisting, tell yourself that if you don't speak up about it, *you are choosing to show yourself that you don't care enough about yourself, that you don't love yourself enough to do this*. And that is why changing this – even in the smallest ways – can bring you quickly to a position of showing yourself that you love yourself and thereby create healthy boundaries for yourself.

Here are some examples of things that others do to us that are a clear transgression of healthy boundaries:

- They keep us on the phone for hours on end with their problems, and because we believe we are their good friend, we believe we must be there for them and listen to all of this, despite the fact that we neglect our own families, or duties, or responsibilities, in order to do so, and despite the fact that we are emotionally and energetically drained when they finally finish
- They expect us to have similar opinions to their own, especially about religion and politics, and especially if they are our spouse
- They expect us to give them things, perhaps not material things such as money or objects, but things we may have worked for during a long time, such as research, detailed knowledge about an obscure subject that was rather complicated to learn, and now they simply assume you will pass it on, some networking or email contacts, or some marketing ideas, or some internet tips, free services (whatever our profession happens to be: dental work, plumbing, French classes, etc.) and they may expect this, simply because they know us socially
- They expect us to spend all our free time with them (especially if they are our partner – see also the chapter on relationships and neediness)
- They expect us to make them happy (see also the chapter on happiness and responsibility)
- They expect us to give up our own needs in order to fill the "family's needs" (clearly *both* needs are important, but if you have poor boundaries, you will not see this), telling us we are selfish if we refuse
- They shout at us
- They are verbally abusive
- They make dates with us and then cancel at the last minute (old friends, new lovers, it makes no difference: either way, by not saying anything, we are manifesting poor boundaries)
- They are overly critical
- They are unkind (this, and some of the other examples given here, may appear to be simply a lack of consideration, and while it is, indeed, a lack of consideration, this becomes a factor in poor boundaries, when you don't say something about it, when it is clearly something that happens frequently)
- They interrupt all the time
- They lie to us
- They are unfaithful to us
- They use us
- They treat us to long silences if we do not behave the way they want us to (these silences have been known to last up to three

weeks and more, and the main reason why the person who uses them does so, is *because up to now, they have given good results!*)

- They use their voice in a threatening way
- They are physically abusive
- They use sex as a tool to keep us in line
- They use money as a tool to keep us in line
- They use their approval of us as a tool to keep us in line
- They want us to dress a specific way and if we don't, they show their clear disapproval in some way that impacts on our existence
- They ask us to do their work
- They ask us for new ideas at work and then take them on as their own
- They don't allow enough time for us to complete our tasks
- They ask us for favors that are not appropriate given the nature of our relationship with them (e.g., your boss asks you to house-sit; your friend asks to borrow an exquisite article you have just purchased for a sinful amount of money, and given the extravagant nature of the article, if she wears it, everyone in your circle will recognize it if you ever wear it in future; your sibling who has an extremely poor driving record, asks to borrow your new car, and so on)
- They get annoyed / angry / disappointed / sad with us, if we try to say anything about any part of their behavior that we think is inappropriate
- They drink too much, take drugs, or otherwise exhibit addictive behavior and expect us to tolerate it
- They are emotional and energetic vampires – I wrote an entire article about this which you can read on my website

This list could go on and on. The tentacles of boundaries that are transgressed find their way into every permutation of the fabric of life, and as long as we are unaware of what is going on, as long as our tenuous hold on an inner sense of well-being depends on the approval or love (if this can be called love) of an individual who treats us in such a fashion, we will not change anything. Understand that your inner well-being – in order for it to be *real* inner well-being, needs to depend on you, you need to make yourself responsible for it by beginning the process of self-love, because then you will never depend on anything external to yourself for your sense of well-being. Imagine the freedom! The kind of love you have known to this point will pale in comparison to the quality of love you will encounter thereafter.

If we go for a moment to the premise of the chapter on relationships, that we can grow most quickly through our relationships if we so choose, then clearly in this instance of poor boundaries, if it is your partner who is trespassing boundaries and manifesting unacceptable behavior, once you recognize your role in this particular dance, you will finally be at the beginning of the process of unlearning this behavior. And in so doing, you will grow enormously. And you will find one of the biggest keys to your inner sense of well-being: your love for yourself. And this would have come about in part due to your frustrations with the relationship.

I also want to add something here that many are unaware of: if you have poor boundaries, and if you therefore allow others to step all over them, specifically because you don't love yourself enough to take better care of yourself, it often also means that *you step all over other people's boundaries*. By not respecting yourself in the ways described, you may have difficulty understanding how you need to respect others' boundaries. Perhaps you are not abusive, but you may take up too much of their time with your stories or complaints about your own life. Think: have you noticed that some people seem to be avoiding you? Or perhaps they've cut you out totally? If so, go back over your contact with them. You may need to analyze how you have been dealing with these individuals.

Back to our main topic: What does learning about poor boundaries have to do with rewiring the soul? Or said another way: why does having poor boundaries keep you away from your soul?

The answer is joy.

When you live with joy and in joy, you are connected to your soul. When you accept joy as part of your divine right, you are connected to your soul. As long as you have poor boundaries, joy is typically not a part of your life. When you *do* experience some joy, it generally happens due to external circumstances, in particular those that involve a partner or other individual, as opposed to emanating from you, from your inner self. Therefore, as you resolve this issue, by beginning the process of loving yourself, accepting yourself, respecting yourself, and admiring yourself enough to grow healthier boundaries in your life, you come closer to joy. Loving yourself and joy are concepts that walk hand in hand.

Dealing With Poor Boundaries

When you begin to deal with your own unhealthy boundaries, as stated earlier, you will typically feel fear. You'll feel afraid because:

- You are beginning something new, something that you've never done before, and crossing new thresholds - that cause anyone to leave familiar comfort zones, the status quo of life up to this point – and as such, is almost always a frightening step

- You don't know the reaction the other person will give you
- One of the reactions the other person may give you is the one you have specifically attempted to avoid all your life by accepting unacceptable behavior and that is: disapproval, criticism, rejection, withdrawal of love, tenderness, approval, admiration, etc.
- The prospect of that reaction: rejecting you, laughing at you, not loving you, not approving of you, abandoning you, and so on, is the one that is making your heart beat in fear as you contemplate taking the first step to ending these unhealthy boundaries.

Because this is all so fraught with fear, I often encourage clients to role play the whole event in their minds first. Remember a past occasion where you felt the twisting in your gut because something was not right, but you did or said nothing. Play it out in your mind in front of the mirror, and then role play your new behavior – your new verbal reaction - as it might have been, had you had the courage that day to say something. Your heart may very well beat furiously as you do this, almost as though it were real, imagining what might happen if you actually talk this way when next faced with such a situation.

But here is a wonderful thing: when you do this for the first time – and perhaps you get a negative reaction from the other person, exactly as you fear will happen – *something else will also happen.* For the first time you will have shown that tiny seed inside of yourself that barely loves itself, that you do, finally, love yourself enough in order to do this for yourself, that you respect yourself enough to do it, and so begins a process of growth for that tiny seed that will flourish under this new found love of you for yourself. *You will feel empowered.* You will feel as though something has broken out of a shell, and although fear will still color your decisions, at least you will have experienced one occasion of insisting on healthy boundaries, and you will have also experienced that even when the worst happens, with regards to how the other person reacts, you, nevertheless, feel miraculously stronger.

Here is an exercise that could also have gone into the chapter on loving the self, which may help you begin to care for yourself in the ways we have been discussing here. Variations on this exercise have been around for years, and can be found in many books.

If you have it, take out a photograph of yourself when you were about five or six years old. Next, if you have a child of that age yourself, or friends (or neighbors) with a child that age, have a look – *really* have a look at that young, lovely and wonderful child so that you can appreciate how innocent the eyes, how *small* the child, how much it needs the protection and love of the adults in its life, how fresh the skin, how lovely, beautiful, and wondrous this little person is. If you have no such child in your life, simply have a good look at one in your supermarket, or neighborhood playground or park, etc. This part of the exercise that I have just described about the photograph and the flesh-and-blood child only needs to be done once.

When you have all of that set clearly in your mind, go to your bedroom, or any other place where you will not be disturbed for about five minutes (it's a short exercise, but you should try to do it every day for at least several weeks). Take a cushion, sit down, and place the cushion on your lap. Close your eyes, and in your mind's eye imagine that the cushion is you when you were little. Again, in your mind's eye, imagine hugging your younger self, caressing your own little self's cheek, touching your hair, saying *I love you so very much*, telling your younger self:

- *You are so beautiful / handsome*, in other words telling your younger self what a good-looking child you are.
- *That dress is so pretty / you look so good in that t-shirt* (or whatever might be appropriate, given your gender and your memories of the way you dressed), the point is to *lovingly compliment* something about the way you; i.e., your younger self looks.
- *What a gorgeous drawing … I'm going to put it up on the fridge / what an amazing paper airplane you made / sandcastle you built* or whatever is appropriate, given your memories of what you used to do as a child. The point is to *admire* something you; i.e., your younger self has created.
- *You know, I am always going to take care of you and protect you and never let anything bad happen to you. I'm going to do that because I love you so very much* (the point is to instill a sense of safety in you; i.e., your younger self).
- That's basically it. Now you can hug and kiss your younger self good-bye – in your mind's eye - and say *see you again tomorrow.*

Now here's the important thing: you have just promised your younger self that because of your love for yourself, you will always take care of and protect yourself. So now you have left the room where you did this exercise, and gone back to your normal life. And a few hours later your spouse screams at you … that's just the way your spouse is. Or your teenage son or daughter has just again been rude to you. Or the person you are just beginning to date and with whom you are out having dinner, is checking out all the other men / women who are entering the restaurant, taking his / her eyes off you each time the door opens. And any of the above that apply (or any others you can think of) create that twisting feeling in your gut. *And you do nothing.* What do you think your younger self is going to figuratively say to you tomorrow when you get back together again? *I can't trust you. You promised to take care of me, and look what you did. You let me feel so bad again.*

Let me reiterate this very important thing to understand: when you have poor boundaries you learned at an early age not to "be yourself" because doing that was dangerous. Being yourself might simply have meant expressing dismay, or hurt, or that you didn't like something. What you did instead was to walk on eggshells around certain people, or you pushed yourself into the background in many different ways, in order to mold yourself into whatever you thought you needed to be in order to be accepted, approved of and loved. It was dangerous to truly express yourself (whether that meant showing others that you loved to paint or sing, or whether it meant saying that you preferred not to accompany your parent to the store, or whether it meant that you didn't want to listen to anyone shouting, but couldn't say so), because if you did, you ran the risk – as said – of not being accepted, approved of, and loved. And so you lived in a twilight zone of unease, anxiety, stress, fear where you may have felt many things, *but you most certainly did not feel protected.*

This is what is called learning a dysfunctional form of love. It's also what happens when we don't learn healthy ways to love ourselves. You might say it's a stunting or crippling process of the pure love nature that a child is born with – and lest you think I'm out on a vendetta against parents, please remember to be compassionate. After all, they (your parents, my parents, *and* you and I as parents ourselves) were often not taught any differently when they/we were children.

Now however, when you begin to "grow" your relationship with your younger, stunted self, and you make a promise of taking care of your younger self, protecting it, cherishing it, loving it, *you must keep that promise if you wish your younger self to eventually grow up to where the rest of you is.* And it will only do so, *if it trusts you!* When we fear for our emotional safety, and therefore take on protective measures such as those described above (and there are many other manifestations as well, but in this chapter I am concentrating on poor boundaries), in order to ensure that we receive a modicum of love and approval, or at least avoid outright rejection, the part of us that takes on the protective measures remains in some fashion child-like and stunted, and this is why, when similar buttons are pushed as we grow older and become adults, we may find ourselves reacting in ways that don't seem to be in accord with the rest of our personality.

We may have developed into highly sophisticated, intelligent, cosmopolitan and professionally adept individuals in most other areas of our lives, but in this one – the one where our emotional safety is at risk – we remain somehow childlike, fearful, withdrawn, perhaps even infantile in our reactions to others, at least with regards to how we react when being faced with the fact that our boundaries are being trespassed. Our *emotional self* has not grown up the same way the rest of us has.

Therefore, once you have begun the exercise of meeting with your younger self on a daily basis, it is very important that you begin to take steps to show this anxious, scared, younger part of you that you are not only to be trusted, but that you come through with what you promise. And so, when boundaries are crossed, and when another says or does something that you recognize – among others because of the twisting in your gut – as a crossed boundary that you need to say something about, say it. Just say it. Say *that is not acceptable*. Say it in a courteous tone of voice. Say that you can no longer accept being treated or spoken to this way. And give a consequence if your request is not met. Having established a boundary, a consequence merely says, "If you do not respect this boundary that I have established, then this will happen."

Sometimes "No" has to be so strong that there are many fences around it to make sure it stays "No."
Rebbetzin Chana Rachel Schusterman

Boundaries need not be harsh or resemble an ultimatum, but they might have to, depending on the circumstances, as these examples indicate:

- To a spouse if both work: If you keep refusing to do the marketing, I will not have time to cook dinner and we will have to eat sandwiches (this should only apply if you like sandwiches and the other person does not ... because consequences are not meant to cause *you* problems or difficulties, only the other person ... see the next example in this sense as well).
- To an older teenager: When you smoke marijuana in this house, you place us at legal risk and it is a fire hazard (apart from potential health considerations), so if you do it again, you will not be allowed to use the car for one month, but since I will not be able to drive you around, you will have to walk to school or your other activities, or use public transportation. This is a consequence of some magnitude for your teen, but not for you, because you will not need to chauffeur him/her around to his

scholastic and social activities. If there is no suitable public transportation he/she can use, then this consequence should not be chosen.

- To a person you are dating: When you phone me at the last minute without having previously made plans with me, expecting me to drop everything in order to see you, it makes me feel as though I have no importance in your eyes, so if you do it again, I will not be available to see you. (Note: there is a difference between being spontaneous and being inconsiderate, or taking the other person for granted).

- From one woman to another: When you dump me two hours before a dinner date with me in order to go on a date with a man who has just given you a last-minute call, you make me feel as though you do not respect and value our friendship, so if you do that again, I will have to re-think our relationship.

- To a chronically late employee: When you arrive late, you make the entire production line lose time, so if you continue to do it, I will begin to dock your pay by half hour increments. If it is then repeated, you will lose your job.

- To a partner who lies: When you lie to me, I feel as though you place no importance on my feelings, so if you do that again, I need you to understand that this is a potential deal breaker for me. (Such a drastic consequence assumes you have a history of being told lies by your partner, and you are now beginning the process of setting up healthier boundaries with him/her).

- To an emotionally abusive partner: When you do such-and-such, it is very hurtful to me. If you can understand that, you will also understand that it is not something I will be able to allow you to continue, so if you behave like that again, I will have to do some deep thinking about the future of this relationship.

Whatever you are willing to put up with is exactly what you will have.
Anonymous

Don't forget the basic tenet of establishing boundaries: if consequences are not set up, then there is no boundary. However, you might want to *explain* your feelings to the other person first, as in these examples, in order that he/she understands what the specific behavior does to you, your family, your health, your safety, your business, etc. And be very careful not to fall into the habit of passive aggression, which is one of the most frequently used patterns by individuals with poor boundaries, as it allows them to vent in a fashion, albeit an unhealthy fashion, where they are doing something to let the other know they are not happy about him/her, but they do so underhandedly, without in fact facing the issue at hand.

But let's imagine you just can't say it yet. The ingrained habit of years, perhaps decades, has left you too debilitated – in this sense – to say anything at all. So do this instead, at least at the beginning:

- Immediately after it has happened (the poor boundary that you permitted the other person to trespass), and after you have felt the twisting, and after you have realized you were not capable of saying anything – *yet* – ask yourself if this is how you wish to be treated.
- After you (presumably) tell yourself that you don't want to be treated that way, oblige yourself to look at the fact that it was not right, not acceptable, and that although you were not yet able to speak up in a healthy way about it (i.e., not exploding, or shouting, or crying, but calmly, and indicating a consequence), you are going to *at least* keep your eye very closely on yourself each and every time you *allow* a boundary to be crossed, asking yourself the same question each time. Keep pointing out to yourself that whatever was done or said made you feel awful and that *you no longer wish to feel this way.*
- Keep telling yourself that you want to be able to love yourself enough in order to stop this pattern in your life.
- Practice some role-play, as indicated above, in front of the mirror
- By so doing, you will be looking the facts in the face as opposed to making excuses or covering them up, and that also, is the beginning of the road to loving yourself, and to keeping your promise to your younger self.
- The more you do this, the more you will come closer to finding the courage to speak up, and the more you do this, *even before you speak up*, the more you will realize that you are now invested in protecting your younger self, in openly demonstrating to your younger self how much you love yourself.

Along the way, as you practice the daily exercise with your younger self, you may even find that during an early part of the process, a young child enters your life, perhaps the child of a neighbor, or the child of someone visiting a friend for a period of weeks, or simply someone you already knew, but who now, curiously, grows closer to you. You may notice that you feel a special tenderness for this child that fills you with joy and that brings you closer to your own younger self. After a time it may be that the child begins spending less time with you, perhaps the parents move away, perhaps the child is now in school and has less time, but then it might happen that an older child, perhaps age twelve or so, enters your life. Jung would term this occurrence an outer synchronous event indicating to you that your younger self has begun the process of growth *because it has felt safe and secure enough; protected enough, to do so.* And after a time perhaps the 12-year-old also spends less time with you and now a 16-year-old appears. Again, growth will have taken place on an inner level, and with increasingly incremental steps, gently bringing your younger self to the chronological place at which you currently find yourself.

If such children as described above don't appear, you may have dreams about children of varying ages, symbolizing a similar outer event (the dreams) occurring synchronistically with the inner growth.

Working on boundaries consciously as a tool for growth can bring you a long way, empower you enormously, and bring you much inner peace and freedom. It also helps you come closer to and reconnect with – through the process of loving yourself – your true self, and thereby brings you to this process of rewiring your soul. Remember, inner well-being, love, joy, gratitude and compassion are the roads that take you there.

When your boundaries are continually being stepped on,
It is a clear sign that you do not love yourself.

Chapter 7

Pain & Forgiving:
Loosening the Grip of the Past

*Without forgiveness life is governed by an endless
cycle of resentment and retaliation.*
Roberto Assagioli

Pain is something that not only occurs in your present moment, but frequently links you to your past, as you relive dark moments of your life. If pain only occurred in the present moment it would cause much less havoc. How so? It is in the reliving of your pain that you become stuck in it, that you become addicted to it (more about this "addiction" in a moment), that you are unable to free yourself from it, and therefore a present moment is lived over and over again at another time in your life, when that erstwhile *present* moment has become your past. Because you do this, you become chained to the pain in ways that impede your happiness in the present moment.

In this regard, Chris Griscom, already mentioned in an earlier chapter, and author of numerous books, including *The*

Healing of Emotions and *Ecstasy is a New Frequency*, refers to the *emotional body,* and Eckhart Tolle, author of *The Power of Now* and *A New Earth* refers to the *pain body*. Here is how Chris Griscom wrote about the phenomenon in the eighties:

> "The seat of the emotional body is the solar plexus chakra, which is in the area of the stomach. Our emotions are registered by the solar plexus ganglia, which trigger the sympathetic nervous system of fight or flight. This alters the blood chemistry in the brain, and the vagus nerve activates physiological responses which actually carry with them an electrical jolt. Everyone recognizes that jolt from experiences where they were taken by surprise – the massive surge of fear and anger which brings us instantly to attention. The jolt spreads itself out in widening arcs which characterize disillusion, shame, and anxiety. *The emotional body becomes addicted to these jolts. It begins to seek people and situations which will re-echo the original charge, even though we become desensitized or unaware of it on a conscious level."*
> (italics mine)

And this is Eckhart Tolle's take on it well over a decade later:

> "As long as you are unable to access the power of the Now, *every emotional pain that you experience leaves behind a residue of pain that lives on in you.* It merges with the pain from the past, which was already there, and becomes lodged in your mind and body. This, of course, includes the pain you suffered as a child, caused by the unconsciousness of the world into which you were born."

> "This accumulated pain is a negative energy field that occupies your body and mind. If you look on it as an invisible entity in its own right, you are getting quite close to the truth. It's the emotional pain-body. It has two modes of being: dormant and active. A pain-body may be dormant 90 percent of the time; in a deeply unhappy person, though, it may be active up to 100 percent of the time. Some people live almost entirely through their pain-body, while others may experience it only in certain situations, such as intimate relationships, or situations linked with past loss or abandonment, physical or emotional hurt, and so on. *Anything can trigger it, particularly if it resonates with a pain pattern from your past.* When it is ready to awaken from its dormant stage, even a thought or an innocent remark made

by someone close to you can activate it."
(italics mine)

Essentially both authors use terms that refer to that part of us that wallows in our pain and remains stuck there, at least emotionally. What, you say? Why on earth would I want to wallow in something painful? The answer becomes obvious. Because *it is a place you know.* Because you feel at home there, as painful as it is. In other words, we have been there so often before, in this place of pain, that when faced with a choice of doing something new and unknown, or wallowing, it is much easier to fall back to the well-trodden path and wallow. We don't really even think about it. We just go there, because it is familiar. And then we feel comfort in the familiarity of the pain. Recognize this? Have you been there? And are you tempted right now, despite what you have read to this point, to go back to your painful thoughts? Does that just feel so much easier? *Become conscious of this process within you the next time you find yourself in a place of pain. Try to remember the steps that took you there.*

> *Pain is inevitable as long as you are identified with your mind.*
> Eckhart Tolle

And there is something else about it, something perhaps even more powerful. The pain body or the emotional body is seductive in its pull on you. It is addictive. You *want* to go there. You want to *stay* there. By going there, you somehow feel right, despite the pain, somehow vindicated, despite not being able to change that painful past you are reliving, and by staying there you are able to see over and over again, in your mind's eye, in your heart, and in your tears, exactly what happened, how it happened, and how, because of how it happened, *you are right in reliving it.* In other words, you tell yourself that *you have a right to* your anger or your pain. Something happened or was done to you that justifies that you continue to feel this way. *If you did not feel this way, it would almost be as though you were telling the world (or yourself) that whatever it was that happened, was not so bad. Feeling the pain, wallowing in it, over and over again, gives meaning to the event. And the event must be meaningful, because it was so painful.* I imagine that you can see how this is, in some fashion, a catch-22.

Another reason people wallow in the pain is because they believe that by going over and over the same situation, they will be able to analyze it and understand it; they will be able to understand why it had to happen as it did, and what this signified in their lives.

While it is not untrue that some analysis and understanding of past painful events may be useful, it is also true that such analysis can be paralyzing, keeping you in a place from which you *are not able to grow*. And if you cannot grow, you will never overcome that past pain.

I often use the example of childbirth to illustrate the point. Many women suffer during childbirth, perhaps less so today than a century ago, but nevertheless, childbirth is associated with painful contractions and so on. If women were to go over and over the moments of the pain they experienced during childbirth, it is highly unlikely that they would ever again voluntarily have another child, and furthermore, the moment of pain would be so indelibly marked in their brains, hearts and bodies, that *it would conceivably rob their present moments – with the child – of their beauty and glory* because of their focus on the past pain as opposed to the present wonder of the child (well, ok, let's be realistic: the exasperation of the child too!!).

This thought is very important: by going over and over a past moment of pain *you rob many of your present moments of their beauty, wonder and glory because you are focused on the past and not on the now* – whatever that now may be. (And if the now is – in your eyes – not good, then you can learn to find beauty in the moment anyway, but this subject is dealt with in greater detail in the chapter on gratitude).

Do you remember our discussion of neural pathways earlier in this book in the chapter about thoughts? So clearly, quite apart from other things I'll discuss in a moment, what you are doing by reliving this painful moment from another time in your life over and over again whenever you think about it, is strengthening the neural pathway that is connected to that event. And the stronger the pathway is, the harder it is for you to *not* think the painful thought or to *not* have the painful feelings whenever the memory arises inside.

How strong is the neural pathway of something innocuous that happened to you several days ago? Probably very weak. Potentially non-existent. Why? Because you have not gone over it again and again as you do with painful events. It was discarded in order to give you more space (mentally, psycho-emotionally, spiritually, you name it) to continue with your life and other events, instead of filling your mind and heart with that particular event. You moved on. You let it go.

But what do we do when we hear a particular song on the radio, when we catch a tantalizing whiff of that familiar cologne, or when we see certain scenes of some movies that remind us of a particular situation? *We go to that place of pain unconsciously because we are not aware of ourselves.* Or we may be aware enough to realize what is going on, *but we have not yet decided to take on our own responsibility for ourselves.* Being responsible for the self, means that you literally assume total responsibility for how you think, feel, act and react.

So of course you would also assume responsibility for what you do when you hear/smell/see/touch/feel that trigger that would normally send you into your emotional body or pain body, as opposed to letting the pain body (your addiction to the painful memories in your life and how they make you feel) take over at that moment. There is much more information about taking responsibility for the self in the chapters on responsibility and happiness, but suffice it to say at this point, that awareness implies a shouldering of this responsibility.

So now I want to really throw an unexpected thought out there at you. If, as I refer to in other parts of this book, our thoughts do indeed influence our body, our cells, our genes, our very DNA, then it stands to reason that by continually re-visiting the past and re-living past pain, we are negatively influencing the very cells of our body. Read some of the work by cellular and molecular biologists Candace Pert and Bruce Lipton, read what scientific researcher Masaru Emoto has to say, look into the writing about quantum research by endocrinologist Deepak Chopra, but whatever you do, don't rest back on your chair, make a puzzled face, and say *I don't believe this nonsense.* Don't allow yourself to say that until you've read the research.

Find a place inside where there's joy,
and then the joy will burn out the pain.
Joseph Campbell

For those of you who still find it hard to believe that thoughts could affect your body, here are some more common *physiological* examples:

- Some individuals are able to provoke tears simply by imagining something and crying because of it.
- Biofeedback has taught us that we can – of our own volition - measurably alter our heartbeat, our tension and stress.
- Some individuals are capable of reaching orgasm simply by their thoughts.

Therefore, *if we know this to be true,* it follows that we need to consider taking cellular responsibility for ourselves. Cellular responsibility?

Part of Your Energy Is In Your Past

How much of you is in "your story" and *would be lost* if you let it go? So then you might have to work on a whole new you ... and depending on how you think about that, it is actually quite exciting ... *you would no longer be burdened by that old, sad awful story you've been dragging around with you.*

You do see that because of *your story about your wounds*, part of your energy, *part of your power* is in your past, in that story about your past, right? If you identify with your story, if that is how you define yourself, then a portion of your power is *there* and not *here*. In order for it to be here, you would need to identify yourself by the *"who" you are now and not the "who" you became due to the painful event.*

Getting Your Fragments Into Present Time

Getting the fragments of yourself into present time is a necessary part of the process of taking cellular responsibility for yourself. So there's bit of you in 1976, and another bit in 1960, and another several parts of you in the early 80's and so on, depending on when in your history things happened to you that continue to maintain a part or parts of you, especially emotionally, there, at that moment in time. Perhaps the events when you were five were very hard, and then again when you were 15, and so on. The anchor that holds you there is the negative emotion that you continue to feel every time that you remember the painful event. That means there are only a few bits of you in the present moment and until you leave those past fragments - that hold so much of your power – behind, you will not be able to get your power back, and you will not be able to take cellular responsibility for yourself.

Who are you, without any reference to the past?
Papaji

Unfinished Business

You know that you have unfinished business with parents, with your spouse or your partner, your kids, your siblings, your friends, your boss, your teachers, and so on, *if you continue to have negative emotions of any kind when you think about them, in particular with regard to past events involving them*. Those negative emotions are the ones that can adversely influence your body and your cells, and it is precisely those negative emotions that can be found at the bottom of what it is you need to begin to take responsibility for, if you want to take *cellular* responsibility for yourself. Finishing up that unfinished business will automatically signify that you will spend a much greater amount of time in the present instead of in the past, and that you will spend far less time focusing on negative emotions from events that took place in the past.

What does unfinished business look like? Unfinished business is typically one or more of the following:

- anger
- resentment
- hurt
- pain
- fear
- guilt
- shame
- anxiety
- depression

What is the quickest way to deal with it? *Forgiving.*

The Importance of Forgiving & the Law of Attraction

Once you can forgive, the unfinished business from the past transforms into a mere memory that no longer carries any negative connotations to pull your power away from the present. It is at this point that you can *begin to take cellular responsibility for yourself*, i.e. you will no longer be harming your body in all senses of the word by keeping alive the connection to that negative power from the past.

Not finding the ability within to forgive yourself or others creates poison, and it's not only poison for relationships and for how you feel about yourself, but it's also poison for the spirit, the self, the soul. By not forgiving much damage is done to the self, to the well of emotions we all carry about within us. Can we challenge ourselves to elevate our capacity to love – others and the self – and thus develop the power of forgiveness? Because doing so is simply no longer something we can put aside until tomorrow. *We must learn to forgive if we wish to heal.* Forgiving is one of our most difficult struggles in the healing process. Forgiving not only others, but also yourself, in order to pull back the valuable psychic and cellular energy you are expending on the memory and re-living of past hurts. If you want to heal yourself, you must learn how to forgive. By forgiving you call back the energy wasted on thinking about past events. By forgiving you return to present time. So by becoming a forgiving person, and letting go of the past, you have, in fact, shifted your relationship with time. You no longer live in the past. You live now.

Some Tools

Doing some of what follows will lead you down the road to cellular responsibility where you will be able to begin to recover your power:

- Become aware of yourself, your reactions to different stimuli, and your subsequent *need* to go into the pain body.
- Decide you *will* be responsible for yourself in all senses of the word.
- Make *better choices* because now you are aware and have decided to become responsible.
- When the pain body surges the next time, now that you recognize it, challenge it by attempting to move yourself in the opposite direction. I don't promise that it will be easy, nor that you will win the battle the first time you attempt it, because a very strong part of you will insist (partially due to those neural pathways again), that you *want* to go down the road to the pain body, but when you do finally win the battle the first time, not only will you feel immeasurably better, but you will find that each subsequent time the pain body attempts to surge, you will find it easier and easier to overcome it.
- Look at your unfinished business with any others in your life – dead or alive.
- Does reliving the past help make anything better?
  - Can you recognize that continuing to hurt about past events won't resolve whatever it was that did not work out well then?
  - Since you are unable to change the pain of the past, do you understand that by choosing to view it differently now, or by choosing to focus elsewhere, as opposed to focusing on the pain each time the memory arises, you will take strength away from the habitual pattern you have created?
- Forgive
  - Whom do you need to forgive?
  - Why are you unwilling to forgive?
  - Recognize that not forgiving holds parts of you in the past.
  - Understand that forgiving does not mean you condone what was done, nor does it mean you now need to have a wonderful relationship with that person ... you may

need to move on, perhaps never engage even in a conversation with that person again, but by forgiving, the hold that the event had over you, will be gone.

- o Forgiving also does not mean forgetting – but it *does* mean, removing the energetic (and negative) *charge* from the memory.

- Gratitude – this is a really big one: see more about it in the chapter on gratitude, but suffice it to say that the more you are capable of being grateful for the smallest things in your daily life, the more you will live in the present, and the less you will spend time on painful memories of the past. This – as so much else – is also a habit that will create new neural pathways in your pre-frontal cortex and that will also bring you to a point where it allows you to keep yourself in a place of inner well-being. Becoming grateful can make a hugely positive difference to your life in just about every sector.

- Mindfulness - this is strongly connected to gratitude because gratitude can be your first step in learning how to be truly mindful; by being grateful for something *right now*, you automatically return to the now, and by learning to be mindful, you will be able to *remain* in the now. For more explicit information about mindfulness, see the chapter on the now as well.

Let's look at how this might work out with a real-life example. Let's focus on the emotional body, or the pain body. Imagine you went through a very traumatic and difficult childhood experience. Perhaps you were abused. Perhaps you were abandoned or neglected. Whatever the case, now as an adult, you frequently find yourself in a very dark and painful place whenever certain things happen. Perhaps when someone you love treats you badly (even if it's just verbally), or perhaps it's when someone you love leaves to go on a trip.

The point is that you feel yourself slipping into this black place in a way that – if your rational mind thinks about it - perhaps goes far beyond what the current situation in actual fact merits. But nonetheless, you go into the dark place. And so you experience deep excruciating pain, and may often ask yourself whether there is a way out. You may ask: How can I forgive?

Especially how can I forgive, if what you did to me was so awful? Anyone whom I tell it to, says I am right and that you were simply awful to me. So how can I forgive you? What you did was really dreadful. I suffered so much. If I forgave you, what would I do with all of that suffering? Just throw it in the trash? Poof - so simple - all gone? I can't do that. You hurt me too much. I have to remember it because it was so bad, and if I forgive you it will all be gone.

What does this mean? It means that I should look at what was done to me as more than just the idea that *you hurt me*. It means that I should look at it like it was part of my *life growth plan*. It means that every person with whom I come in contact in my life *can serve a purpose in my life,* no matter what kind of interaction I have with them.

So even if they do something excruciatingly terrible to me, it can *still* serve a purpose in my life so that I can grow into more of what I really am, by dealing with this situation in a way that allows growth, and not in a way that poisons me and keeps me in a prison of hatred or resentment or pain. But for that to work, I have to look at the painful situation with new eyes. Not so much *you hurt me,* as *how can I grow and learn from this?*

How can I begin to look through such new eyes? How can I stop seeing the pain as something I need to hang on to, because *it defines who I am up to here in my life?*

Simple: *choose* to do so. Nothing else is needed.

But in order for that to happen, you may first need to have an inner dialogue similar to the one described above, and you can only have this inner dialogue, if you have *remembered to be aware.* Remember to remember to be aware! (Go back to the chapter on awareness if you have not yet read it). And remember, as you already read about in the chapter on choice: you *always have a choice!*

Whenever anything negative happens to you, there is a deep lesson concealed within it, although you may not see it at the time.
Eckhart Tolle

Here's how another part of the inner dialogue might sound when a current situation has just pushed you into deep, debilitating pain:

- Is this pain I am feeling all from right now, from the current situation, or could it be possible that there are connections to something in my past?
- If so, do I know what that thing in my past is? Do I know what happened to me back then, when there was something that was so painful?
- If I don't remember, or perhaps if I haven't yet connected the current painful event to the past painful event, I might consider making a life review of my entire life. Do it like this:
    o Take a sheet of paper for each year of your life.
    o At the top of each sheet write the corresponding

calendar year (example: 1996) and your age during that year (example: 21).

- o Underneath that write your place of residence (address or just the city) and the people and pets who lived there with you (parents, siblings, grand-parents, partner, children, nanny, dog, cat, etc.).
- o Under that write the name of any friends you may have had that were important in that year, the kindergarten, school, or university you attended, and your teachers' names (if you remember them).
- o For the time being, that's enough. Leave the sheets (if you are 55 years old, you will have 55 sheets) in a place that you pass often during the day, and each time you recall anything at all that is important for that year of your life, write it down (even if it's something you heard about from a relative or friend of the family, but you consider it important). Just jot it down in bullet fashion, because you don't want to wind up with more than 1-3 sheets per year, and preferably only one. When you make a note in the page corresponding to the year that you began to live in your own place for the first time, without your family, if it was an important step, jot down how it made you feel. Likewise, when you write down that the year you were 23 you met your future spouse, jot down how you felt at first, or why you felt attracted. If there is then, at age 39, a subsequent divorce, write down how you felt, and what caused it (brief bullets only). Likewise with the birthdates of your children, with jobs you have held, important friendships or partnerships, both romantic and business, and so on. In so doing you will frequently encounter something to relate your current pain to. And once you can do that, you are ready to go on to the next step in this inner dialogue.

- Ok, so I know what it was that happened in my past that somehow pushes painful buttons in my present and causes me to go into this place where I hurt so much.
- Do I want to be here? Or do I prefer to find a way out of this morass?
- Here the typical answer is: *yes, I want to be out of here, but it's impossible because this is what always happens now because of what happened then, in my past. I can't do anything about it. I've tried and it doesn't work.*
- So now you tell yourself: "Well, I may not be able to resolve this right now, but I am able to *choose to focus on something else.* Focusing on something else doesn't mean that I'm pretending

this is no longer important, but it *does* mean that by focusing elsewhere I am giving myself the opportunity to come to a better place inside of me, a higher energetic frequency, so that from that better place, I can review the situation."

- I may focus on something I am grateful for in my life, or something I am grateful for in the place in which I currently find myself, in order to bring myself to the *now*, to the present moment, because if I am in the present moment, and furthermore in a space of gratitude, I will automatically feel better even if only for a few minutes. In that moment, in the now, there is no room for thoughts of future worries or past pain.

- I may go for a brisk 20-30 minute walk and during the walk only focus on the sensations in my body as I walk, as well as being grateful for whatever I feel and observe around me, in order to remain in the present by being mindful (see the chapter on awareness as well, for further clarifications about mindfulness).

- Now that I feel better – even if only slightly – I will ask myself if I want to forgive whomever or whatever happened when I was younger that keeps creating present pain.

- My answer may be that what happened to me cannot be forgiven. My answer may be that I want to forgive, but that I can't. I may have tried in the past and found it to be impossible. Or my answer may be that I want to forgive but don't know how.

- In all these examples, the salient point is that *if you do not forgive, whether you believe what happened is unforgivable, or whether you believe that you cannot or do not know how to forgive, the energetic connection to the past will not be broken, and you will continue to feel the pain.* If, however, you decide to take on the process of forgiving *for your own sake and for your own healing, and above all, because you love yourself so much* (or would *like* to love yourself so much) *that you want this to be gone from your life,* then you will do it.

- Here's how, in a nutshell: each time something happens to bring the pain into the present, or each time you remember the event from the past, and hence re-visit the initial pain, tell yourself that your intention is to forgive. *My intention is to forgive. I may not know how, but I intend to forgive. And because I intend to forgive, right now, instead of continuing to focus on the pain (or the anger, or whatever the negative feeling is), I will focus on something life-giving, something I can feel gratitude for, something that keeps me here in the present moment.*

- Each time you do this with awareness and conscious choice, you are strengthening a new neural pathway and weakening an old one. Each time you do this with awareness and conscious choice, you are affirming your love for yourself. And the more you do it with awareness and conscious choice, the more you will have forgiven – for your sake, and for your health and well-being and thus will have furthered the love for yourself and hence this rewiring of your soul that we are so intent on throughout each of the chapters of this book.

> *Forgive the past and it will no longer own you.*
> *Forgive and you will be free.*

Chapter Eight

Self-Responsibility:
Power in Your Life

Be the change you want to see in the world
Mahatma Gandhi

As children, our parents often admonished us: *be responsible! Take responsibility for what you do.* And we took it to mean that if we had chores or homework to do, or if they wanted us to be home before dinner, then we needed to be responsible about completing those tasks or instructions, and not dawdle, or worse, procrastinate so much that in the end they never got done, and we wound up with real emergencies on our hands.

I used to say to one of my sons when he was in his early teens (I found the saying in a long-forgotten article, and after a sweep of the phrase on the internet, I am unable to attribute it to any specific author): *your lack of planning does not constitute my emergency* when he would come to me in the eleventh hour with a paper that had not been written, or a project that had not been properly planned. (Needless to say, he was not overly pleased with me!)

But this is not what *claiming responsibility for the self* is really all about. One thing is to be responsible out there in the world, as described above, and another thing is to claim responsibility for the self. Both *types* of responsibility form part of responsible behavior, but the latter is much less understood, and even less implemented in an individual's life. To claim responsibility for the self literally means to *decide to be responsible for all that goes on within the self.*

> We are all responsible for ALL of our reactions
> to EACH of our experiences.

Here is how it works: we are all responsible for ourselves in all senses of the word. We are responsible for how we feel, how we think, how we act and how we react to any person or event or thought or feeling. We are also responsible for our own happiness as we will see in the chapter on happiness, and we are responsible for our attitudes in the face of anything at all that may happen. So in a nutshell, we might say that we are responsible for everything in our own world.

Not, let me hasten to add, for *all that happens to the self.* You cannot control that. If you live in a police state and are arbitrarily arrested, or if you live in an area often devastated by hurricanes or other natural disasters, or if you live in a third-world country with raging hunger and poverty, or if you are of the *wrong ethnic or religious origin* (according to the powers-that-be) and are subject to harassment or worse, it is clear that you are unable to claim responsibility for that manner of events.

But you can - without the slightest doubt - claim responsibility for the way in which you react to all of that, and therefore, you can claim responsibility for the way you feel about it all, for the state of your being in the midst of such havoc and chaos, and therefore, in a nutshell, you have control of your life. *As long as you are in control of what goes on inside of you, what happens on the outside carries much less weight.*

Not so fast, you might answer. What if ...

- Your boss just passed you over for a promotion?
- The bank declined your request for a loan?
- You've been downsized and only received two weeks' severance pay?

- Your car has been stolen?
- The doctor just told you that if you don't have triple bypass heart surgery very soon, you might not live to see your next birthday?
- The man/woman you love just walked out on you?
- It rained the entire week you spent in Hawaii?
- The girl you asked out on a first date after much self-searching and inner debating due to your fear of rejection, said that she already has a boyfriend, and you are convinced it's not true ... she just said it because she doesn't want to go out with you?
- No art gallery wants to exhibit your paintings?
- Twenty-two publishers rejected your manuscript?
- Your college application was put on waitlist?
- Your wife's iPhone signaled a text message while she was in the shower and you saw it: *Darling, can't wait to hold you in my arms again*?
- Your son has been diagnosed with leukemia?
- Your beloved father has Alzheimer's

In each of these examples something *external* to the self causes frustration, heartbreak, pain, annoyance, anger, or any number of other emotions. And so we explain our negative emotions to ourselves by blaming them on the event or the person. *Obviously we feel that way because of what happened.*

If that is explanation enough for you, then you are willing to give over control of your state of well-being to an event or another person. It is tantamount to saying that you are not in control of your state of well-being. *How can I be when these things happen to me?* You can be in control of your state of well-being by *deciding to be.* It's as simple as that.

Make the decision that when things happen that would normally upset you, you will, in future, look at all the possibilities, all the alternatives of reaction at your disposal. *Of all of these alternatives, one of them is always going to be:*

- I can choose not to get upset
- I can choose to remain calm
- I can choose to keep my cool
- I can choose to remain in a good mood
- I can choose to refuse to let this person or event bother me
- I can choose to grow from this
- Ican choose to look at this as a learning situation and take something positive from it in order to advance to the next place in my life
- I can choose not to participate in this argument

- I can choose to smile
- I can choose to walk away from this situation
- I can choose to laugh
- I can choose to believe in my own value as a wonderful human being
- I can choose to let this person be the way he is, realizing that his way of thinking, or his behavior says nothing at all about me
- I can choose not to worry (because worrying never solved anything at all, and, as Wayne Dyer so humorously said in some of his lectures: if worrying did any good, I'd be out there offering seminars to teach people how to worry better!)
- I can choose to shake hands

The examples of the choices you can offer yourself are endless, but if you make certain that your choices are always roads that take you to a good state of being, that enhance your inner well-being, and that serve you in some way, you are truly taking control, and claiming responsibility for the self.

Recently a friend mentioned the recession to me. His tone was low, he sounded defeated (and he is in fact, in quite a good position financially), and I got the impression he really did not know how he was going to go on. When I encouraged him to speak differently, he admonished me, saying that it is not responsible to not consider the difficulties this recessions brings to most of us on an ongoing basis.

I begged to differ, arguing that concentrating on all these negative thoughts brought no one any good.

- Being responsible has *nothing* to do with thinking dire thoughts about the potentially dire things that could happen.
- Being responsible has *nothing* to do with going on and on in obsessive circles about the problem, in the hope that by so doing you will solve it.
- Being responsible does have much to do with taking responsibility for your inner well-being at every moment of every day.
- Being responsible also has much to do with understanding that your inner well-being depends on what you do with your emotions and your thoughts.
- Being responsible further has much to do with recognizing that even when you are in dire circumstances (e.g., cancer diagnosis, bankruptcy, your daughter is an addict, a hurricane is on the way to your city, etc.), *you are not being more responsible by spending more time thinking about the dire circumstance.* Being responsible means doing your due

diligence, brain storming, trying to find solutions, giving that process a certain amount of time every day, *but then letting the matter rest until the next day* and once you have let it rest, it is time for you to find that good place inside of yourself by using some of the techniques described in this book (and others) to help you remain in a place of inner well-being *despite your outer circumstances.* Furthermore, from that newly-found good place inside of you (which you may need to oblige yourself to find over and over again, until it becomes a habit), you may be in a much more advantageous position to be able to discover – or recognize it when it appears – a solution to your problem!

If your thoughts go to your limitations, and the limitations of your circumstances (which currently for many of us is the global recession), then you will most certainly not be creating inner well-being.

If, however, your thoughts go towards *doubting your limitations*, you are on the road to departing from your comfort zone, to growth, to expansion, and to thinking out of the box. If you doubt your limitations you are thinking on an entirely new level that may take you to places you have never been or to ideas you have never had. *That is being responsible* because it is the beginning of a process that will help you solve your situation with potentially new ways and it is also the beginning of a process that will help you move to a better space inside.

---

*Let everyone sweep in front of his own door,
and the whole world will be clean.*
Johann Wolfgang von Goethe

But let's say you are still not convinced. Let's look at another example in an extremely detailed and very specific way. *What happens when my partner does something hurtful, like lie to me, or cheat on me?*

Here's the quick answer: you are obviously not responsible for what your partner did, but you *are* responsible for how you react to the event. Here's a longer answer: same as above, but add to that the following caveat: as you react to the event, you do so from a totally *aware* frame of mind. In other words, you are not only aware of your perhaps immediate primordial negative reaction, but also your capacity to *choose* to change that reaction. Once you have arrived at that point, you need to bear a number of things in mind and they might be these (or others):

- Is this the first time it has happened?
- If not, how did you react in the past?
- If you reacted from the gut, negatively and blindly, without thinking, perhaps your reaction merely provoked further trouble, taking you into a vicious circle in which you've found yourself so often, and resolved nothing.
- Or were you *aware* of how you reacted?
- In that case perhaps you reacted in a much healthier fashion, and told your partner that whatever it was that he/she did, it is not acceptable. In other words, you took care of your boundaries (if you are uncertain about the significance of boundaries, please take a good look at the chapter on boundaries), and you asked your partner not to repeat this particular action.
- Perhaps some conversation ensued (hopefully) and you and your partner came to some meaningful conclusions about the subject.

> You are only free when your happiness
> is not dictated by your needs.

- In a less ideal world, you and your partner may have simply come to an uneasy truce – still much more positive than exploding or arguing or calling each other names.
- By telling your partner that the action is not acceptable to you and by requesting it not be repeated, you probably also told your partner that there would be some kind of consequence if he/she felt it necessary to continue with that particular behavior.
- So now, as the action has been repeated by your partner, you might wish to pull out the consequence (perhaps you will insist on therapy for the couple, or, if it has occurred repeatedly over a lengthy period of time despite promises to stop, perhaps you'll want a trial separation).
- Or perhaps you will ask yourself some questions on a much deeper level, such as:

    o Why am I in this relationship?
    o What do I get out of this relationship?
    o Is there something I can learn by looking at the potential reasons why this action of my partner's bothers me?
    o Is it possible that what my partner does, more than being something that annoys me or angers me or pains

me is, actually something that reflects a bit of myself back to me? That he is acting as a mirror for me? Not his/her behavior, but how I act or react because of it?

o   If it's showing me something about myself (whether or not the behavior of my partner is acceptable), then doesn't it make sense that I examine that part of myself in order to determine the kind of work I need to do on it in order to *be able to react in a more healthy way in future*? This doesn't mean that I am condoning my partner's behavior – it actually might even be despicable or abusive – but what is clear is that I need to deal with the issue inside of me that is reacting without awareness, from a blind emotional place inside of me, to my partner's behavior. Perhaps my pain at my partner's behavior is showing me that this is a pain I have felt many times before – maybe not only with my partner but with other people, perhaps even beginning with my parents. Might this not be, then, an indication that it's time I dealt with whatever it is inside of me that permits me to feel this kind of pain over and over again (as opposed to being in a state of inner balance)? Probably that part of me that permits this, is a part that does not stand up for itself in a healthy fashion (maybe I have those poor boundaries discussed earlier), or perhaps it's a part of me that is willing to accept pain – no matter how much it hurts – as long as at other times I get a bit (maybe only crumbs) of love or acceptance. If that's the case, if I am that needy, or obsessive, or possessive (also read the chapter on relationships), it all means I need to start loving myself in order to fulfill my needs *myself* instead of being dependent on another for their fulfillment, and therefore in order to also be able to have a relationship at some point in the future, where dependence and neediness are not the glue that hold me in there.

o   Having reached that point in my introspection, I realize that I am beginning to take responsibility for myself, as opposed to blaming others for whatever it is that I am feeling.

o   That means that I may now start down the road of convalescence where I will need to make some decisions. If my relationship is indeed unhealthy, and my partner is giving no signs of taking any steps towards changing, then perhaps I have to end the relationship. The relationship will have served a wonderful purpose in my life. The pain I experienced because of the relationship has brought me to a very important place of learning how to assume responsibility for myself in all these senses. I will have comprehended that the pain I used to feel came about – not so much because the other person behaved badly – but because I had not yet assumed responsibility for my own well-being. An individual who has assumed such responsibility, will not be in such a relationship, because the first time such a painful behavior arises, that individual will clearly state that it's not acceptable. If that is not taken on board by the partner (or prospective partner), the responsible, *self-loving* individual will state in no uncertain terms that since the unacceptable behavior has been repeated, he/she has to apply some consequences for it, and perhaps the ultimate consequence is to remove himself from the unhealthy situation. *Thus he takes care of himself by loving the self and by being responsible for all aspects of the self.*

So clearly, taking responsibility for the self implies a healthy measure of self-love. The chapter on loving the self addresses that topic in great detail, so here it will suffice to say that self-love is what most of us are not taught as children, and hence many spend a good deal of their lives chasing after something *that makes them feel loved from the outside*, as opposed to being loved from the *inside*. Because of that lop-sided (and oft unconscious) stance, many situations like the one described in the previous paragraphs ensue.

We want love so badly that we forget to take care of ourselves. Or we never learned how to do so in the first place because we have been yearning for love since we were small. And we didn't get it. Or we got it but in our *perception* it was never enough. Or we simply could not *perceive* that it really was love. Why this is so as it arises out of our deep, dark past, is not as important as understanding that we can do something about it *now*, in order to improve our present moment, and in order to live a better life from now on.

Looking at our past from the point of view of all that went wrong, and from the point of view that we are victims of whatever it was that happened then (and for you to feel that you are a victim, you do not need to have been abused), *is of little use in this present moment*. It may help in understanding the trajectory of our particular issues, it may help in understanding why those who cared for us did the things they did, or did them in the way they did them, but all of this does little to change the present moment. So in order to change the present moment we have to be willing to accept responsibility for our well-being *now*, no matter what happened in the past, and having accepted that responsibility, be consciously aware of the fact that we have *choices* about how to deal with our lives now. Some of this has been discussed in the chapters on emotions, on awareness, on choice, and on pain and forgiving, but again, all the areas of the human soul and psyche dealt with in this book are so intimately inter-connected, that it is nearly impossible to discuss one of them without delving into all of the others. That is why when you begin to deal with one of the areas, sooner or later all of the others also start to get dealt with. And of course the fact that working on one part of your life causes another to improve as well could be called an added benefit.

You must take personal responsibility. You cannot change the circumstances, the seasons, or the wind, but you can change yourself. That is something you have charge of.
Jim Rohn

So having accepted that we have choices about how to deal with our lives now, and having accepted that our well-being is our own responsibility, we begin to take steps to move ourselves in that direction.

Let's look at another example. Instead of a partner that hurts you, now we are going to examine how to assume responsibility for a low feeling. You're driving along in the car, feeling quite good, possibly even on top of the world, it's been a good day so far, the sun is shining, nothing difficult has cropped up to mar your day, but you have the radio on. A song begins: *Can't live, if living is without you … can't live …* and something inside of you shrivels and goes to a place that is filled with pain.

You no longer see the brilliant blue sky, because you are immersed in the pain of a moment (or many moments) from your past that this song reminds you of. Due to the nature of the song, probably it has to do with a failed relationship that has left long throbbing tentacles of pain. Simply because the song took you back to that place in your memory, it also took you back energetically, because by feeling the way you do, you are fully connected to whatever it was that happened back then that hurt you so much, *as if it were happening now*. You may even feel tears threatening to spill from your eyes.

But you are responsible for how you feel. *No, I'm not*, you respond. *I can't be responsible for feeling the way I do about something that was done to me back then. It hurt so much.* Yes. I understand totally. But here's the thing: if you are going to accept full responsibility for your well-being now, *you also accept responsibility for the places to which your thoughts go*. This isn't about *controlling* your thoughts in the sense of stoically repressing them, or marching bravely on, as though they had not sprung unbidden into mind. Rather, it's about understanding that as long as you are not in charge of the direction into which your unbidden thoughts go, *nothing will change.*

You alone are responsible for how you feel
and for your state of inner well-being.
Decide to be responsible for it!

In chapter one, we discussed thoughts and all their ramifications on your state of well-being. In this chapter we are discussing responsibility in general and also in terms of how you need to become responsible for your thoughts if you desire to live a life of inner peace and freedom. The feelings that arose unbidden when the song began to play on the radio in your car came about partially because of memories associated with that song, and partially because of thoughts that then arose that went something like:

- Why did that have to happen?
- If only …
- I wish …
- I was so happy then …
- I am so unhappy now …

Here are some ways you could deal with it: as you experience the feelings and thoughts associated with the painful memory, and if you are becoming aware enough to catch them almost in the moment of arising (or perhaps you catch them twenty minutes down the road, but the important thing is that you *do* catch them), you immediately begin a brief inner dialogue that might go something like this:

- Nothing has actually happened other than a song playing.
- It was "our" song.
- It triggered memories, both of the good times (that were lost) and the bad times, before and after we separated.
- Those memories are now making me feel almost as sad (filled with pain, angry, despondent, etc.) as I did then.
- I can choose to continue focusing on those memories and difficult emotions, making that memory even more potent,

strengthening the neural pathway associated with that memory each time I choose to spend time on it.

- But I can also choose to focus on something else instead of those memories.
- By so doing I'm not pretending the painful moment and the memory of it did not exist.
- Nor am I pretending that I'm over it, because clearly I am not, otherwise this whole thing wouldn't bother me.
- So what I'll do, is imagine that the painful memory and feelings it has aroused are at my left side, and now, I'll look over to my right side, where I can't see the memory and I can't focus on the feelings, because I now *deliberately and consciously choose to focus on something else* that creates a sensation – even if only slight – of pleasure in me. Here are some ideas: Perhaps a scenario about something you enjoy doing or think you might enjoy doing, perhaps a special trip somewhere. (Traveling on the Orient Express? White water rafting in Costa Rica? Climbing Kilimanjaro?). Or how about writing the software for a new video game? Directing a movie? How about imagining time traveling to the times of Genghis Khan?
- I might also focus with gratitude on something in my immediate surroundings (or just outside the window) that arouses such a feeling of gratitude in me. Again, here are some ideas: perhaps it's the sunshine, a plant, a pet, a piece of furniture you are particularly fond of, a painting on your wall, blue sky, etc. Realize that focusing on gratitude (as you will read about in much greater detail in the chapter on gratitude), brings with it an important advantage: it takes you to this moment, the now, the present, and in the now it is *not possible* to be thinking about the past or the future. Hence, for a moment in time, you will be present, and at peace, not plagued by the pain.
- The point of this little exercise at the moment of your pain, is to realize that by becoming aware of your thoughts as they are involved in the painful moment, and then by becoming aware of your choices, and then by taking one of those choices to focus your attention elsewhere, you are assuming responsibility for the self and how it is feeling and thinking in this very moment. By improving your sense of inner well-being, and consequently by raising your energetic frequency, you are now in a better place inside of you. As you do this more and more often, it will become an automatic response in the same way someone who has developed a fever, will immediately take stock of the situation and determine whether an aspirin is required, a trip to the doctor, or to get into bed. The person with fever does something to mitigate the fever, to balance his health, and you, as you become aware of negative thoughts or difficult and painful

feelings, can also do something to bring balance back into your inner state.

- Taking this kind of responsibility for the self brings immeasurable benefits beyond those just described, because it also, as stated elsewhere, increases love for the self. By taking this kind of responsibility for your inner state of well-being, you show yourself subliminally, subconsciously, and eventually more and more consciously, that *you love yourself enough to do it.* So you begin to show yourself that you respect yourself and that you care enough about yourself to want to be in a better place.

A final example, to better understand how we can always be responsible for our inner state might occur during a moment of road rage. Another driver has nearly caused you to have an accident due to carelessness. You are not only shaken, you are also indignant at his lack of consideration and the fact that he did not even stop to apologize. Just before the near accident you were in a good place inside of you. Now you are in this place of shooting adrenaline, stress, anger, and indignation. As you drive on, you go over the events in your mind, remembering another fact about his carelessness, which angers and annoys you even more. You are accelerating from the inner place of already bad feelings you had a moment ago after the accident to an even worse place now due to your thoughts. And as you arrive at work, you relate the story to several colleagues, and in each telling of the story, you again relive the indignation, stress and fear. Finally, when you arrive home, you again relate the incident, this time to your spouse, whose horrified or consternated reaction adds fuel to your own.

What you have now achieved is creating a day that – counting from the moment of the near accident that morning – has been tinged, and very negatively so, by you, your thoughts and your words. You have done untold damage to your cells by the amount of stress you have produced in your body, and quite likely you will not sleep well tonight.

How would the self-responsible reaction have looked? There are numerous possibilities, but one very good one involves you recognizing that as you re-think and retell the incident, you do yourself harm, and therefore you take the conscious choice to not ruin the rest of your day, a bit of your health, not to mention a bit of the well-being of all who listen to you.

Careful now, this is not about you never being able to talk about things that happen to you. But it *is* about the recognition that where you spend your thoughts and mental energy, is where you will reap your greatest harvest, and in choosing – from a position of awareness and responsibility – to focus on that which brings you the greatest well-being.

So self-responsibility involves making choices that benefit the self from a healthy point of view, always bearing in mind that the manner in which you manage your inner well-being based on those choices, will impact the course of your hours, days, and weeks – it will impact your entire life. Being responsible for yourself ultimately means choosing reactions and behaviors at all times that allow you to live your life on all levels in the most optimal way possible.

We all have the extraordinary coded within us,
waiting to be released.
Jean Houston

Chapter Nine

Your Life Meaning:
Strength to See You Through It All

If you want to live a happy life, tie it to a goal
Albert Einstein

An oak tree grows inside you when your life has meaning in it. This oak will hold you up and support you, and allow you to go on, no matter what, when times are hard. It is the meaning in your life that gives you strength. It is your belief in the meaning in your life that gives you strength. It is your joy in the meaning of your life that gives you strength. And that is why the meaning in your life is equivalent to an oak tree growing inside of you. That is also why – if you want to live a fulfilled life, a life in which your inner state of well-being is optimal under any (potentially difficult outer) circumstances – you need a meaning in your life. Nelson Mandela, about whom I have already written in a previous chapter, makes it abundantly clear in his autobiography that one of the most key elements that allowed him not only to survive the 27 years of incarceration he was subject to, as a political prisoner of the apartheid regime, but furthermore, allowed him to survive without hatred and a desire for revenge, was *precisely* the meaning which he gave to his life. He believed in freedom, democracy, and equal opportunity for all citizens of South Africa, white or black, rich or poor, and that was what he wanted to achieve. The search for this, the movement towards this difficult – perhaps even impossible goal, as it must have seemed at times - gave meaning to his life.

But the meaning in your life must emanate from you. If the meaning in your life comes from your children, your spouse, your family, no matter *how* important these people are to you, if something happens to them, or how they feel about you, or how they behave with you, then that which has supported you to this point, and given you meaning, will no longer be there.

Do you see what will then happen? You will collapse (as we tend to do when we are in love, and the beloved abandons us, if we have not yet discovered the difference between dependent and independent love as discussed in the chapter on love and relationships).

What is the meaning of life? To be happy and useful.
Dalai Lama

We've all known some mothers who dedicated their entire existence to their children, raising them, loving them, and their lives revolved around the children in ways that we might admire – we might think - or people in other generations might have thought, that they were so wonderful because of how much they sacrificed themselves for their children. (On this topic of sacrifice, especially if it is resonating with you in any way at all, please also carefully read the chapter on self-love). But then we have probably also observed what happened to this type of mother once the children leave to go to college or to get married. They undergo a major crisis. And I don't just mean the empty-nest syndrome from the point of view that we all understand that to suddenly no longer live with our children can be very painful emotionally, much as one realizes that they have to move on in order to grow into their own lives. Their crisis is far more existential since they have been left with little or no meaning in their lives!

Similar to the crisis such a mother may have undergone, could be the crisis that many men and women experience when they retire. They have dedicated themselves body and soul to their jobs and now they no longer have those jobs because they have retired.

So what is this crisis about? Clearly, the consuming *activity* these people had in their lives (the children, the job, etc.) and that appeared to give *meaning* to their lives, meant that they did not give any thought to whether that activity gave *real* meaning or not to their lives. In the case of children, as stated earlier, they simply cannot be that which gives us real meaning because although we have given birth to them, they are not something that emanates from us and that therefore can – should we so choose – stay with us the rest of our lives.

With a job it is a bit easier, because the meaning the job gives us could theoretically be continued after retirement. A doctor may decide to volunteer in his chosen field by teaching, mentoring, studying, doing research, etc. A plumber may continue to do all those jobs he loved while he was working, but independently now, simply because he enjoys himself. An accountant may do something similar. For an artist it's even easier and we are all familiar with the stories of so many of them who literally continue to work until they die: actors, musicians, composers, artists, writers, etc. Obviously they do this because *what* they do gives meaning to their lives. A president may become a statesman after he leaves office – Carter, Clinton and Gorbachev are notable examples - because the meaning of what such an individual did while he was in office, is now re-engineered into a related meaning. But if the job gave meaning to the individual's life, mainly because that was how he earned his living, and because it gave him somewhere to go every day, and *not* because he felt an inherent connection and resonance to that job, then when the job is gone, he will be at loose ends. Oh, of course, he may spend some time vacationing, golfing, playing bridge, but if those activities are merely time-fillers, then retirement will be tinged with ever-increasing shades of grey.

Mandela writes eloquently about his love for his family, wife, children, mother, and so on, and on occasion describes heart-wrenchingly that the regime only allowed visits from his wife every six months, and then only from behind glass partitions, and only for half an hour. When he was finally allowed a more humane visit, where the couple was able to sit together in one room and embrace, 21 years had passed since the last time he had held his wife's hand! Letters were few and far in between, heavily censored, with forbidden bits being cut out, leaving the paper in tatters, and at some point even photographs of his family were no longer allowed.

When his eldest son died in a motorcycle accident and later his mother succumbed to a heart attack while he was still being held as a prisoner of the state, he was not given permission to attend their funerals. Clearly this must have been disheartening, to put it mildly. It must have torn him up inside in ways that only someone in his position could understand. But he carried on. And one of the main reasons he was able to do this is because there was a meaning in his life. Therefore if the meaning in your life is to emanate from you, it follows that you first need to understand *what that meaning might be*. It is at this point that many people run into problems because if you have never given much thought to what the meaning in your life might be, you may be totally clueless as to how to begin this process.

There is a magnificent book which is very related to our topic by Mikhail Csikzentmihalyi called *Finding Flow: The Psychology of Engagement with Everyday Life*. In the book, the prolific author, one of the founding fathers of the concept of positive psychology, encourages the reader to find those activities that most flow, that most cause time to pass while engaged in doing them, because they are so pleasurable, so interesting to you. In other words, *they flow*. It might be as you play an instrument, or read, crunch numbers, play golf, write speeches or solve algebraic equations, but whatever it is, it causes time to flow.

> *When you discover your mission, you will feel its demand. It will fill you with enthusiasm and a burning desire to get to work on it.*
> W. Clement Stone

Also, as I tell my clients, try to remember the sense of adventure you felt when you were in the throes of puberty. At that time you probably felt the entire world could still open up at your feet, and there were some things that you really wanted to do. Dust those ideas off, even if you wanted to be a rock musician at 13 and now are a balding 64-year-old, and *see* how you can incorporate some of that into your present life. Perhaps you can take up playing the guitar, perhaps you can write a biography of a world-renowned group, it is only your imagination that will limit you in how you might give this desire of yours from decades ago some life in order to give your life some meaning *now*.

And please remember this: what the actual thing is, that gives (or could give) meaning to your life, makes no difference, the important thing is that you *have* a meaning in your life, and not *what* that meaning is in the eyes of anyone other than yourself! If you enjoy making dolls, writing novels, going on archeological digs, or deep-sea diving, then that is great. If you prefer to become the best tennis player in your club, or have a wonderful kitchen garden that nourishes you and your family throughout the year, or study obscure, long-dead languages, it's totally up to you.

While I believe that this is a great place to start, I would add something else to the process. What happens if you don't know right now, what activity causes you to feel as though time is flowing? What if you can't remember what it was that gave you that early sense of adventure? Or perhaps the only thing you can come up with is sex and/or video games. It's not that there is anything wrong with sex or video games, but unless you are planning on doing extensive research in the field of human sexuality, or perhaps work as a surrogate in a counseling capacity, it is unlikely that sex is going to give meaning to your life. And again, unless you are planning on becoming a video game programmer, designer, or tester, it is unlikely that video games are truly going to give meaning to your life.

So the process has to be broader and more specific at the same time. Broader, because you need to use the entire world and knowledge of the entire world as your hunting ground (you are hunting for the *meaning* of your life), and not only the areas you have already experienced and that may have created flow in your life, and it has to be more specific, because you are going to zoom in on a part of your *physiological* being to help us in the search.

Scattered throughout this book I've made mention of the importance of your body with regards to information you are receiving. Your brain receives and collates information not only directly from the outside world, but also from another, more local – that is, local to your body – world. There are other parts of you that receive information in much the same manner as the brain, parts of you that contain as many, if not more billions of neural cells as your brain, that collate this information and then send it on to the brain. These other parts of you are called the second and third brain, and they are located in your intestine (gut) and heart respectively.

What follows is the partial reproduction of an article I wrote about this subject in 2006:

> Neuro-scientists have finally done it! They have demonstrated that we have a brain in our heart and another in our intestines. What we have in each of these, in actual fact, is an extensive mass of neurons that behave in a fashion similar to the neurons contained in the brain, and that appear to function at mega-speeds, often much greater than those of our cerebral neurons.
>
> **The Second Brain**
>
> The second brain consists of about 100 billion nerve cells in the digestive tract – a greater number than those in the spinal cord. Professor W. Prinz of the Max Planck Institute

for Psychological Research in Munich indicated to Geo Magazine that it is possible that unconscious decisions may be taken by the stomach network, which are later claimed by the main brain as conscious decisions of its own.

This second brain was brought to light by neuro-biologist Michael Gershon of New York's Columbia-Presbyterian Medical Center, author of *The Second Brain.* When asked if the brain in our heads influences our second brain, he replied that it does, and that we get butterflies in the stomach when the brain sends a message of anxiety to the gut. This, in turn, sends messages back to the brain that it is not happy. However – and this is perhaps the most riveting part of it – the brain in the gut can also work in isolation.

The Third Brain

With his revolutionary research the University of Montreal's pioneer neurocardiologist Dr. J. Andrew Armour first introduced the concept of a functional heart brain in the 1990's. This brain in the heart – just as the brain in the digestive tract – may also act independently of the brain in the head. The size of this brain, according to Boulder Creek, California's Institute of HeartMath, is as great as a number of the principle areas of the brain in the head. Studies discussed in *Brain and Values*, have shown that the consistency of the rhythm found in the heart brain is capable of changing – sometimes in spectacular fashion - how effectively the thinking brain functions. *In theory that means that what occurs on a feeling level, has the capacity to deeply influence what occurs on a thinking level.*

In *The Heartmath Solution*, co-authored by Doc Childre and H. Martin, an in-depth look is taken at the heart and its association with the mind and body. This contributes to the newly emerging view of the heart as a complex, self-organized system that maintains a continuous two-way dialogue with the brain and the rest of the body. Research available at the Heartmath website and published in major medical journals demonstrates that the heart has a significant influence on the function of our brains and all our bodily systems.

Imagine the implications of this! Those who live by "their instinct", or who "listen" to their gut, or who make decisions based on what their heart tells them rather than their logical brain, now know that although that may not necessarily always be the right way to go, but all of the information science has now provided us with, clearly demonstrates that in order to make decisions based on *all three* of our brains, they should apply not only that which their logical brain tells them, but also what their feeling brain (heart), and their instinctive brain (gut) have given them to understand.

Keeping up with cutting edge research is a fascinating thing because it means that you are able to discover what is happening in that intriguing world of avant-garde thought and progress long before any of this hits the main stream press. It means that you can begin to apply the information contained therein long before everyone else is talking about it...and of course the only reason that is important, is because it might make such an enormous difference to the quality of your life ... sometimes *just because it changes the way you think about things.*

[...]

Paying Attention to All Our Brains

As a society we have very much undermined and sabotaged the knowing we receive from our feelings and our intuition. Even when we are wont to give such knowing value, due to consistently pejorative and damaging connotations associated with feelings and intuition, we often hesitate to even give them any consideration at all when they arise in us. Therefore, research such as that described in this article is very encouraging, because it may persuade many who might not otherwise do so, to pay greater attention to such knowing, and to begin to use it in their daily lives.

So if we now come back to our original topic of finding a meaning in your life, and you now understand how much information you get from other parts of your body that are not simply neural cells in the brain, wonderful though these may be, you will also understand the next bit: *when you are searching for a meaning in your life, one of the best instruments you possess to determine the area in which this meaning might be found, is right in your heart and gut.*

Here's how it works: Pay very close attention to all the messages your body is sending you. Does your breath quicken when National Geographic or the BBC announce that a documentary about Egyptian pyramids or the history of the African

Zulus will be airing at 8 pm? Do you sit with bated breath as you listen to the introduction? Does your heart start beating overtime when you hear that bridge classes will be available in your neighborhood at a time amenable with your schedule? Do you feel flushed when you listen to the person at your left at the dinner party discussing horse-breeding? Do you feel excitement flooding your veins when you contemplate sitting down in front of your computer, your piano, your digital film editor? Guess what? The combined intelligence of your body – your *other brain* is giving you a discernable clue to what it is that might give meaning to your life. So how would you incorporate that into your daily life? Good question. It would depend a great deal on what you are currently doing, your finances, your time, etc., but the mere deliberating about the subject, and creatively trying to find a place for it in your life, should already do a lot for your endorphins, not to mention the joy with which you get up in your mornings.

This *clue, this voice* inside of you that you so often pretend not to hear – please try to start listening to it. This *knowing* inside of you that you so often ignore – please try to stop ignoring it. This *knocking* at your inner door that you so often turn away from – please no longer turn from it. This *thing* that pursues you over and over again, talking to you, making you think about whatever it is that you continue to turn a deaf ear to, this *thing* is your intuition and your connection to the divine, your connection to your inner self, your possible self!

> *The way you get meaning into your life is to devote yourself to loving others, devote yourself to your community around you, and devote yourself to creating something that gives you purpose and meaning*
> Mitch Albom

Caroline Myss states that self esteem is essential in order to be able to listen to one's intuition - that it is imperative that one hones one's self esteem if one wishes to come into contact one's own divine self, and that seems to make a lot of sense. Consider that we are rarely encouraged as we go through school to pay attention to our intuition. Rather, our rational mind is extolled, and in its continual exaltation over emotions and intuition, we quickly learn to distrust emotions and intuition, and hence, in order for us to even begin to listen to our intuition, we require rather great resolve and self esteem. Albeit from another angle, Clarissa Pinkola Estés also has some insightful thoughts on this subject of paying attention to our intuition in her excellent audio program *Warming The Stone Child*.

In recent years much fascinating work has been done in the world of neuroscience and social psychology indicating that our erstwhile haste to disqualify the non-rational world of emotions and intuition was perhaps not well-advised because inter-disciplinary work by scientists is beginning to indicate that emotions and intuition are not only valuable adjuncts to our rational intelligence, but possibly even prime stars themselves in our quest for a balanced understanding of our world and ourselves.

But why is intuition our connection to the divine? What is the divine? Is it not the eternal part of each of us? Is it not the part of us that connects us not only to all others, but also to all creation? And if that is so, then isn't it *logical* (if I may use such a word in such a context) that somewhere inside of each of us there must be a connection to this divine part? Joseph Campbell, the great mythologist, very much a Jungian at heart, wrote this:

> *The divine manifestation is ubiquitous; only our eyes*
> *are not open to it. Awe is what moves us forward.*
> *Live from your own center. The Divine lives within you.*

So we must be able to connect to this divine part. Meditation is one method. Listening to our intuition is another. (And there are others as well). We know that for most of us things don't come totally naturally. They have to be learned and practiced. And so it is with listening to our own intuition. Begin listening to that voice, to that knowing, to that knocking, to that *thing* that connects you to yourself in a way that reaches far beyond your physical body.

Remember: if your finances are threatening to turn into daytime nightmares, if the relationship with your partner is free-falling off a steep precipice, if your job is wavering and no longer secure, if you are in emotional pain of any kind, having something in your life that gives it a meaning, will allow you to hold on to this strong, stable inner core – *the oak tree* I alluded to at the beginning of this chapter - while you work on resolving the other issues. It will allow you to move on ahead with much less of the usual doubt, fear, and trepidation. All it takes is some decision, determination, and tenacity on your part to find this meaning for your life. And love ... love for yourself because if you love yourself, you know that without a meaning in your life, a fundamental pillar of that same love for yourself does not yet exist. Do this for yourself!

One of the ways to start, even if you only remember one thing from your early youth, when you wanted to become a rock musician, and even if you only have a very faint inkling now about something that gives you a tingle, not necessarily the excitement I described above, is to jot that down on a sheet of paper with two columns. This first one is labeled *Possible Meanings For My Life*, and the second one is labeled *Absolutely Not! Never!* You can begin by writing all those things that you know you could never contemplate as being something that would give meaning to your life in the second column. I very much respect CEO's of large corporations, and all that they do, I even marvel at much of it, but there is nothing in this world that would make me want to think of that as giving meaning to my life. But talk to Richard Branson. He would beg to differ. And look at his life! There are numerous things not only to admire, but also to emulate! And how I admire certain actors and all that they do and are capable of making us feel by their interpretation of a role, but there is nothing that would make me think of that as giving meaning to my life. To begin with, while I have no problem in getting up on a stage and teaching a weekend workshop to large groups, or speaking on radio or television, I tremble inside to think of standing on a stage or in front of a camera and *acting*. But talk to Meryl Streep or Sean Penn and hear their story. And while I again admire surgeons, haute couture designers and engineers, investment bankers and fishermen, to name only a few, for all their different skills, vast accumulation of knowledge and abilities, I would never contemplate having any of those professions or activities giving meaning to my life. So if I were making my two columns, I would already have a lot in the second one, listing what I *know* won't give meaning to my life. What might go into the first one? Gardening, landscape design, forensic psychology, profiling, homicide detective, concert pianist, farmer, illustrator, librarian, and book store owner. And that's only the beginning. These are activities I have often contemplated as pursuing, *if I did not have the meaning in my life that I do*. If things had been different, or if for some reason this – what I do - had not been possible, or became impossible at some point in time, those other activities would be where I would start looking.

> *Every man's life ends the same way. It is only the details of how he lived and how he died that distinguish one man from another.*
> Ernest Hemingway

Let me tell you a story about Desmond Tutu, Archbishop of South Africa, who along with Nelson Mandela was also instrumental in bringing the country to democracy in a peaceful fashion. When he was interviewed by the BBC's Fern Britton, he related with much wit and vivaciousness that when he was young, he wanted to become a physician. This was out of his reach, however, because of the prohibitive cost, let alone finding a way to do it in the apartheid South Africa of the 50's. Then he decided he wanted to be a teacher, but when he was old enough to enroll in college, it transpired that blacks could no longer become teachers, again, due to the apartheid regime. Seeing his path inexorably narrowed – and he laughed as he told this in the interview – he realized he did not want to become a tradesman, or own a shop, and so he opted for the only other alternative: the church.

This is an amazing twist of fate where we might argue that Archbishop Tutu was not able to pursue the dream and meaning he wanted to give to his life, and nevertheless, because of the manner in which he dealt with his options, he *found a meaning in doing that which was ultimately his last choice.* And while he never uttered these words in any clear fashion throughout the interview, we can, perhaps, assume that he set out to be the best seminary student that he could, the best priest that he could, the best monsignor, the best bishop and ultimately the best archbishop. Being the best did not happen because he followed rules and was ambitious, but because he gave of himself in fulfilling his duties, and in so doing, gave meaning to his life.

It was Jung who said: *Free will is the ability to do gladly that which I must do.* My intention here is not to make you think that you must give meaning in your life to something you do not want to do, or even very much dislike doing, but that if you are doing something you do not want to do, and for the time being find it impossible to change, *then it is possible to find meaning in it*, as illustrated above. And if that is not possible, for some reason, then give meaning to your search for meaning or the preparation you do in order to be able to change to another job or activity that *will* give you meaning.

As you look at your own life, realizing that you might choose to change your present profession for an entirely different one, or that you might choose to return to university in order to totally reinvent yourself *if you could*, you also realize that currently it is simply not feasible.

You may have numerous responsibilities, perhaps a growing family, or aging parents, and hence need to continue where you are, at least for now. Please don't despair. Give meaning to this existence as it stands for the time being due to what you are giving others for whom you have taken on responsibility. In giving meaning to your life through this, you may come to experience a very special compassion and love for yourself, for knowing that you will continue in your present circumstances for the moment because you *choose* to do so. And while you live in this fashion, make plans; prepare yourself, for the time when you *can* change.

Having a meaning in your life can come from very simple things: preparing breakfast lovingly for an ill child, reading to an elderly person whose sight is no longer sharp, sitting companionably with someone as you watch a sitcom, an opera, or a tennis match that *they* enjoy. Having a meaning in your life doesn't mean you are meant to sacrifice yourself, but it *does* mean that you are meant to find it in the here and now, as you prepare for the meaning that you intuit you would prefer. On the road from one of these to the other, you may find that your life has become immensely enriched and that you have drawn another step closer to the rewiring of your soul.

He who has a why to live for can bear almost any how.
Friedrich Nietzsche

SECTION THREE:

SETTING THE STAGE FOR PEACE

Chapter Ten

Gratitude and the Now:
Dual Gateways to Inner Peace

*Acknowledging the good that you already have in your life
is the foundation for all abundance.*
Eckhart Tolle

B eing in a state of constant gratitude has a bearing on the quality of the moment; of *every* moment! Recognizing beauty in the commonplace, being mindfully aware with a sense of curiosity and exploration of all that surrounds you, whether it's your physical surroundings, or the events in your life, as well as the reactions those events evoke in you, brings you to an understanding of how gratitude can contribute to the significance of your life in a colossal way. What this means is that you can be in a state of constant gratitude. And *being in a state of constant gratitude* – perhaps you can imagine this better if you visualize the constant gratitude like glorious background music that you aren't exactly paying prime-time attention to, but that is there - *has a bearing on the quality of the moment*, the quality of *every* moment.

You may think this is a Pollyanna approach to life. You may think your life is far too difficult, far too painful, far too sad, far too grey, far too filled with guilt and shame, far too filled with anger, far too filled with unhappiness, far too filled with addiction – perhaps you are in jail – even on death row, to begin to imagine being in a state of constant gratitude, let alone actually implementing such an idea. I would ask you to bear with me, the same way you did in some of the other chapters that may have created an unbelieving reaction in you. Even if you think that what I am proposing is not for you, or is impossible for you, I'd ask you to go into an observer mode, and simply read the next few pages with an open mind. Remember: having an opinion about something you know very little or next to nothing about is not necessarily the most intelligent way to live your life. So at least give yourself the opportunity to learn something about this concept.

> *If the only prayer you said in your whole life was,*
> *"thank you," that would suffice.*
> Meister Eckhart

Research from fields as diverse as neuroscience and mindfulness or cardiology and weight loss or cellular and molecular biology, as well as Buddhism clearly indicates that the better your life is from the perspective of your state of contentment, the healthier you are, and very likely, therefore, the greater your chances at longevity. Research from the field of positive psychology that was "born" at a meeting of the APA (American Psychological Association) in 1998 in Isla Mujeres near Cancun, under the tutelage of former APA president Daniel Seligman, indicates *precisely* that a greater state of contentment or happiness tends to be achieved – *over all and any other factors* that the study examined – by those people who most practice the art of gratitude.

Here's another thing: the more you practice gratitude, the more it becomes part and parcel of your life. Basically it becomes something that you do almost automatically, or rather, it becomes something that you can no longer help doing. You walk down a street and you practice gratitude because of the breath-taking beauty of the riotously violet bougainvillea climbing up a white-washed wall, or the unmistakably soothing sound of palm fronds swaying in the breeze. Or perhaps you practice gratitude for the brilliance of the pristine snow you see as you step out of your house before anyone or anything has left a mark on it, and the numinous silence of the white landscape. Or perhaps you practice gratitude for the crispness of the air and the electrifying sounds of a busy city around you, or the fact that your legs carry you so efficiently from your point of origin to your destination, or for the fact that your car is old, but comfortable and warm, or that you've just heard a child laugh in that contagious way that little kids do, and that makes you recall, with gratitude, the laughter of your own children at that age. You get my point: gratitude can permeate every living moment. *Conscious awareness* and mindfulness can make it so.

As long as you have not experienced this – simply because you have not yet practiced it – you will have no understanding of the difference this can make to the quality of your life. And the higher the *perceived quality* of your life, the greater your experience of a state of heightened inner well-being. And the greater your inner sense of well-being, obviously, the better your life. But here's the incredible thing: your life is better not necessarily because the outer circumstances have improved, but because your perception and experience of what your life means to you have changed because of your practice of consciously aware or mindful gratitude.

Gratitude is another one of those things, since doing it to a large degree also depends on being aware, that can create new neural pathways, simply by doing it over and over, again and again. Many years ago, when I started the practice, I had a beautiful notebook, purchased especially for this purpose. I wanted to write a list of ten things I was grateful for every day, first thing in the morning, or last thing at night. It was something I wanted to do, but I wanted to do it as expediently as possible, and then basically have it out of the way, in order to get on with my day. Somehow it never really worked. I'd forget about it, or sit and mull in front of it for a while and nothing would flash into my brain that I was grateful for, or I'd think of things such as "my children"; "my home", "my health", and while it is very true that I felt gratitude for all of that, it somehow did not inspire me or lead me to any kind of insight or revelation or epiphany, or whatever I had assumed might happen if I started the practice of gratitude.

Man is fond of counting his troubles, but he does not count his joys.
If he counted them up as he ought to, he would see that every
lot has enough happiness provided for it.
Fyodor Dostoevsky

Eventually my not-yet-ingrained-habit died for lack of repetition, and I forgot about it for some time, until finally, during a rather dark and difficult period of my life some years later, during my morning power walk, something I've been doing for decades, I began consciously focusing on the beauty of stones and shells just at the edge of the water on the beach where I walked. At first glance they appeared boring and mundane, and yet, once I focused in more closely on them, I found they were filled with hues ranging from crystalline, brilliant white, to the darkest shades of green and purple, ending in gleaming obsidian black. Of course this was only visible while they were wet, as I often collected some of the smaller, flatter ones to take home with me, and found that once they had dried, they had lost some of that richness of color.

And yet, I returned day after day to focus on them and these amazing colors, and as I did so, a surprising thing happened: as I would stoop to examine the beauty of yet another rock, wanting to add it to my bulging collection, reveling in its magnificence, I would realize that I was also reveling in the sound of the gulls, and the sound of the waves hitting the sand, and the touch of the soft breeze through my hair, and the salty tang of the air, and the warmth of the sun on my face, and the gleam of the same sun on the ripples of the waves out in the distance, and the majesty of the cruise ship way out there, and I realized that by having focused on the rocks, I had begun a process that was allowing me to see, hear and feel beauty in absolutely everything that surrounded me.

There were two very important corollaries to this: In the first place, I recognized very quickly that I was remaining in a very – to me – clear fashion, in the present. By focusing, as I did every morning during my power walk, on the beauty of the rocks, and thanks to that, seeing (hearing, feeling, etc.) the beauty in everything else, I was *conscious of that*, as opposed to being conscious (in a not-so-*aware* kind of way) of the past or the present, and nostalgic feelings, or worries, or thoughts of painful memories, etc. And by remaining in the present, *ipso facto*, by my gratitude for this beauty that I was observing, my inner state of well-being remained in a good place, or, if it had not been in a good place prior to beginning the daily morning process of being grateful for the beauty I was observing, my inner state of well-being (or not-so-well-being) moved to a good (or better) place. So my energetic frequency moved to, or remained in a good place, even when sometimes external things were not so good. What an amazing revelation this was to me!

Why do you think that when we are children our days seem so much longer? When we were children, and we thought of a day or a week, it seemed to stretch endlessly in front of us. It contained such possibility. What happened to that sensation of time as we grew older?

Here is one idea that may help to explain the phenomenon: as children when we did something, or focused on something, we were *all there* with it. We weren't splintered into dozens of facsimiles, with thoughts on what to cook for dinner, on the bills that need to be paid, on the difficulty of that day's yoga class, on the super market shopping list, on the bad hair day we were having, on the remark someone had made at lunch the other day that left us wondering about our relationship with that person, or thoughts about how to re-structure our investment portfolio. On the contrary, as a child, *our thoughts and our attention were totally directed toward whatever it was we were doing*. Building a sand castle? Our thoughts were about that. Reading *The Lion, the Witch, and the Wardrobe* for the first time? Our thoughts were about that. Making a paper airplane? Our thoughts were about that. And so on.

And because your entire being was imbued with being present with whatever it was you were doing, instead of flitting about here and there into other places and times in your life, you vibrated to the energy of that moment. *You were here and now: fully present.* Your moment stretched and stretched and stretched because it was so filled with that energy of your focus and concentration on that activity. And so your moment appeared much longer. It was filled with sensation and energy.

Now however, the person that you have become has lost (or forgotten about) that ability. And so the moments of your life become shorter and shorter – or worse – they barely exist, because whenever you "get" somewhere, or "reach" some new goal, you are already thinking about the next place to "get" to, or next goal to achieve, as opposed to enjoying the one you are at. *We never seem to learn to enjoy the journey*. You can use the practice of gratitude to regain that lost ability, and you will recognize it for the sensation of well-being it gives you and for the manner in which it lengthens the moments of your life.

In the second place, what happened due to focusing on the beauty of the rocks every day during my power walk, was that this: feeling gratitude for something began happening not only during my power walk, but at first at odd moments here and there throughout the course of my day, and then, as more time passed, I noticed that it was happening most of the time. No matter what I was doing, it seemed to be permeating the very fabric of my life. Wherever I looked, there was something for which I could be grateful due to its beauty (which again, *ipso facto* brought me to the present) or any other quality about it that gave me pause and that brought me into that state of gratitude. It became like that continually present background music I alluded to at the beginning of this chapter.

In other words, gratitude had become a habit – not a habit of which I was unconscious, on the contrary, a very conscious one, yet that came about without necessitating work on my part. It had required awareness at the beginning. Had I refused to be aware of myself and what I was thinking about, in order to pull myself to what lay in front of me – in this case those shells and stones that I found so endlessly fascinating – and had I refused to do this on a daily basis during my walk until I noticed some effect of all of this on me and my inner self, then it would obviously not have come about. Perhaps if I had continued with the effort via the lovely notebook and the gratitude lists I had tried to come up with, it would never have worked. And yet by using my power walk as the moment during which to do this, it was easy … not only was it easy, it was totally pleasurable. I found myself looking forward to it every day. At the beginning the reasons for that were not obvious to me, but as time passed, I realized it was – as I stated earlier – because I felt good while I was doing it. It was almost as though time were standing still during that period of time every day. Sometimes it felt like a reprieve from the plaguing thoughts and worries that were normally part of my menu. This process of being aware enough in order to pull my conscious awareness away from whatever thoughts or worries chattered about and cluttered my mind, to the gratitude exercise, was something that I used to call a walking open-eyed meditation, and then I heard of mindfulness, which in many of its guises, is precisely that.

So there you have another neural pathway being formed, growing stronger every day, growing along with other neural pathways described in most of the chapters of this book, that, to use one of the analogies I have mentioned elsewhere, together with all those other neural pathways creates what might constitute a human being that is no longer the same as he/she was before doing all of this.

Genetically much has changed due to a new environment (the perception you have of events in your life now as opposed to before), physically as cells change due to the above, changes can also be observed, first perhaps merely something as simple as better color in the cheeks, later there may be changes in posture, weight, cholesterol levels, blood pressure, stress levels as measured by hormonal activity, and so on. Your telomeres: protective tips that cap the ends of your DNA that shorten each time your cells divide, so when the telomeres get too short, cell division stops, and your life ends, may even increase in length again, something that, according to world-renowned physician Dean Ornish, creates greater longevity.

There are changes in other areas as well: psychologically and emotionally, and as mentioned earlier, neurologically, due to new and strengthened growth in the pre-frontal cortex, particularly in those areas of your brain that increase the sensation of well-being. This is all because you have made some conscious decisions about creating these new neural pathways by changing the *way* in which you think about things, as well by changing the things you think *about*. All of this has to do with becoming aware, and all of this is clearly inter-connected and strongly correlated with everything else in this book.

Choose Gratitude to Move Into the Now

In the current climate of the global economic crisis, natural disasters, poverty, lack of opportunity, lost possibilities, lack of loving relationships, and so on, many people find their lives immeasurably full of worry, sorrow, pain, anxiety and fear.

Here's something you can do to deal with those difficult and dark emotions: as you find yourself immersed in yet another negative or hard thought or feeling, and find yourself succumbing to its way of pulling you into a black quagmire, do this:

- *Choose* to do something different about this today.
- *Choose* to focus elsewhere (*as opposed to focusing* on the worry or fear).
- *Choose* to feel gratitude for something right here and now (a butterfly, the blue sky, a whiff of heady jasmine from the garden next door, your laptop that connects you to the world in such fascinating ways, your child, your dog, that amazing Persian rug you inherited from your grandmother, your capacity to run, etc.). Whatever you feel gratitude for is not important. What *is important* is that you do feel gratitude.
- As you do this, you will find yourself in the present moment *and in the present moment you are not in the place where you were before, when you were worrying or afraid*
- The present moment brings you to the now, where the past or future have no place.
- Remain in the present moment for a while, *choosing to continue to focus on something for which you feel gratitude.*
- Once you notice that you feel better, move to your other activities or duties, but continue this exercise as soon as you find yourself giving way to difficult or dark thoughts and emotions again.

All You Have Is Now

Here's what we sound like when we are talking about the future:

- I can't wait until we go on vacation.
- I'll be so relieved when I lose these last 10 pounds.
- Everything will be perfect when we move into the new house.
- Things will be so much better when I find a new job.
- My relationship will be fantastic as soon as my partner changes.

And here's what we sound like when we are talking about the past:

- I wish I could just have my last vacation again.
- I looked so wonderful when I was 25.
- The house we had when we lived in _____ was so perfect.
- My first job was just incredible.
- When I first met my partner our relationship was so ideal.

So when do we live in the present? *All we have is now.* Yesterday is gone. Tomorrow hasn't come yet, but we insist on filling most of our present moments with wishful thinking of the future (when things *will* be better), or nostalgic thoughts of the past (when things *were* better).

Yet what we could really be concentrating on is *making our present moments* better by using the tools we've discussed about gratitude. By not doing this, we could equate ourselves to the overweight person who moans about the weight, wishes it would be gone, remembers when it was less, but *never does anything in the present moment to improve the situation*. If our present moment is not as wonderful as it might be, one thing to do, therefore, is to actively change some of the things that are not so good in this present moment.

Gratefulness is the key to a happy life that we hold in our hands, because if we are not grateful, then no matter how much we have we will not be happy -- because we will always want to have something else or something more.
David Steindl-Rast

But be careful: that kind of thinking may also take you into future mode, where all you do is spend time on how wonderful things will be when you accomplish this or that.

Therefore, in order to improve the present moment, things must be done in the present *and it is precisely the essence of this that changes your future!* So being grateful for anything at all in your present moment, as simple and small as it may be, has the capacity to make your present moment better and, more importantly, has the capacity to *train* you towards an enhanced ability to live in the present on a regular basis and hence to shift the energy and reality of your future. *Your future is constructed with the building blocks of the present. Therefore make sure that your present is filled with gratitude!*

Think of your positive points. Dwell, for a moment, on all you have already accomplished, no matter what it may be, in order to see – *now, in this present moment* – all that you have inside of you, and *all that you can use* (that is already there, and that has served you well in the past) to make this now moment even better, *in order that future now moments will be similarly improved.* Remember ... you literally throw your life away, if you do not make some of these changes ... life is to be lived now, today, and not tomorrow or yesterday.

Treasure Each Moment

- Are you taking a walk or working out at the gym? Treasure that.
- Are you having your early morning coffee or tea (or lemon water or green smoothie)? Treasure that.
- Are you driving to work in heavy traffic? Treasure that by listening to something truly enjoyable on your CD or iPod (inspirational speakers are my favorite, but you may prefer the latest cutting-edge information about a subject that interests you, or learning a language that you would normally not have time for, etc.)
- Are you taking your children to a soccer game? Treasure that.
- Are your preparing dinner? Treasure that. Remember the magnificent Mexican movie (based on a book by the same name) *Como Agua Para Chocolate (Like Water For Chocolate)* in which abundant food was prepared? Food was the mainstay of the movie, but it was so in order to demonstrate the love the members of this crazy, heartwarming, intertwined family had for each other and which they continually demonstrated by the symbolism of lovingly prepared food.

> *If we didn't learn a lot today, at least we learned a little, and if we didn't learn a little, at least we didn't get sick, and if we got sick, at least we didn't die; so, let us all be thankful.*
> Buddha

The trick (if you can call it that) is to truly begin to recognize that each and every moment of your life offers the opportunity for you to treasure it – *if you so decide.* (And if you're thinking that your life is simply too hard for that statement to be true, please go back to Chapter Five and read about the life stories I included there about people who went through tremendous difficulties). That means you must be fully aware of yourself as well. Good choices are hard to make without awareness. And inner freedom is hard to achieve without making choices that are based on a life lived in the now.

Any time is a good time to realize how blessed you are. Remember this as you go about your day. Remember it every day. Use it as a mantra when things get you down. Think of all your blessings, whatever they may be. Use it *literally as a tool to improve your life at every step of the way.*

This has nothing to do with religion. It is awareness and mindfulness. Thinking of that which is good in your life as a blessing, implies thankfulness or gratitude. Being grateful, or recognizing your blessings, is one of the most successful ways that people are able to maintain themselves in a content and satisfied state of well-being.

Isn't that alone worth it? What a way to begin this new chapter of your life! *What a simple way to make your life better... feel better...live better.*

We are blessed, you are blessed, I am blessed.

Let us rise up and be thankful, for Gratitude is not only the greatest of virtues, but the parent of all the others.
Cicero

Chapter Eleven

Soothing the Self Without Losing Your Way

And remember, no matter where you go, there you are.
Confucius

When life becomes difficult, when rocks are thrown your way, when you don't know where to turn, when crises threaten to undo you – emotionally, financially, physically, professionally, socially, and so on – most generally resort to something that will help you get through the difficult period. That is obvious and normal. You would be counter-productive, if you didn't do that. But what happens to you when you lose your way? You lose yourself. And when you've lost yourself, you have typically listened to advice (from yourself or from others) that told you that the best way to calm down, or to feel better, was to soothe the self by feeling or thinking or doing something that allowed you to lose sight of whatever was bothering you.

So you turn to your work and become a work-aholic, shop-aholic, or you turn to drugs, serial relationships, a frenetic social life for the mere sake of rubbing shoulders or having something to do every evening and weekend, you turn to gambling, to prescription medication readily supplied to many by their well-meaning doctors, to the quest for eternal youth, to films that give you an adrenaline rush, to sports that give you an adrenaline rush, to risky sex that gives you an adrenaline rush, or you become news junkies (that gives you another kind of adrenaline rush), or you become obsessed by the hue of your lawn, or by the number of your published articles in peer-reviewed journals, or by the value of your stock portfolios, or the letters after your name, or the books in your bookcases, the thinness of your body, the sermons you preach from the pulpit on Sunday mornings, the perfection of your skin or the size of your biceps. Whatever you turn to, *if it is something that causes you to turn away from the self, it is, in essence, causing you to lose your way.*

There is nothing wrong, in and of itself, with many of the above activities. It is when they are used to soothe the self, in other words, to ease an inner condition that we find ourselves unable to deal with because we are unable to face the turmoil in our inner world without resorting to something external, that the soothing activities cause us to lose the way. Losing the way means that – at least until we find our way again – we do not connect with our true self, we do not love our self, and hence we certainly do not rewire our soul.

If you realize what the real problem is - losing yourself - you realize that this itself is the ultimate trial.
Joseph Campbell

What Are Your Addictions?

As stated, we use our addictions to soothe the self when we know of no other way to do it. I can just hear you saying: *I don't have any addictions. I don't drink, I don't smoke, I don't snort cocaine, and I certainly don't shoot heroin. I don't have any eating disorders and I don't gamble.*

Good. Glad to hear that.

- How about work? Have you ever heard your spouse, partner or children complain that you spend too much time there?
- How about shopping? Did you ever cringe when the credit card bills came in at the end of the month and you realized that once again you had spent far more money than you have?
- Now how about *judging other people*? You do that more than just a bit? Like quite often? So that's an addiction. Judging other people is something we can get addicted to. If you try to stop you will notice that it is almost as hard to do as saying good-bye to your cigarettes.

- Then there's criticizing others.
- And stereotyping others.
- And being a fitness buff way beyond just being healthy about your body.
- Making money is a good one. There's an addiction that can mask as something totally different ... like being responsible ... or taking good care of your family.
- Socializing to the point of not wanting (or being able) to be alone.
- Being a news junkie.
- *Remaining young.* Better said: *wanting* to remain young. So the addiction is going after whatever it is you believe will keep you young: creams, clothes, injections, surgery, retreats, sports, etc. None of these things by themselves are wrong, it's the desperate and continued and addictive search to remain young that keeps you from your life and your soul.
- Complaining?
- Feeling blue: now how's that for an addiction?
- Feeling like you are a victim.
- Not letting go of old wounds.
- How about being addicted to another human being? Can't be without them? Need their presence? Feel like something is terribly wrong when they are not totally happy with you? This generally means someone we *think* we are in love with, but it could also be a child or a friend or anyone. Stalkers of celebrities are an extreme example of this type of addiction.
- Blaming others. Uff! That's one to write home about. You are allowed to get off scot free, as long as you have someone to blame. And as long as you do, you don't really live your own life, or connect to your true inner self, or love yourself, and you certainly have no way of rewiring your soul.
- Living at any time *other than the now*; always moving into the past or the future in your thoughts. This addiction belongs to most people, at least until we wake up and become aware. We are always waiting for *that* to happen, or for this *other thing* to happen. Or we are always off in our nostalgic past, when things were so much better. Or, conversely, we live in the fear of our future (stress, worry) or in the pain of our past. *But we don't live in the present.* And so we are addicted to living in this other time that is not *now.*
- Addicted to hanging on to bad feelings. We don't release them, we don't forgive those who are connected to them, often because we believe we would no longer be who we are (*who would I be without my wounds?*), if we were to let go of those bad feelings. So we are addicted to them. Re-read the chapter

on pain and forgiving with regards to the pain body and the emotional body. These are *addictions!*

- Being addicted to gossiping. It's truly a *very* useless habit. Becoming addicted to *this* kind of adrenaline rush can actually drain you of your energy in the long run.
- Needing or being addicted to being needed or to doing something to help others. Maybe you volunteer at a charity or soup kitchen, or maybe you are the proverbial wonderful friend who solves everyone else's problems and organizes all the events. Just doing it is cool. But doing it because you are addicted to the look of gratitude you get, or to the fact that you know the others need you, now *that* is an addiction. Especially if you use this to tie them to you.
- Social power. Being addicted to having it. Or being addicted to someone *else's* social power. Basking in the reflection of *their* sun. Rubbing shoulders with them, their social contacts, and the remainder of their entourage.
- Not forgiving. This is also an addiction: you get to hang on to your wounds.
- Excusing others for their bad behavior. Not calling the shots when you should. Having unhealthy boundaries.

No, no, you say. *Those things you're talking about are not addictions. Furthermore, if I judge or criticize another person, I have a good reason:*

- *Look at those racists in that African country.*
- *Or look at the lack of humanitarianism in the members of the regime of Myanmar after the cyclone hit.*
- *Or look at my boss ... he is so unethical ... he simply takes all the credit for work we've all done as a team*
- *And what about my cousin's daughter? She's nuts ... taking drugs and going out with those tattooed guys that wear earrings*
- *And speaking of earrings ... what about those teenage girls that get a diamond inserted into their belly button?*
- *And don't get me started on those women that let themselves go after they hit menopause*
- *And the pastor at my church! He has such an ego. All he wants to do is hear himself speak, so his sermons are far too long, And so boring.*

So you can see I have very good reasons to judge others. I certainly don't do any of that other stuff!

Right. I'm sure you don't. *But you judge others* for doing those things. *And furthermore, you don't seem to be able to stop* doing so. All I'm trying to point out to you is that you have an addiction of judging other people. What does this addiction help you cover up in yourself? Oh, I don't mean bad behavior. I mean you cover up your own inner issues so *you* don't have to look at them. Not taking a careful look at your own issues keeps you safely unaware. And this judging of others – or *any* addiction helps you do that.

Ok, you say, *maybe you're right. Since I have read what you wrote, I actually tried to stop judging or criticizing people – even if it was just in my mind, and I realized that it would be quite hard to do.*

The most common form of despair is not being who you are.
Søren Kierkegaard

As long as you are addicted – to anything – you will not be able to become *what you truly can become*. You will be a fragmented personality. And the reason is because as long as you have addictions – of any kind – you are using the addictions to live your life for you. You use them to cope. You use them to cover up any difficult feelings. You use them to soothe yourself. You use them, in other words, to live your life for you, because without them, you are not able to. Your addictions live your life for you because they make choices for you. And as long as you don't recognize it, nothing changes. So how can it change?

This is not rocket science. If you've been reading the chapters in this book, you'll know at least one or two of the steps: *Become aware* of your addiction/s. *Make the choice* to make different choices each time you become conscious of falling back into your addiction/s. In other words, you make the choice to become responsible for *all of you*. Becoming responsible for all of you literally means *owning* all of what you think, feel, say, and do. *Owning it, means you deal with it in the moment you think, feel, say, or do it, rather than using an addiction to deal with it.*

Let me say that again: *Owning it, means you deal with it in the moment you think, feel, say, or do it, rather than using an addiction to deal with it.*

By applying some will power and tenacity to this process, you will become stronger and stronger in this department, and then *you will do it automatically because the addiction will no longer be controlling your choices.* And you won't need them to soothe yourself. Your neural pathways will have literally changed. And then you are on the road to self responsibility and above all, inner freedom and joy, a place where you reconnect with your true self, learn to love yourself, and thus are rewiring the soul.

But at this point in our quest, while we're not at all yet certain whether we're really interested in connecting with the true self and rewiring the soul, what is of much more immediate importance, and much more useful to our daily life, is understanding that we typically do all of this soothing and losing the self simply because we often have no clue how to use healthy self-soothing mechanisms.

And the whole point of this book, of course, is to show you that once you begin to learn how to be in charge of all those parts of you that threaten to fall apart or dissolve into fear, stress, panic, or pain, you don't really need to soothe the self in those unhealthy ways at all, because you will find yourself, no matter what happens, in a place of awareness from which you will be able to deal with all of those states. You'll come to a point, if you follow through on the information in this book, where you will be your own witness, you'll be the observer of yourself at all times, and especially when you are in a difficult place emotionally. And as you learn to do that, and begin to feel the empowerment that such behavior and awareness gives you, you will come closer and closer to your true self, because you will feel more and more filled with an inner sense of well-being that now, perhaps, is only part of your life occasionally. But it's meant to be part of your life at all times! Not just when you happen to think of it, not just during your walk, not just on Sundays, but 24-7!

And having said that, if you've already read the chapter on meaning, you will have come to realize that there is enormous value – precisely in life's difficult moments – to have a meaning in life that acts as a firm oak upon which you can lean, and the meaning in life is, of course, what you do with your life, how you live your life, the thing to which you dedicate your life. But that is very different from using your life purpose activity to *ignore* the self, to move away from the self, in the same way a bomb shelter, so to speak, allows you to hide away from life's nuclear bombs. The true purpose of a meaning in one's life is very different, precisely because it allows you to *deal with* the bombs, not to *hide* from them.

Coming back to those activities that so many of us undertake in order to soothe the self, let's take a look at Martine (not her real name), who has just finished an excellent education at an Ivy League university, and who now begins her professional career. Maybe Martine has chosen law, or investment banking, or teaching, or stem cell research as a profession, retail fashion, health-care, the movie industry, or the international world of first-class hotels. You might say she has the world at her feet. But a crisis occurs. It's the recession and she is down-sized at her company. Or her older brother dies unexpectedly. She is now faced with deciding how to deal with this crisis in her life.

Back tracking for a moment, let's take a look at what happened in high school and during the university years. Let's imagine Martine was highly motivated and energized to move forward, so she focused – as she was encouraged to – on achieving as much as possible, in order to get into the best university possible. Perhaps in the middle of all of this she fell achingly in love, but lost the beloved to someone else, or perhaps one of her parents was diagnosed with cancer and eventually succumbed to the disease. At such a juncture in life, there are many choices to be made from the point of view of how the situation could potentially be handled, and it's basically up to us, but frequently, because of the way we are socialized, *this*, and by "this", I mean when a crisis hits us, is when we begin to *soothe* the self and simultaneously begin to lose our way.

So Martine, at this point still a high school student, decides to expend energy in physical exercise, perhaps joining the track team, as well as pushing herself more and more on the academic level. In and of themselves, both activities are laudatory, *as long as they are not being used to avoid facing the self*. Soothing the self for a time is also not something that ipso facto needs to be avoided, *as long as the path back to the self is sought by the individual after having overcome the early distress occasioned by the crisis*. But let's imagine she got caught up in those two activities: physical and academic, and basically no longer feels the crisis as crisis. She seems to have overcome the hurdle symbolized by the crisis. That appears to be good. And the fact that the self somehow got lost in the shuffle is not immediately noticeable.

So when Martine goes on to university, and now has a health scare – perhaps she is told she is diabetic, or perhaps she's involved in a car accident, with multiple fractures of the femur – well, that creates another bit of a crisis. So now she gets caught up in the physiotherapy part of getting better, or in ensuring that the diabetes diagnosis does not lead to any further complications, by becoming a bit obsessed with getting all the latest research about advances in diabetes, and constantly being informed about the subject, in such a way, that the chosen method of dealing with the crisis (obsession with the physiotherapy and all it entails or spending an enormous amount of energy on getting the latest medical information, as though by doing that, the potential problem can be kept at bay), becomes a soothing mechanism that again creates a distance from the true self.

By now there may be a kind of pattern effect, and when Martine finishes university and starts working, perhaps gets married, when there is another crisis, as mentioned at the beginning of Martine's story, whether personal, professional, or health-oriented, it is highly probable that the self-soothing mechanisms will again step into place to ensure that no *negative repercussions* – or as few as possible – are felt. The self-soothing mechanisms allow her to focus intensely on something else and thereby to avoid, or side-step any inner process with regards to the crisis. (By inner process I mean that no real attention is given to dealing with the emotion, in this case perhaps, the fear). And that of course, means that it will take a much greater crisis, later on in the life trajectory, to wake such an individual up to the self, and sometimes not even that happens, and more and more *numbing* mechanisms are put into place in order to avoid that which is most feared: the confrontation with the self.

If you have any difficulty imagining that scenario, I know that if I had said – under a similar set of circumstances with the above-depicted moments of crisis – that Martine had opted for alcohol to deal with the problem, or drugs, whether illegal or prescription, you would not have found it so difficult to take on board. *Soothing the self has many faces.* And where we numb ourselves, we lose our path to the place where we are capable of great love of the self, and where we numb ourselves, we lose our path to the self and hence the soul. Remember, an individual who loves the self, who *know* that he/she loves him or herself, *simply would not numb the self.* Because it would be like having a huge mansion, and living only in a small section of the basement, as opposed to having access to all the magnificent reception rooms, the library, the solarium, and the screening room! Numbing the self means that you have cut yourself off from a part – or many parts - of yourself. By wishing to avoid something, and hence numbing the self, you have no contact with a portion of yourself, just as when you are anaesthetized, even if it's just local anesthesia, there is a part of you that you do not feel.

What is important to remember here is the fact that *what* you use to soothe yourself is just as important as *how* you use it. Clearly, using alcohol, drugs, gambling, indiscriminate shopping, overeating or not eating, self harming, risky sexual behavior and so on, are some very unhealthy ways to soothe yourself, i.e., they are unhealthy ways to deal with emotions that you don't know how to handle.

And therefore, by plunging yourself into study, physical exercise, or work, you are undoubtedly using a much healthier way to soothe yourself. But if this healthier way is used to numb yourself to parts of you, those parts that are hurting and feeling things that you don't know how to handle, and you numb yourself in such a way that you are no longer in contact with your inner self, because whatever is going on in the inner self is too hard to face just now, then this healthy way of self-soothing has just become unhealthy. And so a marriage may be destroyed just as much due to alcohol abuse as due to work abuse (or physical abuse – violence), and the relationship between a parent and a child may lose the potential richness of connection just as much due to frenetic social activity (which might be called networking by some), as due to drug abuse.

If, on the other hand, as you plunge yourself into work or study or a creative activity, or something physical such as training or practice in your chosen sport, in order to soothe yourself, while recognizing that you are doing it to allow a healing to take place in order to bring you to a new space from the current crisis, some time down the road, whether hours, days, weeks, or even months, then your approach – the *how* you are going about the self-soothing – has just taken on a very healthy hue. The important difference is that from the outset you are *aware* of what you are doing, why you are doing it, and that once you feel less in need of soothing, you already know in advance, that you will come back to your inner center. Soothing yourself under such premises literally means that each time you do this, you actually have a chance to grow and furthermore, to grow closer to your true self, as opposed to growing more numb and more distant from your true self each time. The process is analogous to taking an aspirin for a headache or fever, and taking it several times over the course of a day or two until the physical symptoms abate, and then, of course, you stop because you know the aspirin is no longer necessary, and you also know, that if you continued taking it, *you would be harming yourself.* Similarly, when you soothe the self, if you are aware of what you are doing, you discontinue the self-soothing (or the numbing over-doing of it) once you have come to a place inside where you are capable of managing life again without the self-soothing mechanism.

There are so many ways of understanding how this happens. We are socialized, not only by our parents, church and school system, but also by everything we see around us in society: billboards, commercials, movies, novels, other people we may have taken on as role models, etc., into believing that our lives consist in doing well at school, becoming successful, being reasonably decent, taking reasonable care of our health, getting married, having children, and growing old. Very little – not even organized religion – gives us another kind of understanding of what we need to do in order to be healthy and vibrant on levels that go far beyond those included in the above description.

So what are we meant to be doing?

I believe it starts with the *cultivation of a connection to the self.* And that of course implies understanding what or who the self is. Is my "self" the part of me that says "I am angry" when something that makes me angry happens? Is my "self" the part of me that wants to be loved by my partner? And is my "self" the part of me that suffers when my partner does not love me in the way I want? Is my "self" the part of me that gets tired in the evening, or that feels kind of blah in the morning? Is my "self" the part of me that wants to make a good salary, or a killing on the stock market, and is it the part of me that enjoys a good movie? What exactly is my "self"?

What it certainly is *not* is the part of you that is afraid, that is angry, that dies. The self does not die. Ever. So the language you want to use with and about the self must of necessity be different than the language you may use when you refer to those other parts that do get angry, afraid and so on, the parts that do die. We could call those parts that die, as many authors do, the body, the ego, and the unaware self. The ego is the self that is not aware of itself. Sorry, I'm not trying to play with these words as much as trying to get you to see and understand what the real self, the aware self, is. You may wish to have another look at the chapter about the ego.

Have you ever been furious about something, perhaps you were just in traffic, and some idiot nearly caused you to crash and total your car? Although all is well, you are now livid. As you scream at the other driver, there is a part of you that is actually observing you harangue and beleaguer him. A part of you that might be amused to see how totally beside yourself you are. Interestingly, this part of you is not angry at all. If you have ever had such an experience, let me tell you that the part that was angry is the ego, and the part that observed was the self / soul.

Here's another example. It is highly likely that when you and your partner decided to join your lives together, was a poignant moment, to say the least. Perhaps as it was happening, and as you realized that the two of you were truly making that monumental decision, filling you with happiness, there was a part of you that was off to one side, observing yourself. As it happened, you observed yourself hand-in-hand with your partner, skipping down the street, or sitting together in that romantic restaurant, or lying in bed, a song in your heart and the flush of happiness on your cheeks. Again, the part of you that was living the immediate emotion was the ego, and the part that observed was the self / soul.

And one final example: you've just been in or witnessed a horrific car crash. Or you've just seen the twin towers being dissected by a plane. Or you just heard the news of JFK's assassination, or you just saw the devastation in Japan after the earthquake and tsunami, or the earthquake in New Zealand, the flooding in Australia, Brazil and Pakistan, the horrific tragedy in Haiti after their earthquake, other terrifying quakes in Chile and Burma, the destruction and ruin suffered by Indonesia after their own tsunami, or by Miami after Hurricane Andrew, New Orleans after Katrina, and so on. You are in shock, horrified, perhaps even petrified, you feel numb, glazed, filled with fear and disbelief. *And you notice that a part of you is noticing the part that is in shock.* Again, the part that was feeling the shock and fear was the ego, while the part that observed it was the self / soul.

If you are stymied by my examples, and have never – at least not consciously – had such an experience, perhaps as you go through the process of becoming more aware, especially as you follow the indications in the chapter on awareness, you will find that soon you will have such an experience in the emotion of some moment. Keep an eye out for it, because it *will* happen.

Here is how Chris Griscom puts it: "As each soul creates a reality, the decision as to whether that reality is an experience of love, light, and God – or whether that reality is an experience of fear, anger, and dying – depends on the capacity of that being to perceive and to recognize choice, and handle the discernment. The enlightened choice creates a reality that promotes, speaks of, and manifests the urge of the soul."

And the soul will never choose darkness. The ego might. But not the soul.

So going back to Martine, our young high school student, university student and young professional, when she begins to use the soothing mechanisms in order to deal with a crisis, the reason a schism is being created that separates her from the self, that self in the above-described sense, the self that is the soul, is *because this "self" is not being taken into consideration.* It is not being acknowledged. It is being cast aside, forgotten about, and above all, not loved and not recognized. Who ever told Martine about this; about the need for connecting with this? Who ever mentioned that by connecting with the real self, self-soothing mechanisms were no longer going to be necessary, at least not in the way described here, because the connection of love to the self would carry her through the crisis?

The connection of love to the self. Once the love connection towards the self has been set up you simply can't lose your way again. You will *automatically* choose from a standpoint of enlightenment to create, as Griscom puts it: "a reality that promotes, speaks of, and manifests the urge of the soul."

To reconnect to this self, also called the divine self, or as Joseph Campbell put it, *the divine inner* self, the self that comes from source, the higher self, is why we are here. Again, in Chris Griscom's words: "The higher self can change the feelings we have towards each other, towards reality, how we perceive. That's why we're here – to bring in the higher self. Each one of us must awaken and know that we are our own teachers, that we are our own healers, that we are our own priests."

Soothing the self can take many disguises. Loving the self is soothing. But the road towards loving the self so that it can become, so to speak, our self-soothing mechanism, is not simple *because of the way we have been socialized.* Most people don't realize how everything else depends on our love for our "self", and therefore, how absolutely necessary it is to come to a place where we begin that process. In the chapter on loving the self, there is much more detailed information about this topic, and suffice it to say that when our self-soothing mechanisms ultimately lead towards this road of loving the self, then they are healthy. When they don't lead there or when they are used independently of any kind of self-love, then they are not.

Looking back, you realize that a very special person passed briefly through your life, and that person was you. It is not too late to become that person again.
Robert Brault

Chapter Twelve

You Are Here To Be Happy

Happiness is the meaning and the purpose of life, the whole aim and end of human existence.
Aristotle

This is potentially one of the most important chapters of this book. If you have understood that happiness is a choice that you make each and every moment of each and every day, then you are well on the road to that loving of the self, to that inner rewiring of your soul, to that reconnection to your true self. You are well on the road to reconnecting with your inner essence, the part of you that is not only infinite and eternal, but the part of you that is here in order to learn this essential lesson. Happiness is a choice. Happiness lies in your own hands. Happiness is not something that depends on outer circumstances, because, as we have already seen in the chapters on choice, on awareness, on thoughts, and on your emotions, *how you choose to react to any and all of the circumstances that surround you, and how you choose to think about any and all of the circumstances that surround you, and whether you choose to be aware of yourself and therefore choose to deal with feelings that arise within you from that position of awareness, will all influence the state of your happiness.* Perhaps the most important consequence of the above sentence is that once you have taken all of that on board, and once you have, in fact, decided to live your life in such a way that you are choosing to remain in an inner space of well-being, no matter what (read again the paragraph about Aimée Mullins in the chapter on choice, or any of the other people whose lives I touch on there), *then you will have begun to love yourself, to have rewired your soul; you will have come to the place you were meant to be in since the day you were born. You are here to be happy!* Joy, happiness and well-being are variations on a theme, but they all underline one central thought: while you may not be in joy if you are imprisoned or undergoing heart surgery, you can, nevertheless, be in a place of inner well-being *by choice.*

We are raised to believe that our happiness depends mainly on what happens in our world. If things are going well, and if we are loved, and if we have enough money, and we are healthy, and our children have developed well, then it is understood that we can have a measure of happiness. Or perhaps we have been raised to believe that our happiness depends also on other outer factors such as how *good* we are to others, how much we *care for* others, how *self-sacrificing* we are, and that if we do all of that well, then we will have a measure of happiness. And while it is true that altruism rates high on scales of happiness, it is much more a question of whether we do it because we really want to, and not so much a question of doing it out of a sense of duty that will give us the measure of happiness referred to above. But let's continue examining this elusive sense of happiness, that drives most of us, but that appears to not be readily available, unless outer circumstances collude to make it possible.

When I first approach people with the idea that happiness is a choice, there is quite a bit of resistance. I am given myriad reasons why it can't be so, and that happiness depends so much on specific conditions in that person's life being just right. These are some of their objections:

- How can I be happy if I can't find a job?
- How can I be happy if I'm not making enough money yet?
- How can I be happy if I haven't yet found the love of my life?
- How can I be happy if I still have to wait eight more months for my vacation?
- How can I be happy if I didn't make the team try-outs?

- How can I be happy if I have to do this inane, boring job, just to make ends meet?
- How can I be happy if my child is sick?
- How can I be happy if my mother is dying?
- How can I be happy if I am in jail?
- How can I be happy if my family lives six thousand miles away from me?
- How can I be happy if I can't afford to go to restaurants?
- How can I be happy if my partner is cheating on me?
- How can I be happy if I am so alone?
- How can I be happy if my dream of working as a model was just torn to shreds?
- How can I be happy if I broke my leg?
- How can I be happy if that car accident left me paralyzed?
- How can I be happy if I missed my flight and can't make it to that important meeting?
- How can I be happy if it's been raining for three days and I can't play golf?

All of these questions – and many more like them – can be broken down into this: *it is impossible for me to be happy because of an external condition that is not the way I want it to be.* The great Spanish painter Picasso was said to have stated: "Everything exists in limited quantity - especially happiness." You can understand that the mere fact of believing something like that quote predisposes you to unwittingly being less happy than someone who does not believe this. And believing one thing or believing the other is equally difficult or equally easy.

Henry Ford said: "Whether you think that you can, or that you can't, you are usually right." *We can choose what we believe. And* we *can choose where our thoughts dwell.*

Becoming Responsible for Our Own Happiness by Looking in all the Right Places

The thoughts we have and what we focus on when things are going wrong in our lives have much to do with how we then deal with these moments:

- Where do you look when something goes wrong?
- What do you focus on when you can't seem to get ahead?
- Which thoughts run through your head when you've just bungled something?

- Which feelings course through you when your world turns upside-down?
- What reactions does your body give you when you *just know* it can't get any worse?

The answers to all of those questions tell you a great deal about the current quality (or lack of quality) of your life, and about the state of your inner well-being.

Looking in all the right places literally means always looking for something to appreciate, love, or enjoy, or something to be grateful for. This appreciation, or gratitude, if you will, as you have seen in the chapter on gratitude, can be highly instrumental in changing your inner energetic frequency, bringing you closer to a place where you might feel much better than you felt before.

It also means looking for something in the situation in which you find yourself, that can help you grow more, looking for something that can teach you to progress more productively, to be more you, and to consistently feel better about yourself – *no matter where you are currently at, and no matter what has actually happened.*

That means that when the fan is full with what hit it, you are focusing on something to appreciate in this situation, something that will create learning in you, in other words, you are looking to find something in *any and all situations life brings you to* that makes you capable of some manner of appreciation.

Imagine just for a moment that you get to choose the things that happen to you. Obviously you would only choose *good* stuff. But let's imagine for a moment that you have a child in first grade. For most kids the good stuff would be recess time and play activities. The not so good stuff might be learning how to read and write. Or math. You get the picture. For the child to progress – although the child might not willingly choose it – he needs to go through some stages of progressive learning in order to become the competent, effective and proactive adult that you are hoping he will indeed grow to be.

Back to you. If you got to choose everything that happens to you, you might only choose the *good* stuff. But let's say there's a part of you that is wiser (as you are – I hope – the wiser adult parent to your hypothetical child in first grade). This part of you that is wiser knows that *in order for you to grow on levels that have nothing to do with reading, writing and arithmetic, you will need to choose a number of situations in your life that will cause you to progress in those directions.*

So if you got to choose, that wiser and older part of you would be choosing experiences that might not – at first glance – look like a lot of fun and games. Maybe you have to live in an orphanage as a young child (like Wayne Dyer), maybe you get sexually abused (like Louise Hay), maybe you are diagnosed with cancer (like Kylie Minogue), maybe you become a quadriplegic after falling off your horse (like Christopher Reeve, the actor who played Superman), maybe you are repudiated by the husband you love because you are unable to bear children (like Soraya of Iran, second wife of the late Shah), maybe you develop Lou Gehrig's disease (like the world-renowned physicist Stephen Hawking), maybe your mother is assassinated in front of the eyes of the world (like Pakistan's Benazir Bhutto's son), maybe you get jailed for 28 years for expressing your political opinions (like Nelson Mandela), maybe you get sent to Auschwitz, the Nazi extermination and work camp, during the Holocaust, and just about your entire family gets gassed while you are in there (like psychiatrist and author Viktor Frankl), maybe your husband is decapitated in a high-speed boating accident (like Princess Caroline of Monaco's second husband), maybe you have to battle drug addiction (like actor Robert Downey Jr.), or alcoholism (like the late Welsh actor Richard Burton, twice married to Liz Taylor), or maybe your young son falls 53 floors from a Manhattan skyscraper (like Eric Clapton's son Conor), or maybe you lose your sister to suicide (like Mariel Hemingway lost her sister Margaux), or perhaps you lose your daughter in a tragic skiing accident (like Vanessa Redgrave lost her daughter Natasha Richardson).

The list could go on and on. I've deliberately chosen famous names so you can relate more readily. You probably have heard of many of these people, can picture them, and have watched some of them via the international media as they were going through their particular *experience*.

Not to mention the millions of nameless who go through tremendous tragedies in their lives, hunger, poverty, slavery, etc., without any of us ever knowing who they were.

So if you could choose what happens to you, and hypothetically, if you choose one of the above painful and difficult examples (*never in my right mind*, I can hear you say ... but just bear with me for a moment here), *wouldn't you have chosen that specific experience in order to gain something from it?*

Again, I can hear you saying: *how could I gain something from such an awful situation?* Do you remember the American couple, Maggie and Reg Green, some years ago, whose young son Nicholas was shot in Italy in a botched robbery while his family was on vacation there? His parents subsequently decided to donate Nicholas' organs and tissues to seven Italians to enable others to live and to have a future that Nicholas was denied. *Their gain* was to see that their young son's life had not been truncated in vain. *Their gain* was to see the joy in the lives of seven families who were able to benefit from their tragedy. *Their gain* was to look beyond the merely obvious, close-down, and personal, to a broader situation where we truly are all one.

So what did they do to get there? I don't know them and am certainly not privy to their innermost thoughts. But I imagine that one very important element was to *focus on the right things, to look in all the right places*. And part of that is:

- What can I do with this?
- How can I learn from this?
- How can I use this to make me a bigger, better person?
- How can this help me grow?
- How does this take me closer to my soul purpose?

Do you doubt that most of the people I mentioned earlier did that? Remember Christopher Reeve's crusade for stem cell research? Or look at Stephen Hawking's zest for life and scientific discovery. Or Mandela's goal to end apartheid without anger and revenge and hatred. Certainly, not all were able to use their experience in the way I'm describing. Nor am I stating that they went about it the way I describe and in some instances the state of their later life attests to having taken another kind of decision altogether. No one says it's easy. All I'm suggesting is that if you give this a try, and begin to *look in all the right places*, you will make your life better *no matter what the external circumstances are*. And that – once again – leads to inner well-being and ultimately, inner peace and freedom.

To live happily is an inward power of the soul.
Aristotle

Neuroplasticity, the Brain & Happiness

Neuroplasticity of the brain, that I have discussed earlier in this book, refers to the fact that the brain is flexible and capable of growth. What grows in the brain are not only new neurons, or brain cells, but also the connections between these, and therefore, as an example, the section of the brain that corresponds to the left hand of a concert violinist, is much enlarged, with thickened and strengthened neural pathways due to the amount of exercise that hand and those fingers get, as opposed to the other hand. The brains of taxi drivers in some large cities have been mapped and the area corresponding to spatial knowledge and navigation in the hippocampus has been shown to be enlarged due to the detailed information these individuals have about routes throughout their respective cities.

When you first learn how to drive a car, you create a new neural pathway that corresponds to the activities you undertake as you drive the car: your hands on the wheel, the gears, the brakes, your attention to the rear-view mirror, the speed, the other cars around you, traffic signals and signs, and so on.

When you start a new exercise regime, perhaps one in which you do strength-training exercises, in order to work on toning your muscles, that you had not worked on to any great extent before this point, then new neural pathways that correspond to those muscles, develop in your brain, at the same time as the actual muscles that correspond to those areas of the body your are toning, begin to tighten and grow in strength.

When you learn how to use a computer, do algebra in long-hand, or conjugate Italian verbs, all of it is always creating new neural pathways. And the more you do the activity that corresponds to the neural pathway in question, the more that pathway is strengthened. And the more you indulge in new activities, the more new and different neural pathways are created, that in turn, connect to other, already existing pathways, demonstrating the immense and seemingly never-ending neuroplasticity of the brain.

Therefore, when you decide – from a position of conscious awareness about wishing to make positive changes in your life – to believe that your happiness is a choice, as opposed to believing in the way Picasso did, that happiness is something that is only available in very limited quantities - then you are creating a new neural pathway in the very same way. (I recall reading a miniature booklet by Stuart Wilde decades ago, titled *Life Is Not Meant To Be A Struggle*, and it captivated me, because *I had simply never thought of life that* way. So reading it created a new neural pathway.

Just as a four-minute mile had never been run before Roger Bannister proved it possible, and after that, many others ran a mile in four, and even under four minutes, *simply because neural pathways now existed in the brains of many people with that belief*, so something changed in me simply by reading about the concept of life not being meant to be a struggle.

New thoughts, new beliefs, and new activities create new neural pathways. And so just by having taken the possibility that happiness is *your right* on board, without rejecting it, and thinking about it every so often – even before you begin to actually put it into practice, your brain begins to change. The flexibility of your brain – its neuroplasticity – is what allows this to happen, whether you are 17 or 47 or 87 years old, and not only does it happen, but the more you continue down the road of this new belief, reinforcing it each time you choose to believe it, despite outer circumstances, the more the neural pathway is strengthened and thickened, *at the same time as the other neural pathway, the one that believed that happiness was only available as a limited supply, is weakened.* When super highways were being built in many nations during the second half of the 20th century, many secondary roads that had been busy with traffic, stopped being used, the petrol stations and cafés that existed there died out, again for lack of use and little or no traffic on those roads, due to the greater use of the super highways, where *new* petrol stations and new cafés came into existence. That is exactly what happens in your brain when you begin to create new neural pathways and then continue to use them over and over again. The new ones become busy and strong and the old ones – that did not serve you well - wither from lack of use.

Do You Have the Right to be Happy?

I would almost prefer to name this section: "Do You Have the *Responsibility* to be Happy?" because being in a place of inner well-being (which is not exactly the same as being happy, but it is closely related), makes such a difference in your life from so many points of view and so you should take it as your responsibility. It influences your physical health. It influences your psychological frame of mind. It has a powerful effect on your emotions and it brings you closer to your soul, it rewires you with your soul because a state of inner well-being that you bring about from a conscious and aware place, literally comes from the soul. When you feel good from inside of you, and not necessarily because something good is going on in your outer world, then you may recognize that this state of inner well-being arises from your soul, and the fact that you are in that state, *no matter what the outer circumstances are,* proves that you have a live and direct connection to your soul.

Being responsible for your happiness and having a right to be happy are concepts that seem to fly in the face of convention. We simply don't tend to talk that way. We tend to believe that happiness *happens* and *not* that it is something that we could *and should* take responsibility for in the same way we are responsible for paying our bills on time. But think about it: why should you not be responsible for your happiness in the same way you are responsible for brushing your teeth? If we began to think that way, if we began to believe in such a situation being normal, you can imagine, for one, how much less depression there would be in the world.

If an individual is prepared to take an aspirin if he develops a temperature, or a headache, i.e., he is used to being proactive about a condition that arises occasionally in the health of his body, he could just as easily be proactive about doing something else when he becomes aware that he is slumping inwardly, feeling down, or losing his sense of inner well-being. If that were the case, he would simply undertake any number of specific activities or would begin to choose different thoughts, or to focus on something different than whatever he had been focusing on to that moment, in order to *shift his inner state.* Imagine what a different world that would be! And I might add that under those conditions, another individual faced with a diagnosis of cancer or heart disease, might then − before considering anything as drastic as surgery or chemotherapy − in actual fact take a deep look inside of himself in order to determine which areas of his life need fine-tuning: where does he need to become more responsible for his happiness and well-being and how? Perhaps by coming to a greater understanding of the supreme importance of loving the self? Perhaps by becoming more proactive about forgiving? Perhaps by becoming more proactive about leaving pain and resentment behind? I imagine you get the gist.* We are not, however, in general, proactive about how we feel on the "happiness" continuum, because we tend to believe that it is not in our hands. So we seek to self-soothe (see the chapter on that), or we medicate ourselves in other ways (making pharmaceutical companies very rich indeed in the process), or we blame others, our situation or the world at large for our lack of happiness.

* Understand that my statements about looking at the self have *nothing* to do with blame. If your health diagnosis is cancer, for example, and you choose to look at yourself, *as well as* looking at conventional medical options, you are doing a similar thing − analogically − as the tennis player diagnosed with tennis elbow, who not only takes the time recommended by his physician for the elbow to heal, but proactively *also* decides to examine how he plays the game, in case that added to the injured elbow.

> *It isn't what you have, or who you are, or where you are, or what you are doing that makes you happy or unhappy.*
> *It is what you think about.*
> Dale Carnegie

The whole topic of whether we have the *right* to be happy is also fraught with preconceived − and very erroneous and unhealthy - ideas about selfishness and sin. Just as we tend not to be too involved in the idea of needing to love ourselves, we are also not very well versed about the idea that we have a right to be happy. Clearly, both concepts go hand in hand. If I know that it is imperative that I love myself, then I am also very much interested in my right to be happy. By loving myself I have instantly moved myself into a place where I take responsibility for my happiness and where I am aware of the state of my inner well-being at all times. That's part of what loving the self means.

But as always throughout this entire book, it comes down again to the factor of awareness. You might have this running dialogue: I must be aware of myself on all levels, beginning with my body, ranging through my psyche or mind and emotions and ending with my spirit. All parts of me must form part of my awareness grid because every single one of the parts influences all of the others and vice versa. I can't forget about the body, because that will sooner or later take its toll in another area, and I certainly can't forget about the spirit either, because that too, would take its toll in the other areas. And so my state of vigilant awareness, perhaps at the threshold of all else I do in all my waking hours, is something that needs to be exercised diligently in order that it may work for me.

But don't lose heart. Exercising it diligently doesn't mean that your life becomes drudgery or unexciting and boring. Each little bit that you invest in paying attention to all of the above, to being aware, enhances the parts of you that have already had a bit of practice in this and thus makes them stronger. And so on successively in geometric escalation. Simply by paying attention, you make it stronger, and *the stronger your awareness becomes, the more being aware will become one of your highest priorities* because awareness connects you to yourself and to your love for yourself. It rewires your soul. It brings you to the place where you always knew – intuitively – you could arrive.

Ever since happiness heard your name, it has been running through the streets trying to find you.
Hafiz of Persia

How Does Happiness Come About?

We've already examined one very important aspect of how happiness comes about: loving the self. But there are many other factors. Because we're not generally taught to love the self, this in itself is a process we have to go through and the chapter on loving the self goes into that in greater detail. But many of the things we do in order to begin to love the self have to do with creating happiness as well.

Here are some ideas:

- Becoming more and more aware every day (aware of yourself in all ways) and using that state of awareness to make good choices for the state of your inner energy (for example, choosing not to continue talking about some event or conversation that bothered you this morning on your way to work, with your colleagues, friends and family, means that because you are leaving the topic to one side, having realized it simply does not merit your energy and negative emotions, you have more inner space to dedicate to feel good, or to be aware of how pleasant life can be).
- Creating good boundaries.
- Remembering to be present, by focusing on the here and now
- Choosing to look at whatever is happening differently.
- Choosing to think about it in another way.
- Choosing to move beyond your current comfort zone.
- Choosing not to remain at the energetic level at which you currently find yourself.
- Choosing to move your energy higher (see the notes in the Appendix for Chapter 2).
- Choosing to recognize that frequently how you feel (a lack of well-being) derives from not having *made the choice* to forgive someone.
- Choosing to focus on something that creates pleasure or well-being or a sense of gratitude, however slight, as opposed to choosing to continue focusing on pain or anger or impatience or jealousy or any other negative emotion. Remembering that by focusing elsewhere does not mean that you are repressing the negative emotion, or pretending it is not there, but that while you recognize that the negative emotion *is* there, and that just now – at this specific moment in time - you are not able to solve it, you nevertheless choose to focus on the other thing in order to shift your inner energy, and hence your state of well-being.
- Recognizing that when you focus on past pains, you reconnect to that past energy, as opposed to remaining here in the present, and therefore making the decision to choose consciously to focus elsewhere instead of on the past pain. The more you do this, the weaker the neural pathways that connect you to the past energy of the painful emotion become, and the stronger the new neural pathways that almost automatically prefer to focus on something that creates gratitude, well-being or pleasure in you become. See the chapter on emotions for more detailed information about this process. Note: As stated, be careful not to confuse this process with repressing the negative emotion. This has been thoroughly discussed earlier.
- Making a habit of daily exercise, even if you only do 30 minutes of brisk walking and using that time to focus on the here and

now, on the beauty that surrounds you, on whatever you may be grateful for.

- Being grateful at all times for *what is* in your life, maybe not *all* of what is, but for some of it and focusing on that much more than the parts you want to change.
- Being aware of beauty at all times and being grateful for it. This can become such a wonderful habit at the threshold of your awareness so that almost without realizing it, you constantly are aware of beauty and constantly are grateful for it. This creates enormous shifts in your state of well-being.
- Searching for meaning in your life (also see the chapter on meaning), if you haven't already found it, and using it to augment the state of your well-being.

Your happiness lies in your hands so much more than you can imagine *until you begin to put some of these ideas into practice.* Then you will understand how much happiness truly is a question of choice!

Nothing can bring you happiness but yourself.
Ralph Waldo Emerson

Chapter Thirteen

Establishing the Inner Connection

Living is being born slowly. It would be a little too easy if we could borrow ready-made souls.
Antoine de Saint-Exupéry

Jung talked about *individuation*, Maslow talked about *self-actualization*, and the way it is used in this book, having an inner connection means that you have a relationship with yourself in the most intimate way possible. You value yourself, you know yourself, you love yourself, you are constantly seeking to understand yourself within a process of growth, but you do all of this while having a valid connection with the world. In other words, you don't expend all this focus on yourself by obviating your connection to the world. The vibrant relationship with yourself takes place within the parameters of your vibrant relationship to the world that surrounds you. Your constantly evolving relationship with yourself evolves in part precisely because of your constantly evolving relationship with the world that surrounds you. You are part of a dynamic inflow-outflow process in which you are totally aware of yourself, but just as totally aware of what is external to you. Your awareness of what is external to you is ruled by your inner connection. In other words, *the manner in which you relate to yourself determines how you relate to all that which is external to you.*

This inner connection carries enormous weight not only with regards to your physiological and psychological health and happiness, but also with your spiritual health. The inner connection literally means that you have rewired the soul, connecting with the part of you that lives on and on, the eternal part of you, the part that does not die, the part that talks to you all your life, although so many never recognize it as such, and put it out of mind by dismissing it as intuition or irrational nonsense or ephemeral coincidence. The inner connection can mean that a life fraught with outer difficulty and pain can nevertheless be good, fruitful, and productive (and I call to mind my three favorite examples: Nelson Mandela, Victor Frankl, and Alexsandr Solzhenitsyn of whom I have made mention throughout this book), and having established the inner connection implies that the individual who has recognized the connection has found the beginning of the road to meaning and purpose in his or her life.

But when the inner connection has not been established – in other words, when the individual has not realized that there can be such a connection, or perhaps may even have glimpsed it, but then decided to let it go – then that person tends to have much more difficulty understanding how we are each in charge of our own inner well-being and happiness, and how it is our responsibility to ourselves to rewire the soul, to connect to the self, to love the self, in order to scale the heights of inner peace and freedom that this connection and rewiring of the soul promise.

People have often told me that they fear being by themselves. That they fear their own company. Or that they dislike their own company. That they will do anything to avoid an evening on their own. Others tell me that while they may not fear being alone, they find it a most boring proposition, and can't quite imagine how to fill the time, other than with TV or a book or some activity. Others refer to being uncomfortable in their own company, and hence, avoid it. All three alternatives lead us to the same conclusion: if this is how you feel about being alone with yourself, somehow you are not connected to yourself – and - more importantly, you have no real relationship with yourself, and therefore, probably don't know yourself.

Why is this important?

Imagine marrying someone whom you fear being alone with, someone whom you avoid spending an evening with on your own. Imagine marrying someone you find so boring, that you would not want to spend time alone with them. Or imagine marrying someone in whose company *you feel uncomfortable*, and therefore, you avoid this person. Sounds like a bad joke, doesn't it? You'd run ten miles before marrying such a person. You'd do *anything* not to have to spend time with such a person. Nevertheless, that's the situation we find ourselves in when we fail to recognize the value and importance of establishing a relationship with ourselves that makes us *enjoy our own company, find ourselves interesting companions about whom we can always learn something new, and who can always lead us to deeper and deeper levels of understanding, and with whom we can have fun and feel excited about.* In a nutshell: someone with whom we find peace and harmony; someone whom we love.

> *I met a lot of people in Europe. I even encountered myself.*
> James Baldwin

Are You Interested in Yourself?

Really? Is such a relationship with the self really possible? It basically comes down to what Jung termed the *conjunctio*, in other words the meeting of two separate parts of the self (generally unconscious) in the process of becoming a whole, or of uniting, and in so doing, of transforming.

But that actually sounds like so much psycho-babble. Who can contemplate overcoming what sounds like such a difficult hurdle? Furthermore, who has the time and money to go into therapy in order to learn about all these things, and explore the deep dark past of one's childhood? In actual fact, it is not so hard, and it certainly *doesn't* depend on whether or not you go into therapy. It has a lot to do with becoming conscious and aware of the self (see the chapter on awareness), with a desire for knowledge of the self, with the intention to love the self, and with the acceptance of responsibility for the self. So basically it has a lot to do with *how interested you are in yourself* and how free you wish to be of all those things that tend to rule your life: unbidden thoughts, emotions resulting thereof, unhappiness, pain, compulsion, stress, obsession, etc.

Carl Gustav Jung, one of the many thinkers who brought us the idea of the integral, or holistic human being, and whose influence is felt in much of the work by Maslow and Campbell and so many others, referred to this holistic human being as one who is understood to be possessed of a body, a mind, and a soul. Jung said that becoming what we can truly be, growing into that which is inherently in us when we are born, is what the process of individuation is all about. This is impossible if we are not in relation to ourselves.

Abraham Maslow, who brought us the *hierarchy of needs* said that in order to self-actualize, we need to become everything that we are capable of becoming. And it follows that we can only become everything we are capable of becoming if we have explored ourselves at depth in order to know how far we can go. Part of it will come due to pushing on in the dark, without knowing exactly where we are going – that leap of faith so much has been written about, but another major part of it will come due to our knowledge of ourselves, due to our discovery of our innermost selves, due to our interest in ourselves, and due to our desire to extend ourselves to the farthest possible outposts.

Joseph Campbell, the great mythologist, said we should follow our bliss. But how can we possibly follow our bliss without knowing ourselves? Without recognizing what it is that creates bliss in us? Without having started out on the inner quest with the intention of finding the inner holy grail, the core, the connection to which brings us into the proximity of bliss that can then be brought out in order to be shared in the outer world? Campbell also writes a great deal about the hero's journey, not only in the classical, mythological sense, but particularly in the highly personal, almost spiritual sense of that inner voyage of discovery, along whose paths we often find the most Herculean tasks that need to be performed, damsels in distress, fire-breathing dragons to be vanquished, and of course, the greatest task of all, the encounter with the self that occurs – almost magically – in the surmounting of those Herculean tasks.

Fear of Being Alone with the Self

If you fear being alone with yourself, perhaps you feel there is so much in you that you hate, or despise, or judge, or criticize, that it is simply a very dangerous – or uncomfortable - proposition to spend time there together with yourself. In other words, it is scary to be with someone towards whom you have these very negative feelings. So doesn't it make sense to get to know this person *that you are* inside and out, and to clean out, if necessary, all those parts that are reprehensible, or, even better, to come to realize that there are actually no really truly reprehensible parts, and that you are, in fact, a rather enjoyable person to be with? But this is only possible if you take the journey inside in order to begin to get to know yourself, more importantly, in order to begin *to love yourself*. The inner connection implies love for the self. It implies harmonic acceptance of the self, including all of its human failings, it implies compassion for the self, it implies the ability to forgive the self, and above all, it implies coming closer and closer to the understanding – and acceptance – of the fact (now demonstrated by quantum physics) that we are all one. Understanding such a thing, that is only possible outside of traditional thinking that forms part of duality (white/black, yes/no, male/female, etc), *can only begin to become possible once the loving inner connection has been established.* Sri Nisargadatta Maharaj puts it beautifully:

> *You cannot transcend what you do not know.*
> *To go beyond yourself, you must know yourself.*

Many of the difficult feelings you may have about yourself can be addressed by using your "energy barometer". Begin by taking stock of your body, asking yourself where in your body you feel anything that may be causing distress or disharmony. I'm not referring to physical pain, but to those things that are the body's language to let us know that something is not in perfect running order in our world.

For example, do you have butterflies in your stomach (solar plexus, adrenal glands, third chakra)? Or is your solar plexus tight and hard with tension? Are you slightly nauseous? Perhaps you have a lump in your throat (thyroid gland, fifth chakra), have a sore throat, are suffering from chronic laryngitis, or must clear your throat frequently before you speak. Do you fear speaking your truth? Perhaps your heart (thymus gland, fourth chakra) hurts, or feels constricted and tight: I mean a real, physically felt pain or constriction, or a stabbing pain, which happens to some people when their feelings have been harshly trampled on. Or perhaps your breathing (lungs, fourth chakra) is shallow, or fast, or restricted because of some felt nervousness, tension, or fear. All of this should only take a few seconds.

Next, take stock of your feelings. Has something been making you feel sad, worried, angry, jealous, heart-broken, frustrated, or anything else that you might classify negatively? Again, just take a few seconds.

Next, quickly scan your mind for negative self-talk that has been going on lately. What are you telling yourself that might somehow be influencing the body and emotional conditions you have just looked at? Note that I am not asking you to do anything about any of these states, I merely ask that you take note. And once again, this should only take a few seconds.

The purpose for doing this is two-fold: first, it allows you to become very conscious where – within your entire system - something is not right, as opposed to simply saying or thinking *what an awful morning*, or *oh, I feel so terrible*, or *I'm so sad*, etc. Secondly, because of the fact that you have taken the time to become aware of some of the potential sources for your current state of being, it allows you to recognize that you have a choice now. *You can allow this state to continue, or you can choose to do something about it.* Much of this was discussed in the chapter about choice.

If a man happens to find himself, he has a mansion which he can inhabit with dignity all the days of his life.
James A. Michener

So choosing to shift your energetic vibration, in other words *deliberately making choices, about what you focus on, about what you think about, about how much of your time you are present, in the now* will automatically take you to other levels where your thoughts and feelings about yourself *will change.* On those other, higher levels, it is so much harder for negative or low energy thoughts to find a breeding ground. When you are feeling good, how often do you dwell on downward-spiraling thoughts? When you are feeling good, you don't want to cry. So shifting your energetic vibration to a higher level is something I encourage you to start practicing *every single day, each and every time you recognize that you are spiraling downward.* This is one of the easiest things you can do to establish the inner connection.

Being Bored with the Self

All of these concepts refer in some way to self-knowledge, but also to *meaning.* You can only be bored in your own company, if there is no meaning in your life; if you have not yet bothered to think about what meaning you could give to your life, and then to actively go about discovering it and putting it into practice. This is generally a lifetime endeavor. I won't delve more deeply into that subject, as it has been dealt with in some detail in another chapter, but I do encourage you to explore it in order to begin to understand how to find the meaning in your life. Following one's bliss can bring great clarification about meaning, finding ways to self-actualize is an impossible task without meaning, and in similar fashion, individuation is also not possible without an ultimate connection to the self and understanding of meaning in one's life.

Being Uncomfortable with the Self

If you are uncomfortable with yourself, it may have much to do with the fact that you simply don't have much knowledge of yourself, and so feeling uncomfortable is similar to how you feel with a comparative stranger, about whom you know little, and who therefore does not create the sensation of ease and comfort a good friend does. Doesn't it make sense to try to become *your own best friend?* Again, in so doing, you will begin to not only appreciate yourself, but also like and love yourself. Even admire yourself. Imagine spending all your time with a friend about whom you feel this way and this friend is you!

I wrote earlier that this process need not be difficult, tedious, and certainly does not require the services of a therapist. It does, however, entail something akin to gardening. When you plant a seed in the garden of your house, or in a pot on your terrace, you know very well that in order for it to grow into a strong oak tree, an elegant palm that sways in the wind, a rose that enchants the senses, a geranium that embellishes the humblest home, sweet-smelling rosemary, or the blossoms of a perfumed jasmine, it first needs soil (preferably rich), water, sunlight, care, and constancy. *Tending the inner garden is no different.*

He is his own best friend, and takes delight in privacy whereas the man of no virtue or ability is his own worst enemy and is afraid of solitude.
Aristotle

Enriching the Soil

Possibly the soil in which you are beginning your process of growth is not particularly fertile at this time. You know that out there, in the external world, you can create a compost heap in order to enrich the soil you use for your plants. In the internal world you can begin to feed your soil (your mind, heart, and soul), with reading and viewing material that will convert into great compost, rather than trashing your garden with leftover junk food and plastic waste (which on the inner level might be likened to the mass media shows and books or magazines that many people like to read and view as a steady diet, and which has little or no hope of ever converting into rich soil). Tend your garden well and watch the lush process of your own inner growth that will take place. Only you can do this for yourself, and only you can make the decision to begin it now.

One of the ways of determining how far you are on the road towards this inner connection has to do with alignment. When you feel uneasy, uncomfortable, not calm, not peaceful, but agitated, mixed up, at cross-purposes, jittery, and so on, you can pretty well count on the fact that you are not aligned with who you really are.

Can you imagine lining up a banana with a walnut? It just doesn't work, does it? One is more or less round, and hard, and brown. The other is elongated, curved, soft, and yellow. They align in the sense that both need their outer shell or peel to be removed in order to be eaten, but other than that, there is little alignment that takes place between the two.

And so it is with you, when you are aligning yourself to some way of life, or to some purpose that has *nothing to do with who you really are* at the core of your being. The feelings of uneasiness, discomfort, agitation, etc. are showing you as clearly as if there were a signpost on the road: *This is not the way to go forward.* And all this inner turmoil, unrest and *disease* indicates a profound lack of connection with your true self.

If we really wanted to unravel the thread from which this whole topic hangs, we would in fact need to look not only to who we are in the flesh-and-blood sense, using all those labels that help us understand who someone is in the greater scheme of mundane activity, but we would also need to look far beyond that. I loved Gary Zukav's term – now much-used – but when I first read it in May 1989 when I discovered his *Seat of the Soul* in a tucked-away-in-the-corner bookshop in Geneva on a business trip, not too many were really using the term *multi-dimensionality* that he liberally sprinkles throughout the book of. We are all multi-dimensional.

Being of this world is part of it. But *we are so much more*, and that is where we often wind up out of whack, so to speak, because we are simply not listening to our inner voice, our inner guidance system, call it intuition or call it what you will, but it's that part inside of us that knows very well what is the best way for us to go each day so that we get to the place we had initially intended to aim for. That wonderful series of books, also in the 80's, by Jane Roberts, about *Seth* discussing *the eternal validity of the soul*, takes the topic one step further.

I know those last paragraphs carry a lot of punch. I won't make it even heavier by going on and on, but consider this: *how do you know that you are just the "you" that you see in the mirror and that you feel when you touch yourself, and that feels something not so good when you are sad or angry? That is your body and your personality and your ego. There's so much more to you than that.* And that other part of you – that you hardly know, if at all - is what gets misaligned when you are not paying attention to it. It's the part that winds up giving you depression, or cancer, or the shakes, or sciatica, or anything at all, in order for you to pay attention to that which is not aligned. The longer misalignment on an inner level is allowed to continue, and the longer you pay no attention to that knowing, that voice inside, the greater is the possibility that your body will create something to make you pay attention.

Having said that, however, does *not mean*, that everyone who has a physical ailment or impairment, is not paying attention on this inner level. Sometimes we go through such a physical process for totally different reasons, and are nevertheless fully aligned. Said another way, inner misalignment will – in many instances - eventually lead to a physical expression of it, to a physical crisis, but physical difficulties or crises are not always the result of an inner misalignment. If this sounds confusing or bizarre to you, you could start with the idea of the *observer, or witness*, as it is often called in yoga, mindfulness, and meditation techniques.

Many authors, including Jon Kabat-Zinn or Eckhart Tolle speak of it and I've referred to the term liberally throughout this book. The observer is that part of you that is observing what you are doing or commenting on what you are doing – to yourself – as you do it, as in: *I can't believe I am yelling at this poor cashier just because she dropped my bag of apples.* The one who yells at the cashier is one part, and the one who observes that you are yelling – and is even amazed by it - is the other part. Or: *Damn, I let go again, and here I am shouting at my husband/wife while I actually meant to behave in a totally different way.* The one who is shouting is one part, and the one who observes that you are shouting – and is rueful at the fact that you had meant to deal with such a situation differently, is another part. Or: *I see that I'm so deeply heartbroken because of _____ and I'm feeling so terrible, I feel so sorry for myself for feeling this way.* The one who is feeling heartbroken and terrible is one part, and the one who observes this, and feels compassion for that part of you is another part. And of course in each of these examples, the observation is taking place *during the* process, and not afterwards, as an analysis of a situation after the facts, might bring you to those conclusions. Observing during the process implies that there is a part of you that behaves or feels in a way that another part of you observes. The observing bit is somehow less attached to what is going on. The observing bit appears to be able to think while the other bit is losing it, verbally, or emotionally, even physically, or in some other fashion. As you explore this path, you will find that the observer is capable of becoming more and more detached from the part that we generally call our body or personality or ego. The observer is a part of you that is not always there in a palpable fashion. In order for you to get a handle on this observer, to come closer to the observer, indeed, to begin to *identify* with the observer, you need to become not only very aware, but also very *desirous of setting up such a relationship to the observer. In fact it is the observer that is the self to which you are attempting to establish the inner connection. The observer is what you are aligning with when you are rewiring your soul.* That's why it starts to get interesting from an *alignment* point of view.

Where does that part of you that you call intuition come from? Out of a mote of dust? A ray of sunshine? The ether? *And where does your inner knowledge that you and Suzy or John have some kind of connection come from, when the two of you have just met right now?* From logical, empirical thought? *And why do you think of your cousin just moments before he calls you?* Was that coincidence? Or ESP? *Or maybe it was a deeper knowing that you have inside of you that comes from a part of you that you simply tend not to pay attention to because it's not considered a priority in this world of external, rational and material results.*

And if that is so, wouldn't it make sense that you need to be aligned with that part? That part that gives you such *normally unavailable information?* That part that somehow seems to *know so much more than your personality or ego part?* That part that is capable of standing apart and observing you (the "blinder" you) as you rant and rave about some disagreement or insult? That part that appears to be connected to an inner knowing to which your outer personality or ego has no access? Imagine it like an extra hard drive inside your laptop that you have just discovered. It's always been there, but you never perceived it. Now you are learning how to read it from your laptop, and now you are beginning to recognize the incredible richness of material already stored on this hard drive that you are only now learning how to access.

Your *eternal self, your observer, your intuition, your inner knowing* can be likened to that other hard drive, and it is right there, *part of you*, and has always been part of you, despite the fact that you may never have been aware of it, or, despite the fact that you may have always denied its existence each time it tried to communicate with you. *It is not separate from you because it is you.*

Simple, really. When you have been sitting for too long hunched over the computer, or on an assembly line, your body screams for a stretch, right? And once you do, your stiff muscles loosen and you feel better. You feel more physically aligned. And being aligned with who you really are is kind of like that.

You go on every day doing things that may or may not be *right* for you, and sooner or later you notice an inner *stiffness*, you notice that something is not right. That's when you are not aligned. That's when you need to consider some of what this is about. Because if you are not feeling right in your skin, it's a message from that same inner part of you that *knows* about the connection with Suzy or John, or that *thinks* about your cousin moments before he calls. That inner part of you is just as much a part of you – if not much, much more – than those muscles that get stiff after too much hunching over the computer.

The difference between it and the muscles is that we have no anatomy books that tell us about it. We have no empirical information that tells us where we can see it, dissect it, or study it. All we can do is go by what we sense, and when we feel misaligned, at least a part of the reason that we feel that way, is because that part of us, *that unseen, but very much sensed and felt part of us*, is not in alignment with what we are doing and thinking and saying in the outer world.

Here's a thought: if you are saying *this is nonsense, I don't believe this, we don't have such a part ... if we did, we would be able to show it, prove it, demonstrate it empirically*, then you might think of the radio, or your TV, or brain waves, or sub-atomic particles. We know there is electricity. We know frequencies allow us to hear the radio, or watch TV. Quantum physicists tell us about sub-atomic particles that change, just because they have an observer, even though they are impossible to see with the naked eye, and cellular biologists tell us that the way we think changes our very DNA, and we believe in all those things *despite not being able to see them. All we see are the results.* So it is with this, our inner sense of knowing and intuition, our inner observer. We can't touch it. *But we can see the results.*

What is the best sign of alignment? Inner peace. It's so simple. And so wonderful once it is achieved.

So how can you get there? Start by paying attention to those feelings of misalignment that come about via your body, your mind, and your feelings. Begin that relationship with the observer. Connect with your inner self on those levels by growing more and more aware. Recognize that you have these wonderful built-in devices that help you figure things out. Don't ignore this treasure trove of information that you get from yourself by telling yourself that it's lacking in empirical proof; that it's not rational or logical. Recognize that this is *a part of you that is eternal and it is giving priceless knowledge to the part of you that is finite and passing.*

What this whole thing concerns is the *alignment and connection of that finite part with the eternal part.* Only by so doing will you establish the inner connection and rewire the soul. That gives inner peace. And inner peace is a prize far more valuable than any that might please your finite, more mundane part. This is another step to inner freedom ... this is one of the most important ones of the many you have encountered in these chapters.

No one remains quite what he was when he recognizes himself.
Thomas Mann

SECTION FOUR:

SETTING THE STAGE FOR LOVE

Chapter Fourteen

Loving the Self:
Portal to Love - Gateway to the Soul

You, yourself, as much as anybody in the entire universe,
deserve your love and affection.
Buddha

Loving the self is one of the most important - if not *the* most important - things we can do for our health: on all these levels - physiological, psycho-emotional and spiritual. Loving the self has very little to do with how we treat ourselves on the outside, i.e., how we live our lives in the mundane sense, if we are not *first* treating ourselves lovingly on the inside. Buying a wonderful car, going on that fantastic vacation, or having the extra piece of chocolate may be ways we have of showing ourselves that we love ourselves, and in and of themselves there is nothing wrong with them at all, *as long as* you are first taking care of yourself in a loving way on all inner levels: psychologically, emotionally and spiritually. This is a habit, just like having a daily shower is a habit, but if you have not made a habit of it in your life, inner peace and well-being and happiness will continually elude you like a butterfly flying just out of reach across a summer meadow, and as long as you believe that you will find inner peace and well-being *once you achieve whatever it is that you believe is missing in your outer life,* you will seek it in vain.

Going back to the analogy of the shower, consider this: would you deprive yourself of food and drink on any given day (assuming you are not in a raw food detox retreat somewhere, or deliberately fasting for a period of time)? Would you neglect to brush your teeth? Have that shower (or more than one) per day? How about not brushing or combing your hair for a day or two, or even a couple of months ... how about all year? *Just ignore it.* Ludicrous, you say? Why? After all, that is what you do with regards to loving yourself. You continually neglect it. Your habits, formed from life-long beliefs (mostly not conscious), and however you have chosen (generally blindly and unknowingly) to treat yourself, have brought you to this place you find yourself now, where loving yourself is simply not something you do with daily attention and care. You would not let mucus run down your face if you had a bad cold any more than you would leave an open wound on your body go untreated. And yet that is *exactly* what you do day after day when you do not consciously love the self.

Loving the self – learning to love the self - is one of the most difficult things that people face in their lives.

There are numerous reasons why this is so hard. Some of those reasons concern:

1. Society and religion.
2. Poor attachment bonds formed in early childhood.
3. Parents who were somehow unable to model self-love.
4. Not understanding that self-love requires awareness and honesty about the self to the self.
5. Not realizing that self-love requires awareness regarding pain in relationships.
6. Believing that loving the self is selfish.
7. Believing that loving the self is a sin.
8. Believing that loving the self is not ethical.
9. Loving the self; thinking about it and talking about it, makes us feel uncomfortable.

Let's examine these impediments to loving the self one by one (and the list I've offered here is by no means exhaustive):

1. **Society and Religion**

Obviously not everyone in society nor everyone in our religious institutions colludes to create difficulties for an easy and healthy process of loving the self. But the fact is that we are much more used to hearing phrases that encourage us to *not* love the self, or at least to regard loving the self as something that verges on selfishness, than we are accustomed to hearing phrases that openly encourage us to love the self. We are often given to understand that loving the self is equivalent to egotism, narcissism, and selfishness. We may even be told it is unhealthy. So while it is true that there is more and more recognition of the fact that loving the self is indeed important for our psycho-emotional health, it is also true that this is not yet the main story most of us hear as we grow up. How we are socialized, what we hear, and hence believe from childhood on, is not impossible to change, but it requires awareness – not only on our part with regards to our own lives, but also on the part of all parents with regards to the lives of their children *and* their own lives. In order to come to a space of inner awareness where those long-held beliefs that do not serve one well are held, a mindfulness practice can be of utmost benefit. For greater detail, please refer to the chapters on awareness, choice, happiness and responsibility.

2.   Poor Attachment Bonds Formed in Early Childhood

The relationship with our primary caregiver in childhood, that is, the main person or persons who are in charge of taking care of us, is largely responsible for how our attachment bonds are formed. By means of an experiment in which children are brought to an office or lab – a place that the children have not been before, and then briefly separated from their parents, developmental psychologists have concluded that there are four main types of attachment that impact our psycho-emotional health, our adult relationships, the manner in which we love, or do not love ourselves, and of course, our concept of ourselves. These are:

- **Secure Attachment**
  These children explore happily while the parent is still in the room, they get upset when he leaves and are comforted when he returns. They also know they can count on the parent for comfort when they are upset because of the way the parent normally responds to the child. If a stranger comforts them while they are upset, they respond well, but clearly prefer the parent. This parent responds well and lovingly to the child at all times.

- **Avoidant Attachment**
  These children explore, but not in connection with the parent. When the parent leaves, they are not upset, nor are they happy when the parent returns and if the parent picks them up they turn away, and show little reaction. If a stranger tries to connect with them they react in a similar –

avoidant - fashion. The kind of parent these children have does not react in loving and helpful ways to the distressed child, and further, has shown the child that he prefers the child not to cry and furthermore, that independence from – and not need for - the parent is a desirable trait.

- **Ambivalent / Resistant Attachment**
  These children distrust strangers, become very upset when the parent leaves but cannot be consoled when the parent returns. There may be low maternal availability in the home or the parent may be inconsistent between appropriate and neglectful behavior. In other words, the child lacks consistent loving reactions from the parent and hence does not know what to expect, which in turn causes him to not know how to react.

- **Disorganized Attachment**
  These children have a lack of clear attachment type. When the parent returns to the room, the child may freeze or rock itself. The parent may be frightened or frightening, may be withdrawn, intrusive or abusive. Because the child feels both comforted and frightened by the parent, it becomes confused and disorganized in its attachment.

If the attachment bond we formed with our parents was not secure, there is a reasonably high chance that we experience some – or much - difficulty in loving the self. This will negatively impact our adult relationships as well, until we seek conscious awareness.

3.   Parents Who Are Unable to Model Self-Love

Much of what we learn when we are children comes from modeling our parents. Clearly, if they are unable to demonstrate healthy love for the self in their own lives, we will not come to the conclusion that this is something we want for ourselves, because we simply won't be aware of it. They may be emotionally unavailable, needy, manipulative, controlling, rigid, or be perfectionists, have poor boundaries, obsessive thoughts or painful emotions. Please note that this is not about parent-bashing! Who can know *how* they, in turn, were raised by their own parents, and so on. This is simply about gaining perspective. No aspect of this type of behavior shows the child of such a parent how to love the self.

We may grow into sophisticated and well-educated adults, with prestigious professions and glamorous social lives and may still not realize that we don't love ourselves. There may be an unidentified nagging of some kind deep inside on certain occasions, but it may take a difficult life transition or crisis - especially in our relationships - before we even come to understand that we are lacking this essential, nurturing and life-giving manner of caring for ourselves.

4.   Not Realizing That Self-Love Requires Awareness & Honesty about the Self to the Self

Imagine the love you feel for someone close to you: your child, your siblings, your parents, or your partner. When we first fall in love with a partner, we rarely see the real human being. We see an idealized version, or a version that appears to us from behind our own rosy-colored glasses, or even a totally false version, often due to our *need* for this person, because of the way we feel when we are with him or her. We call this a projection.

If we eventually marry and then divorce, the decision to end the marriage frequently occurs because we have realized that the real person we are married to is very different from the one we thought he or she was. Nevertheless, sometimes when we *see* the real person, we remain married, and then the relationship often grows greatly in depth and meaning, and of course the love we now feel for the partner, is a love based on a true perception of the other, as opposed to the false one we began with, and furthermore, it is a love *despite this true* perception, i.e., we love the other including all their faults or weaknesses.

When we refer to loving the self, we have to understand that it will only be truly possible, once we are able to acknowledge our true self to ourselves. And that – just as in the example above about the partner – can only happen if we are honest and brave about looking at ourselves, and if we are willing to accept ourselves as we find ourselves, even though later we may wish to work on changing and improving some of those aspects – *precisely and especially because we have come to love ourselves.*

5.   Not Understanding That Self-Love Requires Awareness Regarding Pain in Relationships

Loving yourself is generally just not very high on your list of priorities, nor is it always instilled in you while you are growing up. Only once you begin to realize that it just might be one of those things that is actually holding you back, and you begin to try to work on changing how you deal with yourself, do you realize how potentially difficult it is to achieve. There are many reasons why you may feel you can't love yourself, most of which are absolute myths, but which you typically will firmly believe. What follows represents only a few of these reasons:

- There's *nothing lovable* about me.
- I'm a *bad* person.
- It's a *sin* to love myself.
- It's *selfish* to love myself.
- The Bible says *love thy neighbor.*
- I've spent so much time *not loving me*, that I don't know how to begin.
- I'm so *ashamed* of myself.
- How can I love myself if I don't *like* myself?
- I'm so *afraid* to love myself.
- It *hurts* so much to love myself.
- I'm *not good enough* to love myself.
- My mother/father/partner *told me I'm useless / worthless / stupid / clumsy / _____ fill in the blank*
- I'm *not worth it.*
- I'll love myself *when I get a promotion, lose 20 pounds, make a million dollars, get him/her to love me, etc.*

Let's backtrack a moment. How did you get to this place where you find yourself unlovable, or afraid to love yourself, and so on? Were you born like this? Look at a baby. It may scream when it wants food or is uncomfortable, but wouldn't you say that when it does that, it is manifesting its supreme belief in its *right* to be fed or comforted? And who does that? Only someone who instinctively (we're not even talking about being rational here, merely instinctual) believes he or she is lovable. When a toddler comes up to your knee, sticky fingers on your clothes, and looks trustingly into your eyes, he or she believes he has a right to be there and hence believes he or she is lovable. (Also see the section above on attachment styles).

Love brings you face to face with your self. It's impossible to love another if you cannot love yourself.
John Pierrakos

But – what happens when the baby is not fed or comforted, and just ignored until it cries itself to sleep? Or the toddler gets yelled at, pushed away, and told in no uncertain terms that he is not wanted there because he is dirty, or disgusting, or bad. Or maybe one day the toddler behaves as described above, its sticky fingers on your clothes, and receives a smile, a hug and a kiss, but another day, by doing exactly the same, is scolded, shouted at or slapped. No consistency. Nothing to base himself on when trying to understand which part of him is lovable. You get the picture. I won't go into the hundreds of scenarios, more or less dysfunctional, because many of them happen in great homes, I could describe, because you're probably aware of your own, or at least, you've heard about many of the scenarios that result in a lack of self-esteem, a fear of *being you*, a lack of self-respect and self-confidence, and so on.

Fast forward a few years. The result now is a child – youngster – teen – young adult – who finds it hard to say what he or she wants. Or prefers. Or what opinion he has about a particular subject. Or what he's feeling. And because this individual *finds it hard* to say things of this nature, he allows others to say or do things that are not right, that are unacceptable, maybe just not *quite* right, but nevertheless, something *not right is being allowed*. All of that describes behavior by a person with poor boundaries as opposed to healthy boundaries. And before you jump at me, I'm not necessarily talking about hard-core abuse here, it can be much less, it can even just be something the first person *perceives*. Partially this behavior stems from his assumption that by saying what he wants or prefers, etc. (as opposed to what the other person is saying), he will not get what he most wants: love and appreciation, that commodity that somehow was missing part of the time when he was little, so it is better to say nothing, because then he just might get some love, some few crumbs of love.

> *To love yourself right now, just as you are, is to give yourself heaven. Don't wait until you die. If you wait, you die now. If you love, you live now.*
> Alan Cohen

So we now have a person with low self-esteem, or a feeling of shame about the self, or a lack of self-love, or respect, and hence we have a person with poor boundaries. And this of course perpetuates into adult life *as long as it is not recognized and dealt with as an unresolved issue*. And it can do untold damage to the unfolding of the life of the person involved. His or her lack of belief or love in the self is forever perpetuated by the people subconsciously chosen to participate in the life, because these are *precisely the sort of people* who are able to enact the kind of behavior that persons with poor boundaries should object to, or speak up about, and yet they do not. We might say – in Jungian terms – that the infinite intelligence of this person has attracted such people into his life in order that he/she may work on these issues. And although I am pointing towards the past in order that you understand where the poor boundaries originated, I am not suggesting that you spend *any time* whatsoever on determining exactly what happened then. That is not nearly as important – if at all – as it is to *change your present behavior in favor of yourself so that you may begin to love and respect yourself* and in order to do so it is important to understand the role relationships play – and have played – in your life, as you will see in the next chapter.

6.   Believing That Loving the Self is Selfish

Much of this has its origin in the somewhat erroneous or skewed interpretation of scripture by the bastions of most organized religions, as well as ideology, philosophy, and ethics. To illustrate this point, I will repeat here something I have already written about in the past, but which is very illuminating about the topic. It comes from Erich Fromm, the author of *The Art of Loving* in his 1939 article titled *Selfishness and Self-Love:*

> "Modern culture is pervaded by a taboo on selfishness. It teaches that to be selfish is sinful and that to love others is virtuous. To be sure, this doctrine is not only in flagrant contradiction to the practices of modern society but it is also in opposition to another set of doctrines which assumes that the most powerful and legitimate drive in man is selfishness and that each individual by following this imperative drive also does the most for the common good. The existence of this latter type of ideology does not affect the weight of the doctrines which declare that selfishness is the arch evil and love for others the main virtue. Selfishness, as it is commonly used in these ideologies, is more or less synonymous with self-love. The alternatives are either to love others which is a virtue or to love oneself which is a sin."

We have been socialized into believing that if we profess to love the self, we are being selfish. *Nothing could be further from the truth!* To understand this better, let's look at some definitions of selfishness: self-centeredness, egotism, state of only having concern for one's own self. But *loving the self does not preclude having concern for others*, it simply means that you take care of yourself first, in order to be able to take care of or have concern for others *better than if you had not taken care of yourself first.*

A case in point, that I often use to illustrate this with my clients, are the instructions given by airline personnel when they show passengers the use of the oxygen mask. In the case of need, they say, if you are traveling with children, *put your own mask on first* (so that you don't run the risk of falling unconscious before you can help them). In other words: *take care of yourself first.* Most people upon hearing this simplistic analogy get it immediately and recognize that there is not one iota of selfishness in the act of loving the self first.

Fromm becomes even more damning as he continues his assault on our societal mores concerning self-love:

> "The doctrine that selfishness is the arch-evil that one has to avoid and that to love oneself excludes loving others is by no means restricted to theology and philosophy. It is one of the stock patterns used currently in home, school, church, movies, literature, and all the other instruments of social suggestion. "Don't be selfish" is a sentence which has been impressed upon millions of children, generation after generation. It is hard to define what exactly it means. Consciously, most parents connect with it the meaning not to be egotistical, inconsiderate, without concern for others. Factually, they generally mean more than that. "Not to be selfish" implies not to do what one wishes, to give up one's own wishes for the sake of those in authority; i.e., the parents, and later the authorities of society."

Please read the foregoing paragraph again because for those of you who disagreed with my earlier statements regarding theology, philosophy, and ethics because we are no longer living in the Middle Ages, or because your family did not go to church, etc., you may have now seen glimpses of yourself in this second Fromm citation. *Not because your parents were reprehensible, but because they knew not what they did*, and anyway, they were probably the fruit of the earlier socialization by their own process of growing up as described above. But no matter how you look at it, we are again faced with the implacable wall that indicates that we are selfish if we dare do what we think is right, or what we want ... imagine the heresy ... *doing what we want* ... even if it is something like desiring to study art instead of law (which might be what father wants). Examples abound. This is also the starting point for many unhealthy boundaries in people ... unhealthy boundaries mean that the individual allows others to cross limits that should not be crossed ... all learned in childhood by learning *not to be selfish*, or by learning to *please another.* (Note: poor boundaries also have other origins).

7.   Believing That Loving the Self is a Sin

I am confident you can understand from the above statement, that many members of generations upon generations of

Christians* have learned that *to be fond of oneself, to like anything about oneself is one of the greatest imaginable sins ... identical with selfishness or false pride.* Again, nothing could be further from the truth! Think of this: imagine you have a small child. Imagine you determine to make that child a God-fearing, responsible, and hard-working adult, and you decide to do so by following the above tenets, by not being fond of that child, by not loving that child. Do you think that child would prosper? I don't mean that it would die, but I do mean that bits of it would shrivel up and die, or at least, disappear, *because that child would need to be loved.* And so do we all – we need to love *ourselves* in order to be healthy on all levels.

* Of course it is not the Bible that forbids love of the self, but *how* the Bible has been interpreted.

Self-love, my liege, is not so vile a sin, as self-neglecting.
William Shakespeare

---

8.   Believing That Loving the Self is not Ethical

Fromm, whom I referred to above, also mentions Kant:

"According to Kant, it is a virtue to want the happiness of others, while to want one's own happiness is ethically "indifferent," since it is something which the nature of man is striving for and a natural striving cannot have positive ethical sense. [...] love for oneself, striving for one's own happiness, can never be a virtue. As an ethical principle, the striving for one's own happiness "is the most objectionable one, not merely because it is false,... but because the springs it provides for morality are such as rather undermine it and destroy its sublimity..."

I believe no further comment is necessary.

9.   Loving the Self – Thinking About It, Talking About It - Makes Us Feel Uncomfortable

Examining this more closely, we find that most of us feel somewhat (or very) uncomfortable when we consider loving ourselves *before* others, even more uncomfortable, if we consider saying such a thing, and equally uncomfortable when we think about or refer to things like needing to love ourselves first in order to be healthy inside. *Why do we feel uncomfortable about this?* One prime reason has become apparent from what we have been discussing to this point: everything we have heard about the subject since we were born makes us feel uncomfortable to talk about loving ourselves. At best, there were many mixed messages. At worst, we heard that loving the self was bad, selfish, etc. When we hear such things as children - at a point in life when we don't yet have use of reason in order to weigh a statement and be able to determine whether it resonates with us - we accept it blindly, and therefore take it to be the truth. And consequently we feel uncomfortable when we contemplate loving ourselves until we have become aware of the origin of the belief, or the reason why the thought makes us uncomfortable. Being aware is the basis of everything.

Are you beginning to see where civilization has taken us, by following such guidelines in theology, philosophy, and ethics? *We are not to love ourselves,* we are told. If we do, we are selfish, we sin, we are not virtuous. Small wonder then, that so many generations have spent their lives in pursuit of external things such as fame, money, fortune, prestige, honor, beauty, power, etc., or pleasing others while simultaneously being filled with resentment, in attempts that are frequently in vain, to generate a feeling inside that lets you feel good, but *that you can only get from yourself, by loving yourself, and that you cannot get from the external things, wonderful though they may be, or from other people.*

It is heart-rending, when you look at it from that point of view. Fromm's statements referred to earlier are an eloquent testimony to the reason why so many people in the world need psychotherapists such as myself, or spend years on medication, or why so many people in the world are so desperately unhappy. Think about it, and understand that your reticence, your difficulty, your reluctance and feeling of discomfort when you attempt to begin to get around the idea of loving yourself, may all have their roots in statements of the above type.

Understand also, that the process of beginning to love yourself is *precisely* that: it's a process through which you will unlearn well-ingrained habits and thought patterns, as well as unlearning emotional trigger points calculated to make you feel guilty, and just like unlearning any other habit, it will take some time, it will require some discipline, and results may not show up immediately. Do you get toned triceps the first day at the gym? But the results *will* show up and they *will* change your life, and they *will* create a sense of well-being such as you may have never experienced before.

So how do you actually begin to love yourself? Literally follow the chapters of this book one by one. Learn to be sufficiently aware to keep yourself in a state of inner well-being by choosing to take on the responsibility for your inner well-being and happiness at *all times*. Doing it just occasionally is not enough. It *must* become a habit. Learn to be aware of your emotions and thoughts in such a way that you are able to have a conscious choice about where they are leading you. Learn to be aware of what healthy boundaries are, and what you need to change in order to have them in your life. Learn to be aware in order to live in the present and in a state of gratitude. Learn to be aware of your pain, where it has come from, and how you can be free of it by making the conscious choice to forgive. All of these steps – and decisions – will lead you to a closer and more loving relationship with yourself. In so doing you are connecting with yourself, loving yourself, and rewiring your soul.

Don't forget to love yourself.
Søren Kierkegaard

Chapter Fifteen

Relationships:
Loving Others

*Everything that irritates us about others can lead us to
an understanding of ourselves.*
Carl Gustav Jung

Relationships are the place where we can grow most quickly. Relationships are the place where we can most learn about ourselves. Relationships are wonderful tools, not only for love, joy, happiness, and satisfaction, but for speeding up the coming to recognition of all our issues, *if we so desire*. In other words, when relationships start to go sour, or when they lose their early rosy-colored hue, as they are wont to do, at that point is the place when we can begin to use them alchemically, to transform ourselves, or, to put it into the words of renowned mythologist Joseph Campbell: *"through the alchemical cooking [...] the gold is brought out. And the gold is your own spiritual life [...]. The ordeal is a gradual clarification and purification of your life."*

We tend to believe that relationships only exist to make us happy, to complete us, and to make our lives better, and if they do not fulfill these purposes, we tend to quickly discard them. Both psychologically and spiritually, however, the real purpose of relationship goes far beyond that, as stated above, because it is precisely through the problems and difficulties that we encounter in our intimate relationships, that we can grow the most, and furthermore, grow most rapidly.

However, this only happens if we are willing and capable of looking at ourselves *before* we look at the partner with blame. It isn't a question of taking on the blame yourself, perhaps your partner has truly behaved atrociously or unacceptably, but of looking at what it is within yourself that has drawn you to this or that partner, and once you see that which you consider unacceptable, and which you have not been able to *change* in your partner over weeks (or decades) of trying, then you must ask yourself *what is it in me that has caused me to hang on for weeks (or decades) despite finding this type of behavior atrocious or unacceptable, or even just very annoying?*

It is the honest answer to questions such as these in the throes of relationship difficulty that leads you to insight into the self and consequently, to the potential for growth. So the answer to the question – if it is to lead to growth – will never concern the other nor will it have to do with blaming the other, it will only concern the self.

Here are some typical answers that concern the *other* and that therefore do *not* lead to the kind of growth that is the promise of all relationships, *unless we decide to do something about the part of ourselves that says these things about the relationship*:

- My partner needs me.
- My partner is such a wonderful person inside, and I *know* that if I love him/her enough, and that if I show him patience and understanding, that wonderful part that I can see will eventually shine through.
- I am afraid of what he/she might do if I take a stand about this issue.
- I am afraid of what he/she might do (to him/herself, or to me) if I leave.
- I couldn't do this (a new type of behavior as opposed to whatever has been done in the past or up to this point in the relationship) to my partner.
- I've done that (showing some boundaries) in the past and it has not changed anything in the way my partner treats me. He/she will never change.
- My partner is inconsiderate, rejecting, emotionally unavailable, needy, aggressive, violent, controlling, obsessive, abusive, rude, unfaithful, etc.

- My partner will get very angry if I do this (react in this new way).
- My partner would never understand that kind of behavior.
- My partner will never forgive me if I do this (react in this new way).

All of these examples show that the person who is saying or thinking them, could be learning something new from the problem that has arisen in the relationship, or that has existed in the relationship for a long time already, but because of the things this person is saying or thinking, it always has to do with the other, i.e., there is always either an element of *not being able to do this to the other* or *of blaming the other*. There is no looking at the self to see what is going on inside in order to try to understand one's own role in the dance. Because there always is a dance. When couples have come to see me and I begin to unravel their particular "dance" for them – by which I mean the steps each one of them takes in order to maintain a specific status quo in the relationship - instead of changing things - they then often begin to understand how *subconsciously both members of the couple are somehow invested in keeping everything the same*, although on the surface, both may be screaming bloody murder!

> *Problems in relationship occur because each person is concentrating on what is missing in the other person.*
> Wayne Dyer

And before you start thinking: *oh no, another subconscious thing that I am never going to get at without attending a very expensive workshop or buying some gadget that will cost a lot of money or going through years and years of therapy*, let me reassure you, that although what keeps you in this "dance" may be subconscious, you can quickly bring it to consciousness by beginning to become aware. There is that word again, that has been so stressed and reiterated in this book already. By becoming aware of yourself at every moment of every day on all possible levels: physical, psychological, emotional, spiritual, you will soon be able to comprehend what keeps you in the dance. Awareness alone will not pull you out of the dance, but it is a beginning, a very important beginning of just about everything that ails you.

Here's part of what happens: when something goes wrong in a relationship, we often tend, as stated, to believe it is the other person's fault. We may then attempt to reason, cajole, manipulate, or force the other person to change, perhaps back to the way we thought they were before, or simply to conform to whatever we believe would be a better form of behavior, a behavior that would suit our own purposes better. Naturally we don't necessarily look at it like that, but if you analyze any past relationship difficulties you may have had, much of the above is what probably happened. And by the way, however it was that our partner was before (or how we thought he/she was before), generally has much more to do with our *own* projections and needs, than with the reality of our partner.

Carl Gustav Jung had a lot to say about the *anima and animus*, the inner and hidden feminine side of a man and the inner and hidden masculine side of a woman, respectively. Nevertheless, these hidden parts of ourselves are what tend to attract us to our important life partners *and it is in the unveiling of these hidden bits, bringing them to consciousness, that we are able to begin to deal with our relationship issues and that we begin to understand that what we blame so much in the partner, or what pushes our buttons so much about our partner, has less to do with the partner, than with earlier circumstances in our own lives that set the stage for the dance.* In other words, it has to do with our inner opposite gender self – anima or animus. June Singer, a Jungian analyst, wrote an entire book about the fact that there are four people in every relationship: the physical man and woman and the inner man – *animus* – of the woman, and the inner woman – *anima* – of the man, all of which play major roles in the unfolding of the relationship. All of this applies equally to same-gender relationships, by the way.

Going back to our attempt to get our partner to behave the way we want them to, we then either achieve our partner's acquiescence, or we find ourselves faced with an impasse. In the case of the former, all is well until we have another contretemps, at which point this entire scenario may repeat itself, but in the case of the latter, we may now spend weeks, months, years, or even decades, trying to convince our recalcitrant partner that they are at fault, and that they need to change. There may be recriminations, tears, insults, threats, punishing silences, and so on. If these two individuals do not separate or divorce, all of this may – if nothing changes - eventually morph into resentment, apathy, depression, a debilitating and poisonous atmosphere in the home, or a deep-rooted pain on the part of the partner that wants the other one to change – all of which, of course is blamed on the partner that is doing the so-called "bad" thing or not behaving the way the other partner wants him/her to behave or to revert back to behaving the way the other believed this one was before, "when we met".

Unfortunately the problem with this scenario is that, as stated earlier, while it may very well be true that the "bad" partner is showing unacceptable behavior, or being atrociously unkind, rejecting, inconsiderate, or outright cruel, the other partner, the one who considers that all that is going badly in the relationship is the "bad" partner's fault, has never stopped to look at the self and ask *why do I allow this? What has brought me to this point in this relationship?*

When I ask that question in my private practice of such a partner, the answer is typically: "Oh, I don't allow it, but my partner pays no attention to me. I've told my spouse / partner over and over that I don't want this, but he/she never changes one iota. I've begged and pleaded and cried and shouted and ranted and raved."

And while this is generally absolutely true, it still does not take into consideration *why the aggrieved partner allows it*. And of course the kind of allowing I am referring to has to do with this: what *issue* is there inside of you that means that you are unable to change what is going on? And when I say "change", I clearly am not referring to changing the partner - that is never anyone else's responsibility. The only responsibility you have is to change yourself.

Holding on to anger is like grasping a hot coal with the intent of throwing it at someone else: you are the one who gets burned.
Buddha

Here are just a few common examples of what that issue in you, that prevents you from seeing your part of the dance, might be:

- Lack of self love, self respect and self esteem
- Co-dependency
- Fear of being alone
- Emotional neediness
- Unhealthy boundaries
- Dysfunctional parenting
- Perception of having received insufficient love in childhood

All of these (and many others) tie in directly with the first one, the most important of all, and the one that generally underlies all of the reasons we have not yet become connected with our true self, and in the process become rewired with our soul. A lack of self love, a lack of self respect, and a lack of self esteem, all create such a fundamental problem in our lives, and permeate everything else, that we can safely say, that if we work on that issue first, and only on that, eventually all other issues will resolve themselves. *Isn't it wonderful to know that??*

In this example, when the partner who starts to look at the issue, and actually recognizes an issue, he/she has now arrived at a new place inside. The possibility for real inner change now exists. As this inner change progresses, beginning with self-love, not only does the personality grow and expand, but the soul begins its process of rewiring, because through this course of action the individual commences the road that brings him closer and closer to his true inner self, the one he wants to connect with, the one that he truly is, as opposed to the one that suffers so much and so needlessly. In so doing, he automatically begins to experience a much higher level of inner well-being.

> *It is time to see that we are all in energetic relationship to each other. If the people around you are sick, you can get sick.*
> Barbara Hand Clow

So there you have it: one example of how a relationship difficulty can eventually bring both partners, and more typically *one* of the partners, to greater self-knowledge and self-understanding. The lesson to be learned here is not how to figure out what all the different examples might be, because then we would have to write books and ever more books only about that, but to realize that when a problem arises in a relationship, it is up to each person to look inside, as opposed to blaming something or someone outside, *no matter what has transpired.* And in this process of looking within, seeds will be sown, buds will emerge, and oak trees will begin to dot the inner landscape.

Now let's look at the other side of the coin. Let's say you have begun the above-described process, or you are already familiar with it. You now know that relationships do not exist to make you happy (although they may, indeed, be the source of much happiness), but that your happiness is your own responsibility. You also know that relationships do not exist to fulfill your needs, but that you are responsible for fulfilling your own. Therefore, knowing this automatically means that as you move towards that inner goal, you will gradually come to a relationship from a position of *independence*, as opposed to one of dependence.

When you *need* the relationship to supply you with happiness, or when you *need* the relationship to fulfill any of your needs, then you are dependent on the other person for your well-being, which therefore means that in the moment that the other person does not behave the way you would wish them to, you are no longer happy or fulfilled. But when you are in charge of your own happiness, and when you are in charge of fulfilling your own needs, then, of course, you come into the relationship as an independent human being who does not *need* the other in the traditional sense of the word and who realizes and recognizes that when those inner needs arise, they are not to be placed in the lap of the other, but they must be resolved in the self. This by no means signifies that partners don't help each other along this road, but that kind of support - grown from an understanding of the need for growth in the self – is very different from depending on the partner for those things.

How many times have we not fallen into the trap of believing we love someone because we need them? And yet it is this very need that makes us dependent on the other person, and hence we are no longer free. Freedom in a love relationship does not imply less love, on the contrary, the quality of love that comes from a position of independence, as opposed to one of dependence, is far superior, as anyone who has experienced it, will attest. Coming from a position of dependence means you are together out of neediness of some kind, as opposed to coming from a position of independence, which means you complement each other. Complementing vs. needing. That brings you to a whole new partnership level. One that we can term spiritual partnership.

But before I turn to spiritual partnerships, I would like to address the subject of need in relationships with more detail.

Why is it that so often when we feel we are in love, we also feel we are in bondage if anything happens to shake the feeling of "security" in the love? Why does love so often make us dependent on the other person? Shouldn't love be a marvelous and freeing feeling rather than these other sensations of need and fear and dependence? We need that person *to be able* to stay alive, at least figuratively speaking. Without the person we love, we believe we are nothing and we cannot bear to live.

And while we all know that this is not exactly true, most of us have certainly been in the position of feeling something akin to those words. So what does it mean? Does it really signify that loving someone implies that we need the other person so much that we simply feel we cannot go on without them? Or could all that be a fallacy?

Let's examine what happens in a typical *love* scenario. As already stated, Carl Gustav Jung said that our psyche is so infinitely intelligent that it *attracts* us to certain individuals (just as their psyche causes them to be attracted to us) in order that we *experience precisely that which we need to grow* by virtue of the difficulties we will eventually have with those individuals in the relationship.

We don't yet know it in those early days of attraction and love, but what we will be dealing with in those relationships that become the important ones of our lives, will be those unresolved issues from our childhood that somehow re-emerge in those adult relationships once the initial honeymoon stage is over. It is through our partners that we re-visit those childhood issues, that we were unable to resolve then, and are given the opportunity to do so now … if only we can recognize it!

So how do we typically grow? By going through an experience of some sort that may not be easy. We grow at school by learning, studying, and taking exams. We grow in life by becoming more aware, and we generally tend to become more aware when some life experience obliges us to do so.

By extrapolating, we might say that in relationships we grow most quickly through situations and experiences that are not necessarily easy. And going back to Jung and his clear proposal that throughout the course of our lives it is our psyche that in its infinite intelligence leads us to be attracted to *precisely* those individuals who most have the potential to be instruments in our individual growth, we need to understand that in order for that to work, evidently we first have to be fully *in relationship* with those people. So we fall in love, we begin to feel that our happiness depends in some measure on the other person, and so begins our *need* of that person.

An external need, in others words, when we depend on something *external* to ourselves for our well-being, frequently carries within it the seeds of failure. In the case of a relationship, it may often be the cause of power plays between the two people, the less *needy* one being the one to dominate the relationship, and the *needier* one to resentfully accept this dominance due to his or her need for the other partner. But although on the surface it may not appear to be so, have no doubt that the dominant partner needs the needy partner as much as the other way around!

Power plays are not the only manifestation of relationships mired in mutual need. Another frequent expression is obsession or possessiveness, or a need to control. And you can imagine – if you haven't been there – the kind of resentment and negative feelings that this can generate on the part of both people. Akin to any substance addiction, obsession or possessiveness or the need to control can take people to hellish places in their hearts and minds that few of us would wish to visit. I have created an entire workshop on this topic, because although this type of addiction is often masked by a veneer of sophistication, it occurs more frequently than most people suspect, and makes the existence of those that suffer from it a living nightmare.

So why do we become needy in relationships? Of the roughly 40% males and 60% females from over 20 different nationalities that come to my private practice, many would initially answer that 'needing' your love partner is how it should be. But why should love imply a feeling that almost always develops into something negative, and at best, makes those who feel it, as said earlier, that they could not live without the beloved, thus 'proving' in their minds, that this is really love? Is that really what love is all about?

Wouldn't it make more sense to assume that love means freedom rather than independence? So what does needing our partner tell us?

Let's start with the falling in love part. What are we actually falling in love with? Stated simply, we fall in love with those bits and pieces of *ourselves* that we have not yet recognized, but that we find (via projection) in the partner. Is she tender and understanding? Is he funny and the center of the party? Is she strong and enterprising? Is he confident, with a great sense of integrity? All of those qualities may well be part of your partner's character, but the fact that you fell in love with those specific traits, tells you that they are actually part of your own character *as well*.

> *Remember that the best relationship is one where your love for each other exceeds your need for each other.*
> Dalai Lama

Since you do not yet manifest those qualities, because you have not yet recognized them in yourself, you need your partner to be able to 'be in touch with' that part of you. That is what 'hooks' you on your partner. Your partner's presence in your life gives you contact to those parts of you that you have not yet developed, making you feel that your partner is absolutely indispensable to your well-being. Another element you get hooked into early on in the relationship *precisely* because most people have not yet learned to love themselves, is the wonderful feeling of being loved by the other.

I hope that you are able to recognize that while feeling so good is understandable, legitimate and logical on the one hand, on the other, *if we already loved ourselves the way we are meant to*, we would not be so easily be swayed by this good feeling of being loved (or desired) by the other, and *regard the other with slightly more objective* eyes at the beginning. Our lack of love for ourselves makes us crave the love we perceive that is directed at us by the other. It makes us feel so good in part because we don't already supply it for ourselves. The removal of that love, either because the relationship is no longer working, or because the partner has gone, is what causes so much of the agonizing pain (even physical pain and nausea) we feel, and yet, if we already loved ourselves, that *self-love* would be of great comfort and would allow us to maintain an inner balance and some healthy measure of well-being *despite* the outer situation.

So then, when something happens to the relationship, or your partner leaves, or threatens to leave, is when the strong feelings of need arise. This is the time when you should realize that these strong feelings of need are a vast red flag letting you know something is going on inside of you *that only you can do something about*. If you ignore it, or translate it into "*I was deeply wounded by my partner*", or "*my partner did not return my feelings when I most needed him/her, so I guess that means I always choose the wrong people*", or "*next time I will choose better, so that this kind of thing never happens to me again*", then instead of resolving your inner dilemma, you will merely perpetuate it by maintaining the status quo inside of you, falling in love with yet another person that puts you in touch with bits of you that you have not yet recognized in yourself, and thus setting yourself up to be 'needy'.

So what is the solution? Simple to state, less simple to execute (mainly because it requires some of that inner discipline that most of us don't want to exercise): work on those bits of yourself that *you catch a glimpse of* in the beloved. Examine yourself to see where they might reside in you. Work at developing them; growing them. If you do this, I guarantee you that the next time you fall in love, it will be with a smaller degree of external need, and hence, a greater degree of internal freedom. Or, if you remain with the same person, your love will grow into something infinitely more loving.

Spiritual Partnerships

Now let's get back to spiritual partnerships. Some of the ways to define spiritual partnerships might be these:

- You complement each other as independent individuals who know they are fully responsible for themselves, as opposed to needing each other and hence continually entering the *dance* I referred to earlier, that brings about so many of our blind reactions.
- You are each invested in working on yourselves, alone, as well as within the parameters of the relationship, in order to grow into the richness you know you have within.
- You are both aware of the fact that one of the best ways towards bringing about this growth, is through a conscious and aware relationship with a loving partner.
- You are fully conscious about *wanting* to do this, to behave this way in this spiritual partnership, because you know it will lead you to yourself, and ultimately to your soul. There is nothing religious about these ideas. There is nothing abstemious about this. There is nothing in this spiritual partnership that does not allow you to live all the love and sexual and sensual richness that you may desire. Indeed, a spiritual partnership will lead you to greater richness *and* depth than you may have ever dreamed possible because there is no reason for passion to die the way it tends to in blind and reactive relationships!
- You both recognize the fact that the ego often rears its ugly head, wanting to be right, wanting to be more powerful, wanting things

its way, and hence using manipulation as a tool to keep the partner under control, and that in order to circumvent the ego, so that ultimately each of you is in charge of your own ego, as opposed to the ego being in charge of each of you and hence in charge of the relationship, you both do your utmost to remain aware at all times in order to – from a position of awareness – be able to thwart the ego (see also the chapter on the ego).

▪   This means that when either of you comes under the grip of those typical emotions that cause havoc in relationships, such as jealousy, insecurity, fear, anger, impatience, etc., you will make the conscious effort (which will require some discipline at the beginning), to remind each other of your goal: to remain aware, and to *not fall into the typical relationship traps of reactive blindness.*

▪   You both recognize that healthy boundaries are one of the relationship's priorities, and that in order to maintain such healthy boundaries, both of you will need to learn to respect the other *as well as the self.* You may – especially at the beginning – often forget about respecting these boundaries, and hence, precisely because this is the nature of a spiritual partnership, you will remind each other with love, tact, and compassion that your boundaries have been transgressed. When you do so, contrary to what will then occur in a blind and reactive relationship, the partner who is being reminded will be grateful for the reminder, and even if he finds himself momentarily caught up in a "blind" reaction, he will be able to catch himself simply because this is what he *consciously* wants to do, and because it's what you both signed up for, so to speak, when you agreed to enter this spiritual partnership.

▪   You are both aware of the necessity to grow your own love for yourself in order that the relationship may be more loving. Because of this, you will no longer tolerate your own moods, for example, recognizing that they are a sign of an unaware individual who has not assumed responsibility for his/her own inner well-being, nor will you tolerate the moods of the other. However, not tolerating means that you will each kindly, lovingly, and gently remind the other – when the need arises – that by having a mood he/she has forgotten about loving the self.

In a nutshell, in a spiritual partnership you most certainly will continue to run into snags. You continue to wish certain things were different. You may feel jealousy, and anger, and all those other emotions that typically make our relationships so fraught with problems.

But there is one enormous difference: you are aware that you are in the relationship – the spiritual partnership – not only to love, but in this process of love, to grow through whatever comes up for the two of you in the relationship. You are also aware of the fact that by dealing with whatever comes up by looking at the self - *each of you* looking at the self – at *your own* self - you come to an entirely different way of dealing with those problems that arise, than those that were used in the scenario painted in the earlier part of this chapter. By so doing, you grow the self. Growing the self means you love the self, reconnecting to your true inner self and that reconnection causes you to rewire your soul.

Boredom between two people doesn't come from being together, physically. It comes from being apart, mentally and spiritually.
Richard Bach

Chapter Sixteen

Compassion:
Loving the World

If you want others to be happy, practice compassion.
If you want to be happy, practice compassion.
Tenzin Gyatso, 14th Dalai Lama

We tend to associate compassion with thoughts of children dying of hunger in Darfur or the Sudan, or with thoughts of handicapped and crippled orphans in Haiti, thoughts of young boys and girls forced into sex slavery in numerous countries of our so-called *modern* world, thoughts of genocide in too many other countries of our so-called *modern* world, or thoughts of people losing their homes and livelihoods thanks to financial sleight-of-hand on Wall Street and in the City in our so-called *modern* world. We may feel compassion for the beggar we see on the street, or the homeless person protecting himself from the cold with cardboard. Our compassion may know no bounds when we consider those who are less fortunate than we are and when our eyes remain fixed on the difference between them and ourselves from a financial, health, or bereavement point of view. A mother who has just lost her only child, a mother who is dying of AIDS and has no resources, a friend who has terminal cancer, our neighbor whose spouse just died from an aneurism, the family whose home was foreclosed because the father lost his job, the child who lost both his legs in an accident, and so on.

However, when we sit in judgment on our colleague at work because he has just taken the credit for what was originally our idea, or on our teenage child whom we caught smoking marijuana in his room, or other judgmental thoughts go through our mind when we see the woman with the skirt that is just too tight or too short (or both), or the couple who is drinking just a bit too much at the bar in the country club and whose behavior is now raucous and slightly unacceptable, or the girl at the next table in the café with black fingernails and lipstick, and several rings in her nose and lips, or the self-important man in the Armani suit impatiently tapping his fingers as he continually checks the time on his watch - when we sit in judgment on these people, we are not generally aware of the fact that compassion, rather than judgment is what should be filling our minds.

> *The major block to compassion is the judgment in our minds.*
> *Judgment is the mind's primary tool of separation.*
> Diane Berke

Why compassion? Because we can *choose* these reactions about our fellow human beings, and compassion is filled with so much more love and joy (which bring us closer to our true selves), than judgment. How do we feel when we sit in judgment on others, or when we criticize, or feel holier-than-thou, or self-righteous, or better than, or any of those emotions that separate and divide much more than bring us – the human family – together? When we entertain such thoughts and emotions, we do not feel good. We may feel smug. Or "better". Or justified. Or self-righteous. But we certainly don't feel joy. *Just by the lack of joy, or some measure of good feeling that is related to joy, we can already know that what we are feeling does not serve a purpose that serves us well. And what serves us well? Anything that brings us closer to our true selves. Anything that moves us towards the process of love and of rewiring our souls.*

So thoughts or actions that produce love and joy would qualify. But thoughts and actions that fill us with these other emotions don't. You might look at it from the perspective that one moves us closer to ourselves and one does not. Several years ago I posted a brief talk on YouTube called *Emotions: Your Road to Inner Freedom*, because if you learn to use your emotions as a barometer for that which serves you and that which does not - and you begin to continually move yourself into the direction of those emotions that serve you - you have come a long way towards understanding what to do in order to rewire your soul and in the process find inner peace, love, joy and freedom.

Where does judgment or criticism take us? To a place that is not connected to love and joy. The whole purpose of this book is to take you closer to your innate sense of love and joy. Therefore each chapter of the book shows you different paths to take you there, in order that you come to realize that *absolutely everything you do in life can bring you closer to love and joy. You get to choose!* There can be joy in all manner of things that are not typically joyous. There can be joy, for example, in death. Have you ever read the 1997 book *Tuesdays With Morrie* by Mitch Albom? It's a true story and recounts weekly meetings of the author with an older man (Morrie) who is dying. In these meetings Morrie gives Mitch, who was once his student at university, lessons about life. But this older man who is dying, does so with vim and vigor. He embraces death, he embraces what is left of his life, having been diagnosed with Lou Gehrig's disease that is slowly wasting his life away, in order to continue to be alive – with joy – as long as he still has life in his body. The book tells the story of that last chapter of Morrie Schwartz's life.

I had a similar case in my own life. A friend - although she and I were not close in the conventional sense - but nevertheless our relationship went far beyond being mere acquaintances, gave me the exquisite privilege (for which I will forever be grateful) of allowing me to see her die. I don't mean her actual death, but her *process of dying*. The way she dealt with it. Her thoughts about it. Her thoughts about the fact that she was not going to be able to continue in this life of ours. She was my age, she had been diagnosed with cancer, and just before the diagnosis, had met the love of her life. With the diagnosis – despite the diagnosis - their love deepened, he took her to live with him in his country home, and she tried to live. But it was not to be. Well-meaning oncologists convinced her that surgery and chemotherapy would help her, they mutilated her, and it all came to naught. In the end she was under palliative care with a local hospice, although she eventually spent the last weeks of her life back at home with her wonderful partner and daily palliative outpatient care provided by the Spanish national health care system. During those last weeks, both at the hospice, and later, back at home, I visited her and thereby was able to see her death process. She clearly did not want to die. She would have dearly loved to have remained here, to be able to live together with this man she loved so much, and die many years later, at a ripe old age. However, she knew that was not happening. And so she *embraced* her upcoming death. She planned for it with joy. She divested herself of the things she loved the most: her books, her paintings, some of her clothes. She gave of herself and talked about her death. You might say that we chatted about it in the way we might have chatted about an upcoming trip --- a very important upcoming trip - to a country she did not yet truly know. Or perhaps she knew the country very well, but had not yet been able to remember it. She was filled with love and joy despite all of this.

So the point of this story is to share with you that while we generally consider love - and especially joy - to only form part of our lives when all is well, when our lives are running smoothly, when we have no major problems, this is in fact, not the case. Love and joy can be found in Robben Island, in Auschwitz, in the Gulag, in a weekly meeting with a dying man, or in a country residence here in southern Spain looking into the smiling face of a dying woman. We are the ones who are responsible for ensuring that love and joy form part of our lives *no matter what*. And there are tools that help us maintain such a frame of mind. One of these is compassion.

> *... when we finally know we are dying, and all other sentient beings are dying with us, we start to have a burning, almost heartbreaking sense of the fragility and preciousness of each moment and each being, and from this can grow a deep, clear, limitless compassion for all beings.*
> Sogyal Rinpoche

So when we are in a judgmental or critical frame of mind, compassion might be one of the ways that enables us to move back to love and joy. Forgiveness is another. Compassion is such a fraught word. Some people think compassion means *feeling sorry for,* others think it means having to *feel everything the other person who is having a hard time feels,* yet others think it means *needing to do something for the one who is suffering.* The word in fact comes from a Latin root and means *to suffer with.* Many philosophies consider it a great virtue, and the major religions of the world consider it the greatest virtue.

The Buddhist concept of compassion *wants others to be free from suffering,* and this is the manner in which compassion is being used in this book. Consider that suffering is not only being nailed on a cross, or dying from disease, or losing your money, but suffering is also being impatient, unkind, untruthful, haughty, self-righteous, angry, jealous, etc. In other words, when you see a person behaving in any of those ways, you could begin to look at them from the point of view that something inside is causing them to suffer and that is why they are behaving like that. *This does not mean that you should tolerate it, but by being willing to choose the possibility of taking such a stance, it does mean that you might be able to muster some compassion for them.* The Gospels say that true compassion should extend to all, even including your enemies.

Let's look at bullying for a moment. How does a bullier do what he/she does, if it is not from a position of suffering? Perhaps the bullier wants power, or recognition, or followers, or popularity of a sort. All of these "needs" come from a place inside that is suffering and in pain about something. If an individual wants to be strong, that is not a need or desire that comes from suffering, but if an individual wants power, then that comes from a position of need. Perhaps this need has arisen in order to be able to lose the feelings of inferiority or fear of what others think. The need may be fueled by hatred. (And by the way, this kind of a need qualifies as an addiction, as we discussed in the chapter on self-soothing because as long as you seek power because it allows you to thrust those other feelings about yourself under the carpet, you are self-soothing in an addictive way). So it stands to reason that the bullier needs our compassion. *Not* our tolerance, but our compassion. This means that *both* the bullier *and* the rest of us need to learn about empathy. With empathy for another it is not possible to judge the bullier nor for the bullier to bully the other person.

Empathy and compassion go hand in hand. And while this book is not a treatise for schools and the manner in which bullying needs to be addressed, it is becoming more and more clear that quality time needs to be allowed in classes for teachers to be able to interact with students on a human level, creating a sense of cohesion, particularly in the early grades, promoting personal interaction that goes well beyond class work, where issues such as bullying and compassion and empathy – as well as many other age-appropriate issues - can be discussed, and where – if bullying is in fact actually happening – it can be immediately addressed in the classroom, in that socially and emotionally intelligent interaction between teacher and students. Such an opportunity for learning, for understanding, for developing a sense for open discourse, for *seeing the other's point of view*, for internalizing the idea that there is always a choice, and that we are each responsible for our own behavior, is invaluable, and certainly much more important – for healthy and potentially joyous living throughout the life trajectory - than memorizing the date of a battle that was fought during the Civil War, or learning to differentiate grammatical terminology used in syntax. Doing this - using our schools for the furthering of such interaction - our society has not only an opportunity to promote empathy and compassion from an early age, but has an even more important opportunity of offering young people understanding and skills that will not only serve them throughout their lives, but will serve all those whose lives they touch, and hence the larger, societal whole.

So back to the fact that compassion might be one of the ways that enables us to move back to love and joy. Let's examine what happens when you are contemplating (or telling your therapist, friend, or parent about it) how much your partner, companion, or spouse has hurt you, cheated on you, lied to you, deceived you, manipulated you, changed on you (as compared with how he/she was when you met), disgraced you, or abandoned you, to name only a few possibilities.

We've already seen in the last chapter about relationships that it *does* take two to tango (so, for example, if he/she did such-and-such to you, why did you let it go on for so long?), and further, that *no matter what* "relationship crime" the other party has actually "committed", he/she also deserves some compassion because who can know what has happened in their life up to that point (and particularly in their early life) in order to bring them to behave in such a despicable way? (I know these last statements may raise the ire of all those who believe there is no responsibility in cases of abuse on the side of the abused. Please let me state here and now that I firmly believe that abuse of any kind should not be tolerated. However, in an ideal world we would all be responsible for ourselves (I am excluding the very young, although again, in an ideal world, they would be taught these tenets as early as possible) and hence, when someone behaves in an inappropriate fashion, we would *recognize* it for that and would be capable of setting up healthy boundaries. Since we do not live in an ideal world, and since people are not taught this from early childhood on, we clearly need to protect those who are abused, or potentially abused).

When I venture such opinions to clients, this will occasionally merit me a baleful glare. But often I also see a glimmer of understanding, or even of agreement. Sometimes I think it's their way of assuaging their own angry thoughts at themselves for having fallen in love with the other person at all, of justifying to themselves that there *was* something wonderful there for them at the beginning (as indeed there tends to be), and that therefore it is not necessary to view themselves as total relationship failures for having chosen so badly. Indeed. But there is more to be looked at.

Why we might feel compassion for someone who has hurt us seems to be easy to understand. They may have become the way they now are; this awful way they are behaving with us, in other words, because of, as mentioned earlier, difficult traumas in their childhood, perhaps painful relationship patterns prior to meeting us, or a myriad number of other plausible reasons that might allow us to get a glimpse into the inner makings of this other person.

But *how* do we go about feeling this compassion, when what we really would like to do is wring their necks, or never let them see the children again, or take the investment portfolio plus everything that's in the bank, leaving them without a penny, or make them pay in some other way that will truly make them realize just how much they have hurt us?

How do we find it in ourselves to bring to the table any measure of compassion when they obviously are such absolutely awful people? These are people who have perhaps hurt us more than anyone else ever did. And they did this deliberately, hatefully, viciously. A betrayal of this nature, where once there was love, and now there is only blackness, is perhaps more difficult to deal with than any other kind of betrayal because we see it from the position of deliberate calculation on the part of the other person. Even if they did not want to hurt us, they nevertheless did so knowingly.

While major religions spend a great deal of time preaching compassion, religion is by no means the only method to find your way to compassion. Rather, I would venture to say, the first step might be by taking a look at yourself. By seeing what is inside of you. By getting to know yourself, your intentions, your desires, your needs, your fears, your vanities, your pride, your ego, your priorities, your patience, and your degree of self-awareness.

Self-awareness is such a tricky thing. If you don't have it, you generally don't know that you don't have it, and when you begin to acquire it, you keep forgetting about it until you make a discipline of it, of obliging yourself to be self-aware at as many moments as possible in your daily life. Only then does it have a chance of becoming second nature, and thus of you gradually becoming self-aware at almost all times. This implies that you begin to take responsibility for *everything you feel, think, say and do* (see also the chapter on responsibility), and as you take on responsibility for all that, you begin to understand that what another person has done to you is his/her responsibility, his/her problem, his/her issue to be resolved, and that no matter how much you may rant and rave or crave revenge, you will never be able to change the other. *You can only change yourself.* As we absorb the truth of this statement, we begin to understand that what others do unto us is truly only interesting and important from the point of view of *how we react* to their words or acts. Please read that last sentence again!

And *how we react* depends in large measure on our degree of self-awareness. It is at this point that the possibility for compassion enters the picture. The more self-aware you are, the more you know you have choices and alternatives at every turn of the road. Therefore you begin to understand that someone who has hurt you (hurting others generally implies, among other things, fear in the one who hurts; fear of feeling insecure, fear of chaos, fear of loss of control, fear of vulnerability, etc.) has done so from a position of blindness, of a lack of self awareness.

Careful now, I am not suggesting we simply excuse all these people and say, "oh, they didn't know what they were doing, so it's ok". Of course it's *not* ok (*please* see the chapter on boundaries). But because you are now capable of understanding where they are coming from; in other words, from blindness, and because you are aware, or are becoming aware, you are now able to *choose* to feel compassion. How they resolve their own issues that cause this behavior on their part, is their problem. Perhaps you will want to be supportive in helping them shed light on it, perhaps not. You may need to oust them from your life, perhaps even press legal charges etc. But in the meantime, you have resolved an enormous issue of your own, by looking at yourself, by resolving to become self-aware, and by choosing the path of compassion rather than the path of hatred, anger, self-pity, or revenge.

Compassion for others does tend to have a ripple effect. Try it and observe what happens, not only with others, but most particularly, inside of yourself.

> We can strive gradually to become more compassionate, that is
> we can develop both genuine sympathy for others' suffering
> and the will to help remove their pain. As a result, our
> own serenity and inner strength will increase.
> Dalai Lama

As you begin to *allow* compassion into your life, as you begin to make different choices about those individuals, organizations, groups, religions, ideologies, or governments you would have previously pitied, derided, criticized, judged, or hated, and as you begin to be more and more aware that this is truly all in your own hands, you will also begin to see the first fruits of such decisions and choices impacting the quality of your own life. How does pity, derision, criticism, judgment, and hatred make you feel? Isn't it true that none of it ever makes you feel good? What I mean is that although it may make you feel self-righteous, or justified so that you can say to yourself you are doing the right thing in criticizing or judging (see also the chapter on self-soothing), it certainly does not offer you a feeling of joy. Nevertheless, as you begin to allow compassion into your life, you will notice a totally different type of feeling flood through you. Compassion in and of itself has been shown to increase well-being in those who feel it. Due to the fact that

Western psychology has not yet defined compassion in the same way in which it defines depression or social phobia, it has not yet in fact studied the phenomenon of compassion in the same way other psychological states have been studied. However, due to the high importance placed on compassion in Buddhism, and the ever-growing dialogue between positive psychologists, scientific researchers, and Buddhists, particularly Buddhist monks, as well with an ever-growing number of neuro-scientists, there are more and more studies revolving around the positive psychology of compassion.

There is another corollary to compassion – paradoxically both a consequence of it and a way that leads to it: compassion leads to a sense of connectedness with others, with *all* others. The more we try to forget about the differences between ourselves, the more we come to feel compassion, and the more we feel compassion, the more we feel connected to all others. This topic is discussed at length in the chapter on establishing the inner connection.

Compassion is on the same continuum as caring and love, and in some ways it includes both. While you may believe that when you feel compassion for another who is not connected to you in a personal way – perhaps the compassion I feel for the clients in my practice and with whom I have no other ties, or the compassion you may feel for the bully in the school yard, or the panhandler on the street – it does not include the emotion of love, it does, in fact, include it. It's a less personal love, a love that exists because the foundation of your compassion holds that love, and it signifies that you are one with the other person, and being one with the other, implies that you love the other. Compassion viewed in this light is very different from pity or charity or volunteer work for the good of others. Compassion, by its very nature, does include love, and I suppose the lesson for all of us in this is that if we are not capable of acknowledging and accepting this love inherent in compassion, then perhaps what we are feeling is not compassion, but one of those other "do-good" variations mentioned above.

If you want others to be happy, practice compassion. If you want to be happy, practice compassion.
Dalai Lama

In fact, there is another very important element to compassion that helps us discern if what we are feeling is indeed compassion or not, and that is lack of duality or separation, and while there will be more about this subject in the chapter on intermingled molecules, let's just say this: the nature of duality (seeing things as black/white, good/bad, day/night, light/dark, you/me) is something we all live with. Attempting to move beyond that is not easy, but without it, we'll never truly be capable of compassion. Which is the same as saying if we are all one, there is no you/me, there is no separation. But before you guffaw or get irritated with me, don't think I'm pretending to know it all and be there already. Quite the contrary. This is one I grapple with every day. I'm nowhere near that ideal state I've just described. But that's ok. The important thing is to know that it exists, and that it's your goal. Or if it's not your goal yet, just consider that you might like it to eventually be your goal. And so each step you take, choosing to make choices that firmly propel you in that direction, moves you closer to that goal.

Love and compassion are necessities, not luxuries.
Without them, humanity cannot survive.
Dalai Lama

Chapter Seventeen

Intermingled Molecules:
We Are All One

We are all responsible because we are all one.

H ow can we believe we are not all one? In other words, how can we not believe that we are all interconnected? That where I end and you start, is, in a sense, only an optical illusion, because we are so interconnected that we are connected. The field of energy from whence we spring, and about which so many have written so eloquently (e.g., Einstein, Rumi, Deepak Chopra, Lynne McTaggart, etc.) is not only around us, but also in us, and continues beyond us to all else, including everyone and everything else. There is no you and me in the classic sense of the word, but there is *we*. With so much information shooting out at us from disciplines as varied as quantum physics (that tells us that we are all intermingled molecules in a universal energy soup and that what we think about and what we intend, creates, in actual fact, our visible reality), and cellular and molecular biology (that tells us that how we perceive something in our environment, whether that is a tiger chasing us for lunch, or a car bearing down on us, or how our partner has just spoken to us, or how we react to a song we are listening to on the radio, influences the very make-up of our cells and DNA), and neuroscience (that tells us that we can change old neural pathways in the brain – whether we are 78 or 18 years old - and create totally new ones, just by changing our habits and the way we think, and *especially* by meditating or practicing mindfulness), even though most of this may not yet be mainstream knowledge that people chat about around the dinner table, it is, nevertheless, out there as easily accessible information for anyone interested enough in these topics on the internet and in many books that are being published. Let's have a look at some of these ideas more closely:

Quantum Physics:

Many of us (back in the dark ages of the mid-twentieth century) learned at school that the atom was the smallest bit of material substance in the universe. Then we heard about subatomic molecules, then about quarks, and finally (late 80's and early 90's) we learned that as we descend further and further down into the subatomic field, we find that we end at a space of nothingness. At least, there is *nothing* there in the sense that there is *no thing*. What *is* there, however, is pure vibrating energy, but what this energy does and how it appears, depends very much on whether someone is observing it or not, and who that someone is, that is observing it, and what that someone has on his or her mind, and what the *intentions* of that someone might be. All rather confusing, but endlessly exciting, having opened up so many possibilities that we had never been aware of prior to these discoveries. Max Planck, quantum physicist, said in his Nobel Prize for Physics acceptance speech in 1927 that beyond sub-atomic particles there is a field. At another speech in 1944 in Florence, Italy, titled *The Nature of Matter*, he said:

> As a man who has devoted his whole life to the most clear headed science, to the study of matter, I can tell you as a result of my research about atoms this much: There is no matter as such. All matter originates and exists only by virtue of a force which brings the particle of an atom to vibration and holds this most minute solar system of the atom together. We must assume behind this force the existence of a conscious and intelligent mind. This mind is the matrix of all matter.

And as we continue examining this pure vibrating energy that is at the bottom of everything, so to speak, we discover that quantum physics does not conform to the same type of laws that we had heretofore believed governed our physical reality. We learn that all of this vibrating energy extends on and on to everything and everyone in such a way that the energy connects it all, or, said in other words, that everything there is in our world – vegetation, such as plants and trees, man-made things such as tables or computers or cars, and also structures, such as buildings or bridges; inanimate things that occur in nature, such as rocks or mountains; and every animal and human being on earth - are all made of this energy, are all part of it, and are all connected because of it, in such a way that we are all one. We might liken it – as many have done - to a drop of water that is made of the same liquid substance that is the ocean, and therefore that drop of water is also part of the ocean and is furthermore connected to all other drops of water that compose the ocean. *We are all one.*

Taking this one step further, and continuing within the realm of quantum physics, we discover that the subatomic world changes and rearranges itself due to our observations and intentions. It is in the observation of subatomic particles that we (or whoever it is that is doing the observing) actually influence the physical process of these particles. It was Einstein who said: *When you change the way you look at things, the things you look at change.* And taking that one step even further, if we are all one, and if our observation of the particles actually influences their physical processes, we can begin to understand how we all participate in co-creating our reality.

That, of course, begs the question: what happens to this process without consciousness? What happens when the great majority of the observers are not aware of our one-ness, potentially not particularly interested in the topic, and are furthermore, not at all aware of their own inner state? If we are all part of a great pool of energy, and we all influence the creation of this common reality, then what you think and feel and say and do, has an energetic effect on me and vice versa. So if you are not aware and I am not aware, what are we creating? And how are we affecting each other? Absolutely everything is resonating on the quantum level, including our bodies, our thoughts and all that surrounds us. It is all part of, as Lynne McTaggart puts it, one gigantic energy field where everything resonates at different frequencies. We are all one and we all form part of this process of co-creation and we all influence the field in some fashion. Rumi said: *Out beyond the ideas of wrongdoing and right doing there is a field. I'll meet you there.*

Having come this far in this book, I am confident that you recognize that your greatest responsibility is to be as aware as you can possibly be each and every day, not only to improve your own life and inner well-being, but to add to the advance of the entire world, and all the people therein. If we all sweep in front of our own door, as Goethe put it, the whole world will soon be clean!

Cellular & Molecular Biology

The field of biology has brought us some amazing discoveries as well that fly in the face of much of what was conventionally accepted and taught in universities up to the last couple of decades of the 20th century. In another chapter of this book we already examined the fact that more and more biologists, notably Candace Pert, concur that *every thought and every feeling produces a physical molecule.*

> *My research has shown me that when emotions are expressed--which is to say that the biochemicals that are the substrate of emotion are flowing freely--all systems are united and made whole. When emotions are repressed, denied, not allowed to be whatever they may be, our network pathways get blocked, stopping the flow of the vital feel-good, unifying chemicals that run both our biology and our behavior.*
> Candace Pert

Led by Bruce Lipton other biologists have further demonstrated that genetic determinism is a fallacy, one that has been taught at medical schools for well over a century and hence has influenced generations of physicians and clinicians all over the world. Essentially genetic determinism implies that if an individual carries the genetic markers for a given disease or disposition, that person has a much greater likelihood for developing that disease than does the rest of the population. How many times have you completed medical histories that ask the question whether either or both of your parents (or other members of your family) had cardiac disease or cancer? *We all knew this.* If it has happened in your family, *it runs in your family*, and there is a better chance than usual that you may also get it. (As an aside here, my mother died of uterine cancer in her mid-fifties and my only brother died of malignant melanoma when he was just 31. If I had bought into the fallacy of genetic determinism, I might have brought myself – in my mind over all those years after their respective deaths, only 36 months apart - to a deathbed labeled cancer, and yet, *even when I was diagnosed with uterine cancer myself* in my early fifties, over 30 years later, I was absolutely convinced that cancer had no place in my body and that it and I had no relationship, despite this family history. So I worked on the thoughts in my head, I worked on my feelings, I worked on what gave meaning and purpose to my life, I contemplated the love in my life for my three sons, my family, and my friends, I did not discuss my diagnosis with anyone except people who had a strong hold on themselves and could therefore support me in the way I was dealing with it, as opposed to commiserating with me, or pitying me, or getting sad and crying, or worrying about me, and I carried on – *business as usual* – and three months later there was no cancer in me. Would events have turned out differently, had I entertained a mindset influenced by genetic determinism? We'll never know empirically, but I'm betting on the answer to that question probably being yes.)

So genetic determinism has been shown to be a fallacy, and while it is not yet universally accepted by scientists and physicians across the board, it *is* becoming more and more mainstream, particularly if you understand how it ties in so closely with what both quantum physics and neuroscience are and have been discovering. But there is a caveat. If you have the genes, the markers, and your mindset is essentially one of impotence, in other words, a mindset where you believe that this will, in all likelihood, be your fate, or that genes are genes, and there is nothing you can do about them, then, despite genetic determinism having been shown to be a fallacy, the chances that you will succumb to whatever it is your genes are determining may be much higher. But – and this is what biologists such as Lipton and Pert discovered, that is of such relevance to our discussion and the content of this book – if you realize that you can influence your environment (your inner, genetic environment and your inner, psychological, emotional and spiritual environment, and your outer, physical environment, such as your body, the air you breathe, the food you eat, how and whether you exercise, and so on), then all of this that you do to influence this environment, *including your thoughts and your feelings*, and your love for yourself, will bring about changes in this genetic possibility that you were born with. Almost – in very simplistic fashion - like you were born with muscles, but what you then do with them will decide whether you have muscle tone or not.

> *I was exhilarated by the new realization that I could change the character of my life by changing my beliefs. I was instantly energized because I realized that there was a science-based path that would take me from my job as a perennial "victim" to my new position as "co-creator" of my destiny.*
> Bruce Lipton

Neuroscience

Each of these three fields: quantum physics, biology and neuroscience is fascinating, and it's hard to decide which is more so, but the field of neuroscience is so close to us in the sense that it feels almost as though it were the easiest one to apply; it is, ultimately, all about our brain, although all three fields are interrelated and connected. What happens in one; what you do to affect one, affects the other two, and so on.

The field of neuroscience has been enriching the world with more and more information that directly impacts our lives with leaps and bounds. First – after the world had long believed that the only brain cells you will ever have are the ones you are born with, and when you begin to lose them, they were gone forever – it was discovered that while that may be so, the *connections* between those cells – dendrites and synapses could increase – at any age – (this was discovered with geriatric research in the aging population, again in the 80's and 90's), *depending on what one did*, and especially if one did something new, such as learning how to play an instrument, or learning a new language, and so on. This, in and of itself, impacted the field enormously and the importance of those findings could not be minimized, because it meant that in some fashion, our brains do go on growing, and it demonstrated that aging did not necessarily have to mean cognitive decrepitude and decline. Almost simultaneously, it was found that some areas of the brain can take over for others, if needed, perhaps if after an accident, something is no longer working the way it should. Thus when the use of the left hand is lost through paralysis, for example, brain function that heretofore had only been related to functions on the right side of the body, might now be rewired by the brain in order to give some fashion of movement to that part of the left side that no longer functions properly.

Amazing work in this direction is related in a book by the psychiatrist Norman Doidge: *The Brain That Changes Itself*. All of this gave rise (in the latter part of the 20th Century) to a term now known as neuroplasticity (already used by William James in the century before, but largely discarded by the scientific community until much later) which merely refers to the flexibility of the brain, not only to continue growing, but also to be multi-functional, we might say, depending on how it is needed and used. An interesting point, however, is made with respect to neuroplasticity, and it is that *paying close attention* is essential to it. In other words, when the brain is being trained in some way, and we are stretching it, so to speak, in order for something new to be learned, or something no longer useful to be *unlearned*, it can be done, and it can be done well, but only if we play close attention to what we are doing while we are doing it, which is the same as saying we must be *aware and mindful*.

Eventually scientists discovered that not only can connections between existing brain cells continue to multiply and grow, but that neurogenesis can actually take place – new brain cells or neurons, can grow – again, depending on the activity that the owner of the brain undertakes.

Here are some examples of the activities that promote a greater proliferation of dendrites and even new growth of brain cells:

- Walking just 30 minutes a day six times per week
- Learning something new (a musical instrument, a foreign language, the use of a new technological or digital gadget, a field of study, cooking, fishing, video-editing, you name it, if it's new to you, it will stimulate neural growth)
- Changing long term habits for other, new and more positive habits
- Becoming self-aware by practicing mindfulness and remaining present

Awareness of the self, compassion for others and the self, forgiving others and the self, assuming responsibility for all aspects of the self, including your inner environment (how you feel, what you think and what you focus on), as well as what you say and do, and finally, loving the self, all form an integral part of the coming to consciousness of the inter-mingled nature of our world, and all of us who inhabit it.

Bearing all of this in mind, should we not begin to concern ourselves with understanding the inter-connectedness of the tapestry into which we are all woven? I can hear you saying: *"But that is all very complicated. I can't possibly begin how to understand all of that. It doesn't really make any sense in my life."* Perhaps you can't understand it all because just the idea of it is so foreign to your current way of thinking, but what you most definitely *can* do, is to begin some work on yourself on the individual level in order to improve not only your own life, and how you feel about yourself, but also how you feel about *life in general* all day, every day for the rest of your life. If you begin today, your life will begin to change today and if that happens, then the way you behave with other people will also change and therein lies the secret for global change at the very individual level. *That is what you can do about it.* Just by becoming responsible for yourself in all the ways we've discussed in this book so far, you can change the world. As can I. As can each of us.

Fascinating studies are being carried out on the use of psychedelic substances: some hallucinogens, involving psilocybin, the psychoactive ingredient found in certain mushrooms for depression in cancer, for obsessive-compulsive disorder, end-of-life anxiety, post-traumatic stress disorder and addiction to drugs or alcohol, as reported in an article in the New York Times. Permission has been granted to scientists to study – as others had in decades gone by, until it was prohibited – the potential of such drugs for use in the treatment of problems in mental health, as well as for illuminating the nature of consciousness.

What has particularly fascinated scientists is the similarity between experiences arising from the use of hallucinogenic substances and experiences that are often life-altering, as recounted in the history of humanity by religious mystics and long-term meditators. *Researchers have identified such similarities in neural imaging studies.* One study that examined subjects with no major physical or psychological problems – and no prior history of hallucinogenic use - who were given psilocybin, found that the drug was able to induce what these individuals portrayed as a profound spiritual experience.

Similar studies carried out since then, in particular with individuals dealing with cancer and depression found that these people reported "an improved outlook on life *after an experience in which the boundaries between the self and others disappear.*" They talked of "their egos and bodies vanishing as they felt part of some larger state of consciousness in which their personal worries and insecurities vanished. They found themselves reviewing past relationships with lovers and relatives with a new sense of empathy." In fact, according to one of the study's directors, it appears likely that the wiring of the human brain is such that we are meant to experience such "unitive" experiences where we feel attuned with others. Participants in the study further reported that while under the effect of hallucinogens, they were able to "transcend their primary identification with their bodies and experience ego-free states."

Due to my understanding of some of the numerous advances in recent neuroscientific research, I now believe that we can, in fact, come to the same place these hallucinogens promise us with their lure of "easy" psychedelic adventure, *by full awareness, by the practice of mindfulness, by centering - so to speak - on the self, on that part of us that leads us to the sense of one-ness, compassion, empathy and love*, as discussed in this book.

Thoughts and Reality

It comes as no surprise that over the course of the last years amazon.com (in its global sites) has frequently included in its top 15 bestselling books or DVD's items pertaining to the intention of thought, and similar inclusions have been noted in the lists published by the New York Times.

Emerson said it, Epictetus said it, the Buddha said it, Christ said it, Thoreau said it, James Allen said it: *Your thoughts become your reality*.

Now however, in the 21st century, it is not only philosophers, metaphysicians, religious figures and other esoteric thinkers who say this, but also quantum physicists, biologists, and a host of other empirical thinkers and researchers. *So there can no longer be any doubt: our thoughts do indeed determine our lives.* If you still are reluctant to believe it, remind yourself of the group of people who wanted Copernicus arrested and jailed for proclaiming that the earth revolves around the sun instead of the other way around! Sometimes it is hard to believe what differs from that which we've been hearing all our lives, but just because it's *different and strange*, does not mean it has no merit, and should be summarily dismissed.

Understanding the concept behind such simple words that thoughts have power, can change the very foundations of your life. Let's look at an everyday example. Suppose you and your partner or spouse are continually bickering. When you met, fell in love, and got married, you were ecstatically in love, and couldn't wait to be with one another. Now, well, let's just say that things are different.

Remember: our goal is to understand the power of thoughts. So just as an experiment, I'd like you to try an exercise for the next week. Make a list of about ten qualities or aspects or characteristics about your partner that you really enjoy and appreciate (even if lately they seem to have gotten lost in the shuffle). Look at that list on a daily basis. Think about the items on the list, remember some of the times in the past – before your current bickering - when they were in evidence on a regular basis. Whenever you find yourself thinking about the unpleasant aspects of your partner, or what he or she said or did (or didn't say or do) last week, the other day, or this morning, *deliberately* change your thoughts towards your list, and think about the good things about your partner, rather than about the negative ones. Focus on the good traits. Refuse to think about the negative ones. Just for one week.

I would love to hear some of the results of this little experiment, but my guess, judging by the results achieved by my clients, is that a good number of those who try it will be surprised to realize that things went better than usual. They may even say that it was just one of those weeks that was less difficult than others. Hmm. Could it be possible that it had something to do with the thoughts that were being focused on; the positive aspects of the partner rather than the negative? Could it be possible that the more you think about something … *anything* … the more precisely that will appear in your life? This is, after all, what all the afore-mentioned thinkers and researchers have said. Focus on the negative aspects of your partner, and your life will be filled with them. Focus on the positive ones and note the difference in what happens.

I invite you to try similar experiments about whatever it is that plagues you. Do I hear someone saying that this is impossible? A pipe dream, because thoughts creep unbidden into the mind and one can't control them? Did I say this is easy? How did you learn how to use your computer? How did you grow nearly non-existent bicep muscles into a hard, firm, well-toned upper arm? How did you learn that foreign language? How did you learn how to play tennis? Was it not with some practice and discipline? Of course. And so it is with this. Realize that in order to grapple with your thoughts; in order to find some measure of control over them in such a way that they *speak the language* that most approximates whatever it is that you wish to see or realize in your life, you must practice *changing* the thoughts that do not lead you in that direction into another kind of thoughts.

And this is only possible with practice. Just because we are talking about your thoughts and not muscles or the grammatical structure of a new language, does not mean that discipline isn't an important aspect of it. For a time, particularly at the beginning of your journey down this wonderful pathway, you will need to spend a good portion of your leisure time practicing this endeavor. Reminding yourself of it. Recognizing over and over again, that once again you forgot, and then, just like a child who is learning how to walk, and falls, and gets up, and falls again, and gets up again, and again, and again, and again, you also, will get up as often as is necessary, in order to come to a point, where this new way of thinking becomes a well-ingrained habit. And of course, as indicated in the chapters on thoughts and emotions, use your feelings to get a handle on your thoughts. It is much easier to pay conscious attention to your inner state of being, than to your thoughts. But – your feelings will inform you very explicitly about what's going on with your thoughts. And that's the place where – from a position of awareness – choice, self-love and self-responsibility can come into play in order to change the tenor of those thoughts.

Although there are times in life when thoughts are necessarily dark, when people one loves have died, when difficulties visit one in unexpected ways, there are, nevertheless, ways of dealing with these times that continue to be positive. You might ask: what can I learn from this? How can I use this experience to become a better, more all-rounded person? Read books such as those written by Victor Frankl, Nelson Mandela, or Alexander Solzhenitsyn (all of whom were discussed earlier in this book) or listen to inspirational talks by many others mentioned in this book and listed in the Appendix and Bibliography, in order to better understand this philosophy, as evinced by individuals who survived despite horrendous pain and suffering – and who survived without bitterness and hatred in their hearts.

And during less difficult times choose to think only those thoughts that lead you in your desired direction. Think only those thoughts that raise your energy. Think only those thoughts that cause you to come to a more balanced and loving inner state. This is not easy. At least not at the beginning. Keep reminding yourself. Remember the little child that continues to get up even after falling down twenty times. Make good use of the sources available at the end of this book, take care about the kind of conversation you choose to participate in, scatter reminders to yourself about thinking this way about your house and office, and remember, this is just as easy or just as hard as it was to build the muscle or learn the vocabulary of a new language. The difference is that this doesn't just give you a better looking body or a way of communicating in another country, but a way to change your entire life. Going for it will create sweeping changes in a short period of time.

So let's consider once again the connection between the power of your thoughts, how you feel because of those thoughts, what this implies about your effect on those who surround you, or whose lives touch yours, and how this leads – in you – to a greater understanding and internalizing of the fact that we are all one. At this point the process reminds me of the mythological ouroborus, the serpent that is depicted with its own tail in its mouth, thereby forming a perfect circle. The ouroborus symbolizes – in alchemy, Gnosticism and hermeticism – the cyclical nature of things, transformation, and a return to the origins, which again reminds me of the T.S. Eliot quatrain reproduced earlier from *Little Giddings*:

We shall not cease from exploration
And the end of all our exploring
Will be to arrive where we started
And know the place for the first time.

The reason this is so, is because when we finally reach the point where we can understand and internalize the fact that we are all one, then we truly know that all we think, feel, say and do is part of the field in which we are all intermingled molecules and hence it all affects each and every part of the field. The higher we maintain our individual energetic frequency, the more we influence the energy of the entire field and thus come full circle. In other words, we not only take responsibility for ourselves in the broadest sense of the word, but begin to understand that in so doing, we also take responsibility for the whole, because of the fact that we are all one. Only then, do we consciously participate in – as opposed to blindly act – the co-creative process in the field that affects our entire universal reality.

Conclusion:
The Possible Human – The Possible Self

You were born with wings, why prefer to crawl through life?
Mawlana Jalal-al-Din Rumi

We can be so much more than we think. This refers not only to outward, worldly accomplishments as so many inspirational authors and speakers encourage us to believe, but specifically to inner progress and growth of a kind that allows us to reach unimagined heights of freedom, peace, harmony, and joy. If this is indeed so, that we can become so much more than we think, and if this applies both to our outer *and* inner growth, then it seems logical that in the same way we are encouraged to seek out role models in our chosen profession and outer goals in the world of matter, in order to study and emulate their steps towards success, so we can also seek out a model of an ideal inner state, a model that we might term *the possible self or the possible human* and upon which we can pattern ourselves as we strive to reach a higher level in our evolving consciousness.

Thoughts: Gateway to Awareness

Such a person – *the possible human* – has come to realize that by using thoughts to remain focused and in charge of the inner world, the outer world begins to shape itself as well. But even if it doesn't, the inner world will nevertheless afford such a person peace, harmony and inner freedom and joy. In affording this heightened awareness and higher consciousness, we are led inexorably to a closer connection with our soul. For such a person negative thoughts simply don't fit into his agenda. Oh, they may arrive at his doorstep occasionally, but he is so aware, that he catches their intrusion almost immediately and begins to focus elsewhere in order to ensure that the inner order of things in his being – the inner stability and well-being – is not shaken. And - if necessary, when such negative thoughts intrude – he begins a process of self-questioning (from a place of inner well-being) in order to become aware of why such thoughts have arisen and what needs to be done about them. Such a person does not spend hours or days at a time asleep, in the sense that one is asleep when one is not aware.

A person asked Buddha:
"Are you a God?"
Buddha's reply was "No."
"Are you an Angel?"
"No."
"Then what are you?"
"I am Awake."
Anonymous

And therefore such a person is vigilant about remaining awake, knowing that this is the only way to remain in charge of that inner order of things. This person always uses his thoughts to further the joy, well-being and inner balance and harmony in his life, no matter what the outer circumstances, and hence this person always chooses thoughts that allow this joy and well-being to be. Self-defeating thoughts – when they appear, are taken care of immediately, by recognizing – not that this person is so perfect that everything is already solved - that he can choose to have another kind of thought and that he can choose to dwell on difficult parts of life or problems for designated amounts of proactive time (and then pass on to other matters, *at least on that day*), as opposed to letting the negative thoughts rule his entire day or his life. Such a person knows that it is the quality of his thoughts that can make or break his life, and knowing this, consciously chooses – at all times – to remain in charge of his thoughts and to choose thoughts that further this agenda. Such a person knows that one of the keys to loving the self and to reconnect with his soul, to rewire his soul to its highest purpose and function, is by learning how to be aware of his thoughts and to consciously choose those thoughts at all times. He does not throw down the towel if this mission seems hard at the beginning because he knows the rewards are enormous. He persists, and eventually sees the immense benefit this has on his daily life.

Emotions: Keeping Your Energy High

Such a person – *the possible human* – knows that she needs to remain vigilant about her inner energy. In other words, she takes a reading, so to speak, of her inner energetic frequency at intervals throughout the day – at least until this becomes second nature – to ensure that this inner energy continues to vibrate at a good level. However, if by any chance, it decreases to levels that she had previously decided upon as being unacceptable, she immediately undertakes measures to raise that energy, understanding that it is her entire responsibility to maintain it at healthy and balanced levels for her own good, and she accepts that those healthy levels of the state of her inner emotions shall never again depend on outer circumstances. She consistently makes energy-raising choices about what she feeds her body, eyes, ears, mind, heart and spirit. She chooses – within her means – an energy-raising environment to live in because her home enhances her inner state. She chooses the media she listens to, reads, or watches, and she carefully chooses her friends and the conversations she has with them.

Therefore, when this individual wakes up one day and finds that her spouse of 20 years has decided to leave her for a much younger woman, or her business partner has embezzled funds that belong to the firm, or her doctor tells her that she has malignant melanoma, she immediately takes action in order to maintain a healthy and balanced inner state of being, despite these outer circumstances.

She realizes that this is her responsibility towards herself. It is a measure of her love for herself, to decide to take care of her inner well-being in such a way. And precisely because she recognizes that it is her responsibility, she knows that the way she initially feels when something happens that is not to her liking, is not the *final* way she has to feel. The way she will eventually feel, will come about through a linked chain of choices that she takes to keep her energy balanced. This will in turn lead her to that place inside of herself where she knows she will always be able to return to. It's a good place, a safe place, a place that allows her to breathe in peace even when her world is falling apart. And because she has understood this, she knows that she has to cultivate this place by paying close attention to it every day.

The Ego: Who Is In Charge?

Such a person – *the possible human* – recognizes when his ego is talking or taking charge of his thoughts, feelings and actions, and therefore strives to eliminate such an intrusion on himself. He knows that when he is being judgmental or critical, making unfavorable comparisons between the self and others, being self-righteous or holier-than-thou, boastful, envious, helpless, full of doubt, angry, or jealous, or when any other emotion or feeling takes over that does not enhance his sense of inner well-being, that it is his ego that has once again taken charge of his life, and therefore, he consistently strives to purge its insidious power and control from his life. He knows that being aware of himself at all times is the only way to be successful in such an undertaking, and therefore, time after time, he does all he can in order to increase his moments of full awareness in present time; in the now. He knows that his ego is not beneficial to his inner well-being, nor is it beneficial to any whose lives he touches, and he is filled with the desire to sever the ties that link him to it. He does this over and over again until the ego has been loosened and finally lost all hold on him. Once this has happened, *the possible human* is free to engage with the world and all others without any negativity. Without the ego there can be no negativity in the self, and when negativity comes from outside of the self, without the ego, the inner response can never be negative.

He *looks* for the observer, for that part of himself that emanates from the soul and that is capable of observing egoic behavior in order to come closer to being that observer self at all times, and in order to not fall back into the grasp of the ego. He does this because he wants to, because he prefers to, because he loves himself, because he has come to recognize that living his life from the position of the ego, will always be a blind life, an asleep life, and what he wants and desires is to be as fully awake and conscious as possible.

Awareness: Becoming Conscious

Such a person – *the possible human* – has begun taking a great many steps towards being conscious and aware. She has understood that doing so implies assuming responsibility for her growth into awareness *by her diligence* about growing in that direction a little bit at a time, every day, all the time. And taking responsibility for being diligent about doing that means having recognized that it's a constant question of choices. Do I choose to use this moment - this now moment – to increase my awareness of myself? Perhaps right now I am very angry, or very sad, or very jealous, or very impatient, or very annoyed, or in much emotional pain. The possible human understands that she needs to use each of those moments to gain greater awareness. And to do so means that she needs to continuously remind herself to do so – at the beginning at least - until a habit and new neural pathway is formed. By gaining greater awareness, and by continuously reminding herself to do so when she starts out on this path, she notices that emotions and states of being that before might have caused her great concern or problems, and where she might have reacted blindly or negatively due to others pushing her buttons, now no longer have that same power over her, and she realizes that she is becoming more and more the master not only of herself, but also of her life.

Because she knows that gaining mastery over her life will lead her to a state of mind and being filled with peace and joy, as well as inner freedom, she also knows that evolving daily in awareness and consciousness is one of the most important things she can do for herself. She uses every single opportunity that appears in her life to grow even further, by looking at how someone's behavior, for example, or an external event of some kind makes her feel. She then uses that "feeling", by examining whether it is a feeling that leads her to greater inner freedom, harmony, peace and joy, or if it is a feeling that takes her down a very much more negative path. In that case, she then uses this understanding to continue moving herself to greater awareness by the very consciously chosen use of her inner dialogue about the negative place in which she currently finds herself. Looking at herself in that way allows her to see herself in ways that were not possible prior to undertaking the task of bringing herself to awareness.

She is also very aware of the company she keeps, the information that is permitted to enter her being via her eyes and ears, as well as what surrounds her in her home because she knows that all of these elements impact on her life and inner state of being. She is no longer blind to the fact, for example, that she might do well to go on a diet about the daily news because of the impact this can have on her state of well-being, or to choose to spend less time with friends whose conversations revolve around gossip or complaining about their lives. She chooses to eat healthier foods and exercises because of the impact it has on her state of inner and outer well-being, as well as on her mood. Choosing to become aware is something that impacts each and every sector of her daily life.

Choice: Portal to Freedom

Such a person – *the possible human* – knows that exercising his right to choose brings him to freedom from pain and negative feelings more quickly than *any* other way. In the very moment he feels down, or in a bad mood, or angry, or in pain, he recognizes that he has a choice about these. Precisely because of the fact that he has chosen to be responsible for himself, he chooses to figure out what he could do at that moment in time – from a place where he is present, as opposed to living in the past or future - in order to change the state of his inner well-being to one of greater balance and harmony. He understands that to achieve this, he needs to practice this over and over again in a mindful, intentional and aware fashion, and because he loves himself, he is willing to do precisely that. He does not try to fool himself into this better inner state by pretending that the situation that is the apparent cause of his feelings does not exist. He knows it exists. He also does not pretend it is the fault of the other or the fault of the external event because he knows that no matter what the other has done, or the external event may have been, it is *his reaction* to all of this that is important. Thus he chooses to focus differently. He chooses to look at the alternatives available to him in order to choose the best one possible. The troubling situation is not now under some rug or buried in the sand – rather, he is viewing it from another focus, using another lens, so to speak.

He also knows when faced with a belligerent or manipulative or demanding individual, particularly when that individual is someone close to him emotionally, that it is his choice to permit this or not. He chooses to closely protect his boundaries because he loves himself and knows that his health – on all levels – and inner well-being depend in large part on his choices, much more than on external circumstances and other people. He knows that while he is unable to control those outer circumstances, he *is* able to be in charge of his choices about those circumstances – *if he so chooses*.

Boundaries: Path to Empowerment

Such a person – *the possible human* – has understood the importance of healthy boundaries and has therefore learned to create them in such a way that they contribute to her inner well-being and to the manner in which she responds to the world because she loves herself and has recognized that without healthy boundaries she is unable to live well, and without healthy boundaries she will forever be filled with pain and resentment and unrequited needs. This person has acknowledged that one of the best paths to empowerment is precisely by establishing healthy boundaries and by practicing – if necessary – over and over again, a new way to respond and react to those others who attempt to transgress those boundaries. While so doing – responding in this new way - the possible human has learned to shake off the erstwhile fear and stress that are provoked by behaving in this new way, and can rejoice in the new-found feelings of strength and freedom within.

When she is faced with someone in her life who attempts to take over any part of her life – inner or outer – by behaving in unacceptable ways with her, she is able to state in no uncertain terms, and without fearing the outcome, that she will not tolerate such behavior, and that if it continues, there will be a consequence. She knows that if she does *not* do this, she is continually showing herself that she does not love herself sufficiently to take good care of herself in this way. She knows that part of the price to attain inner peace is demonstrating clearly to others where her boundaries lie, not from a position of defensiveness, but from one of self-love.

She clearly understands the strong connection between healthy boundaries and self-love, and knows that as long as she is not caring for her boundaries, she demonstrates to herself over and over again that her love for herself is not yet strong enough to overcome this dilemma. Therefore, when faced with boundaries of any kind that have been assaulted by another, she *uses* the situation to practice and to show herself that she is fully embarked on, and determined to continue on the path to self-love.

Pain & Forgiving: Loosening the Grip of the Past

Such a person – *the possible human* – knows that in order to free himself from the connection to the past and in order to free himself up for all that such a connection prevents him from doing, he needs to forgive. Having the intention to forgive begins the process of freeing him from bondage to the past. Having the intention to forgive *over and over* again, frees him step by step, each time he consciously chooses to do so, a little bit more, until finally, one day, he realizes he can think of the painful event with no more energetic connections attached to it. The painful event simply no longer has control over him.

This person knows that now, due to that process, he has much more energy and power available to himself to be used towards creating his reality, than he did before he chose to intend to forgive. He now looks proactively for any further areas of his life where he needs to forgive, and chooses to intend to do so. And when – at a future moment – someone does something, or some event occurs, that would have put him into the painful mode of his past, where he would then mull over the pain over and over again, creating ever stronger connections to that painful moment, pulling fragments of himself into that moment more and more and more – when such a moment occurs now, he knows how to let go of it immediately. He does that because he loves himself and because he no longer has any need or desire to hold on to it. He continues to live in the now, as opposed to visiting that past moment again and again, and hence no longer creates any new energetic connections to it.

By so doing, and by so choosing from a position of awareness – he has freed himself from the tyranny of pain and memory. He has freed himself in order to be able to live his present moments – his life – from a position of full presence – in other words, from a position where *all of him* is actually present, not just some of the fragments, and hence he is able to live his life in ways that he could only dream of before.

Self-Responsibility: Power in Your Life

Such a person – *the possible human* – assumes full responsibility for how she thinks, feels, acts and reacts to absolutely everything that occurs in her life. Was she just insulted? She chooses a reaction that is beneficial to her inner well-being, as opposed to one that is focused on getting back at the other person. Was she just told how wrong she is about some expressed opinion? She again chooses a reaction that is beneficial to her inner well-being as opposed to one that focuses on showing the other person how wrong *he* is. Was she just turned down for a job promotion? She chooses a reaction that is beneficial to her inner well-being, perhaps focusing on what she still needs to learn, or what experiences she needs to get under her belt in order to be considered for this promotion, or determining that perhaps it's time to move to another firm, as opposed to focusing on how unfair the world is, for not allowing her to be promoted. Was she just diagnosed with cancer, lupus, heart disease or diabetes? She chooses a reaction that is beneficial to her inner well-being, perhaps deciding to examine her habit of judging others or her need to work so compulsively more carefully, recognizing that perhaps these are areas where she still needs to improve – and then doing so with full awareness - as well as considering where and how she spends her time (inner and outer) every day in order to be able to promote change on levels that impact her very DNA (apart, of course, from making appropriate physician-directed choices). Whatever it is that brought her to this place is something that merits a closer look and by so doing has the potential to bring about change.

At absolutely every step of the way she chooses reactions from this position of taking full responsibility for herself that are in her benefit. She does so not from an egotistical point of view, but from a position of awareness and self-love, where her ego is not in play. She does so because she is fully connected to herself and knows that each situation that appears in her life is there for a reason and is potentially instrumental in furthering her on this path of self-development and growth.

Your Life Meaning: Strength to See You Through It All

Such a person – *the possible human* – has spent some time in deciding what it is that brings meaning to his life. He may have had to spend more than just a few days or weeks in this process, but because he knew that it was imperative to find a meaning for his life, he persevered. He examined himself, his interests, his response to things in his world, *he paid close attention to everything he reacted to in positive ways*, and ultimately came up with a meaning for his life.

He knows that his choice is not only something that excites him, but that it also brings him closer to himself, as well as furthering his chosen process of growth. He continually chooses – from that same position of awareness that pervades everything else in his life – from among a vast array of possibilities, those that are most closely aligned with this meaning he has found. He knows that without this meaning in his life, he would be far, far less than that into which he has grown and evolved.

When moments of hardship enter his life, from any source at all, he is able to reap strength from this *thing* that gives meaning to his life. Because he believes in its value and because he knows that without it he would be so much less and so much weaker, he has made it a central point of his existence. And while it may evolve and grow and eventually morph into something that looks quite different from his initial conception, it continues to give this essential meaning to his life.

Gratitude & the Now: Dual Gateways to Inner Peace

Such a person – *the possible human* – consciously uses any element of beauty or wonder around her to continually ground herself in the now moment. She knows that focusing on something with gratitude takes her there and allows her to live her life in a much more peaceful, free and joyful way. She takes the time to make a daily practice of this, using everything in her environment as well as in her mind to focus intentionally and with gratitude.

She knows that by so doing her inner energetic frequency remains at, or is continually raised to, levels that are highly beneficial to her body, mind, heart and spirit. She has learned to live her life mindfully, because she has made the choice to learn how to do so.

Her awareness of the effect of living like this, and her desire to continually raise her energy to higher levels, is what has given her the determination and strength and perseverance to do so.

She knows that every moment that passes during which she has consciously focused on practicing gratitude and mindfulness brings her closer to that inner goal of fully loving the self and rewiring her soul and she also knows that such moments, strung together as priceless pearls that compose the necklace of her lifetime, give her joy in immeasurable degrees. And that is precisely what connects her to her soul.

Soothing the Self Without Losing Your Way

Such a person – *the possible human* – always recognizes that needing to calm himself down with a substance or addictive behavior when he is undergoing a difficult situation in life, would be counter-productive to his well-being *even if it made him feel better for a few hours or a day or two.* This individual considers the wellness of his own inner state the main priority of his life, and therefore seeks to soothe himself in ways that are not detrimental to that. So he might focus on breathing, on walking or other physical exercise, perhaps interval training in order to elevate the amount of oxygen in his system, understanding that this is simply one of the tactics he can use to calm and soothe the self. He chooses to focus on being mindful, on being highly aware of his own body and his current surroundings in order to be conscious of the beauty there, in order to experience gratitude there, in order to be present, and come into the now, because all of this – as not only Eastern thought and religion has taught us, but also scientific research in the field of neuroscience is demonstrating - is calming and soothing, and allows him to view his current difficult situation from a slight distance, instead of being caught up in it in such a way that all he is capable of is reacting blindly to it.

He knows that soothing the self is something that ultimately must originate from inside of himself and not from the outside. Hence he knows that retail therapy, food or substance bingeing (or, conversely, food control), exercise bingeing, gambling and other risky behaviors, etc. will only mask the symptoms for a time, but never resolve them, requiring, therefore, an ever-growing concentration (or riskiness) of the soothing activity in order for it to work.

Because this person loves himself – or is evolving on an ever-continuing path in that direction, and does so consciously and with conscious intention by virtue of his daily choices from the smallest to the largest decisions – he knows that whatever soothing mechanism he chooses, it must be one that will work for his higher good. It must be one that will eventually move him forward in his quest to find inner harmony, peace, joy and freedom.

And so he begins to build up a library of inspirational audio CD's, music, books, and movies that not only raise his energy, but in so doing, help soothe him in difficult moments. He is also continually aware of the activities in which he participates and the people in his life people and conversations in his life that raise his energy and soothe him in order to make choices consistent with that awareness. He knows it is his responsibility to learn how to soothe himself in the healthiest and most life-giving ways possible.

You Are Here To Be Happy:

Such a person – *the possible human* – knows that one of her primary purposes in life is to be happy, or to learn how to be happy. She knows that everything she does every hour and each day of her life, must be locked into this goal. She understands that being happy implies that she will maintain a healthy state of inner balance and well-being that is not generally shaken by the outer circumstances of her life. Therefore, in each of those hours and days she continually works on perfecting the well-being of her inner state precisely because by so doing, she demonstrates her caring and love for herself.

She knows that if happiness is something that she leaves to chance, or if it's something that happens only when her outer circumstances are favorable, she will never achieve the possibility of a truly good life, nor the connection to her soul that she desires.

The way in which she works on perfecting her inner state at all times, in the first place, is to be continually aware of herself and her thoughts, feelings, words, actions, and reactions, and secondly, to *adjust* – even if only minutely – that inner place where her energetic frequency is held, if she recognizes that she is not traveling in the desired direction. She makes a priority of this *task*, this mission, because she knows that by so doing, she affects each and every other sector of her existence.

Establishing the Inner Connection

Such a person – *the possible human* – actively seeks a rich relationship with the self in much the same way he would seek one with another individual in whom he has become interested. He *enjoys* spending time with the self, he *is interested* in the self, and he knows that one of the best ways he can be in touch with the self on an on-going basis, is by frequently checking in on his *energy barometer*, his inner state of being, his feelings, his inner balance, in order to connect with where he is at in any given moment. He knows that the relationship with the self is one of the most important – if not *the most* important – relationship he can make in his lifetime. He notices when he is not in touch with himself by becoming aware of feeling misaligned or of feeling as though something is off. If so, he then recognizes that he has been self-soothing or partially asleep for a time and gently begins the process of tending the inner garden again.

He is continually aware of his responsibility to build a rich connection with himself through all that with which he fills his awareness: surroundings, people, work-related activities, conversations, music, books, art, theatre, sports, politics, community work, mass media, etc., because he knows that whatever he fills his awareness with, is what he can use as a solid bridge to the self or a rotting and broken one that will never lead to the self.

He is not only aware of his inner voice, but he actively listens for it and to it. This inner voice or intuition is a gateway into his "self" and his enthusiasm for a constant connection with this voice is evident in the way he responds to it as opposed to neglecting or dismissing it. He observes himself as often as possible, while striving for it to occur at all times, not in an analytical, clinical way, but in order to come closer to the self that is the observer and not the ego.

Loving the Self: Portal to Love - Gateway to the Soul

Such a person – *the possible human* – takes every possible opportunity to demonstrate to herself that she cares for herself. If her boundaries are being transgressed, she takes the appropriate steps – just as she would if her small child were being hurt – to erect healthy boundaries and maintain them in place with consequences for the offending party, should those boundaries be passed again. She knows she has to do this for herself – because she loves herself and she knows that if she does *not* do it, she will be sending an unmistakable message to her inner self that states that she does not care enough about herself.

If the events of her day are not optimal, she takes the appropriate steps to soothe herself in healthy ways that will simultaneously serve to keep her inner energetic frequency, her sense of well-being in a good and balanced place. If her ego has taken over again, she realizes her love for herself must take a stronger role and by so doing, becomes very aware of her ego and shows herself yet again that her love for herself can overcome its pull. At the beginning she may not yet have achieved this perfectly, but because she loves herself, she is patient with herself in this process of growth towards that ideal, and praises herself for every small step taken.

By taking on responsibility for her happiness, by choosing to learn how to use *tools* that will aid her in this quest, by choosing gratitude as one of her most potent tools, and by choosing compassion when she notices that she has become annoyed or angry at others, she continually proves her love for herself to that inner part – her eternal self - that needs to know that she is doing this consciously.

She is equally proactive about taking on the responsibility of making healthy choices at every step of the way, based on her love for herself, in order to remain in the best state of inner well-being possible. If she wakes up in a dark mood, or if she runs into impediment after impediment in her day, she knows she needs to continue making choices that will aid her movement up the energetic frequency ladder and will take the necessary measures to do so because of her love for herself. As she continues to show herself that she loves herself in step after step throughout the hours and days of her life, that which she emanates - her vibration; a vibration of love – is precisely what will attract other kinds of events and situations to her as opposed to more negative ones she may have been experiencing prior to engaging in such a practice of self-love in her life. She knows that the more she loves herself in this way, the healthier she will be and the more her life will be able to have a positive impact on the lives of all those whose with whom she has contact.

Relationships: Loving Others

Such a person – *the possible human* – views all the relationships in his life as gifts. He knows that the place where his greatest growth can occur is precisely in his relationships, not only with those people who are close to him, his family, loved ones and friends, but also with others, the taxi driver, the newspaper vendor, the shoe cleaner, the policeman who stops him when he is speeding, and the super market clerk.

However he also knows that it is in the relationships that involve his emotions with those individuals who are closest to him, where he will find not only his greatest challenges, but also his greatest opportunities, and he knows that in order for this to be able to occur, he needs to remain fully aware of himself, his feelings, his thoughts, and his reactions in those relationships. Therefore, remaining aware at all times is one of his biggest goals.

It is his conscious desire for everything that happens in his relationships to be utilized by him for the purpose of growth, and in order for this to be so, his intention must remain constant and he is continually vigilant that this is so. He has proactive conversations with the people in his life in order to promote such an understanding, and he asks his loved ones to support him in this endeavor. He notices that he is less and less interested in spending time with those who continue to live their lives blindly, and although he may support them if they wish to move forward, if that is not the case, he prefers to spend his time with those who are moving on a path of spiritual partnership and conscious evolution as he is.

Compassion: Loving the World

Such a person – *the possible human* – knows that understanding and using compassion in the benefit of not only her individual and personal relationships, but also our collective ones on the global level, we will have a much better opportunity to survive, than if we refuse to use this nearly miraculous *tool* – compassion - at our disposal. This person knows that the best way to influence the whole is by changing the single unit, one unit at a time. That unit refers to each of us, and because of this, such a person chooses each and every day, to make a habit and practice of compassion. *Especially* when she notices that she is on the verge of judging or criticizing, *especially* when she notices she is on the verge of being impatient or angry, because compassion used in such an instance – as opposed to only when someone is obviously suffering – will assist in bringing about changes on that individual level that needs to be honed in order for the whole to change.

She is aware that because she loves herself when she makes use of this tool she feels much better and vibrates at a much higher energy than when she allows herself to judge, criticize or be angry. She is aware that she desires such a state of higher energy to form part of her daily life and therefore chooses to become mindful about her way of interacting with others in order that compassion may be a salient part of her existence.

Intermingled Molecules: We Are All One

Such a person – *the possible human* – sees himself in all others. Such a person – *the possible human* – knows that there is nothing that separates her from all others. This *possible human* is still an ideal for which many strive, but few, if any, other than some very enlightened and spiritually advanced teachers, throughout the ages, have achieved.

Such a person continually endeavors to think and feel in terms of *we are all one* as opposed to me and you. When such a person catches himself doing those things that separate – judging, criticizing, disliking, deriding, despising, comparing, being envious or jealous of – he immediately reminds himself that *we are all one*, knowing that by doing so, he helps himself transcend those attitudes and that behavior, and that one day he too will truly *know* that we are all one.

Such a person does everything she can to remain conscious and aware at all times in order to curtail thoughts of duality and separation, in her quest to arrive at an inner place where she can see that *we are all one*. This person knows that while he may not achieve the perfection he seeks immediately, his continual and conscious intention to do so will take him down the right path. Such a person never loses sight of the belief that she will be able to achieve this goal because she knows it is precisely why she is here.

****

Do you doubt for even one moment that this *possible human* who has taken on the awareness of and responsibility for his thoughts, emotions, and happiness, and who makes conscious choices at all times, who seeks to keep a firm hand on her ego and ultimately disengages from it, who recognizes his boundaries need to be kept healthy by himself, who continually does all she can to remain aware, who knows that the pain in his life will be gone if he only decides to forgive, who has moved her life in the direction of that which gives her meaning, who knows that by practicing gratitude he remains here and now, as opposed to in the past or the future, who sees clearly that he needs to be highly aware of the manner in which he soothes himself in moments of difficulty, and in so doing has established a firm connection to herself, has learned to love the self, has learned to see his relationships not only as potential sources of much happiness, but also a potential source of much growth, understands that compassion applied properly brings us all closer to the potential of surviving as a global community, and knows that in order for the next step in our collective evolution to take place, we *must* strive towards understanding and internalizing the fact that *we are all one* – do you doubt that such a *possible human* will be successful in life?

He will be successful not only in relationships, profession and finances, but also in that true inner success that comes from having found inner peace, freedom, and joy in true love for the self leading to the rewiring of his soul. This possible human resides within all of us, just as surely as the butterfly resides in the caterpillar. It is our heritage to be at peace, free and in joy, and our very DNA will be instrumental in helping us reach those goals as we move in the direction of rewiring our souls.

> *What the caterpillar calls the end of the world,*
> *the master calls a butterfly.*
> Richard Bach

APPENDIX

Chapter 2: Emotions: Keeping Your Energy High

27   http://www.brucelipton.com/biology-of-belief/embracing-the-immaterial-universe

28   http://www.brucelipton.com/book-excerpts/the-world-according-to-new-edge-science/

http://www.brucelipton.com/wisdom-of-your-cells/the-wisdom-of-your-cells/

29   http://www.huffingtonpost.com/mariana-caplan-phd/spiritual-living-10-spiri_b_609248.html

35   The following list of suggested websites where material may be downloaded (legally and generally free of charge) is taken from the right sidebar of my blog: http://www.RewiringtheSoul.com

Please contact me if you know of other such sites (especially in English and Spanish) that you would like to recommend

All url's were last verified May 26, 2011

60 Minutes
http://www.cbsnews.com/sections/60minutes/main3415.shtml

Abraham Hicks
http://www.abraham-hicks.com/lawofattractionsource/mp3downloads.php

All In the Mind
http://www.abc.net.au/rn/allinthemind/

Animal Planet
http://animal.discovery.com/

BBC Documentaries on YouTube
http://www.youtube.com/results?search_query=bbc+documentary&search_type=&aq=1&oq=BBC

Brain Science Podcast
http://www.brainsciencepodcast.com/

Brain Sync: Theatre of the Mind
http://www.brainsync.com/podcasts.html

Bruce Lipton
http://www.brucelipton.com/

Caroline Myss Free Media
http://www.myss.com/CMED/media/

Charlie Rose
http://www.charlierose.com/

Coast to Coast Radio
http://www.coasttocoastam.com/

Conscious Media Network
http://www.cmn.tv/

Conscious TV
http://www.conscious.tv/

Crimson Circle
http://www.crimsoncircle.com/

Culture Unplugged
http://www.cultureunplugged.com/

Daniel Siegel, MD
http://www.drdansiegel.com/

Deepak Chopra, MD
http://www.chopra.com/

EnlightenNext magazine
http://www.enlightennext.org/magazine/

Explore Your Spirit With Kala Radio
http://www.exploreyourspirit.com/shows.html

Fora TV
http://fora.tv/

Google Talks
http://video.google.com/googleplex.html

Hay House Radio
http://www.hayhouseradio.com/

Harvard Business Review
http://hbr.org/

Her Place
http://www.herplace.com/

Institute of HeartMath
http://www.heartmath.org/

Institute of Noetic Sciences
http://www.noetic.org/

Integral Institute
http://www.integralinstitute.org/

Intelligence Squared (Australia, UK, and USA)
http://www.intelligencesquared.com/
http://www.iq2oz.com/
http://intelligencesquaredus.org/

Intuition Network
http://www.intuition.org/

Life and Love TV
http://www.lifeandlove.tv/

Live Station
http://www.livestation.com/

More than Sound: The Art & Science of Mind
http://morethansound.net/wordpress/

Natural News
http://www.naturalnews.com/

News For the Soul
http://www.newsforthesoul.com/moreshows-registered.htm

Norman Doidge, MD
http://www.normandoidge.com/normandoidge/MAIN.html

Open Culture
http://www.openculture.com/

Open Culture Podcast Collection
http://www.openculture.com/2006/11/arts_culture_po.html

Open Culture Intelligent YouTube Channels
http://www.openculture.com/smartyoutube

Open Culture Top Cultural and Educational Video Sites
http://www.openculture.com/intelligentvideo

Oprah & Tolle: *A New Earth* Class Syllabus (ten 90-min. sessions)
http://www.oprah.com/oprahsbookclub/A-New-Earth-Syllabus

Oprah y Tolle: Las 10 clases de *Una Nueva Tierra* en español
http://www.youtube.com/profile?user=eckhartencastellano#g rid/playlists

Oprah Soul Series
http://event.oprah.com/videochannel/soulseries/oss_player_980x665.html

Oprah Soul Series Season 2
http://www.oprah.com/oprahradio/Oprahs-Soul-Series-Webcast-Archive-Season-2

PBS Nova Movies online
http://www.pbs.org/wgbh/nova/search/results/page/1/sort/dc.date+desc?q=&facet%5B0%5D=dc.type%3A%22Program+Video%22

PBS Public Broadcasting System
http://www.pbs.org/

Radio 4 All
http://www.radio4all.net/

Rewiring the Soul (my weekly internet radio show that aired 2009 and 2010)
http://www.blogtalkradio.com/rewiringthesoul

Santa Barbara Institute for Consciousness Studies
http://www.sbinstitute.com/

Science For Life Radio
http://www.scienceforlife.net/

Skeptiko: Science at the Tipping Point
http://www.skeptiko.com/

Sounds True
This site has many wonderful audio CD's (for purchase) by most of the "big names" in the field of spiritual development. I particularly recommend the audio and video programs by: Wayne Dyer, Caroline Myss, Eckhart Tolle, Deepak Chopra, Bruce Lipton, Candace Pert, Clarissa Pinkola Estés, Gregg Braden, Brian Tracy, etc., among many others too numerous to list. Sounds True also offer free interviews for your viewing
http://www.soundstrue.com/shop/Welcome.do;jsessionid=Ky J4f3pKffIFSQjSTWCb.app02

Spiritube
http://www.spiritube.com/

TED Conversations – one of the most stimulating sites around, with some of the talks translated into dozens of languages!
http://www.ted.com/

The Monthly
http://www.themonthly.com.au/

Thinking Allowed
http://www.thinkingallowed.com/

Trans4Mind
http://www.trans4mind.com/

Vimeo
http://vimeo.com/

Wayne Dyer
http://www.drwaynedyer.com/

Chapter 4: Awareness: Becoming Conscious

50   ***Additionally it is not typically possible to talk to the child:*** it is, however, possible to speak to children, even small children, about big emotions, as well as about mindfulness. See Daniel Siegel's book: *Parenting from the Inside Out.*

53   ***Shirley MacLaine:*** The book I first read in which Shirley writes about The Light Institute and Chris Griscom, was *Dancing In The Light* (see Bibliography)

55   ***It's a Full-Time Job:*** visit YouTube to hear my radio show talk *Emotions: Your Road to Inner Freedom* http://www.youtube.com/watch?v=7I2pYKJXdOs

56   ***Making Conscious Choices:*** I have adopted the concept of 'the intention of your attention' from Daniel Siegel as he uses it in this 2008 interview on the Brain Science Podcast http://www.brainsciencepodcast.com/bsp/2008/8/22/meditati on-and-the-brain-with-daniel-siegel-bsp-44.html

59   Siegel, Daniel J. *The Mindful Brain.* New York: W.W. Norton, 2007

Chapter 5: Choice: Portal to Freedom

67   ***Sabriye Tenberken:*** http://www.time.com/time/asia/2004/heroes/hsabriye_tenber ken.html

71   ***Choosing to focus on polishing your CV:*** See the entire list of suggestions under Chapter 2 above

72   ***(Caroline Myss has written extensively – and brilliantly – about this topic and used the term "woundology"):*** specifically see her book *Why People Don't Heal*

Chapter 6: Boundaries: Path to Empowerment

76   ***Another thing that happened was that you did not learn:*** Clarissa Pinkola Estés has a wonderful audio CD: *Warming The Stone Child: Myths and Stories about Abandonment and the Unmothered Child* that addresses the issue of learning to ignore the signals and intuition we receive from

the body. You can find it at *Sounds True* (see the link above under Chapter 2)

Chapter 7: Pain & Forgiving: Loosening the Grip of the Past

89   Griscom, Chris. *Ecstasy is a New Frequency*. New York: Simon & Schuster, 1987, p.14. (italics mine)
Tolle, Eckhart. *The Power of Now*. Novato, CA: New World Library, 1999, p.29. (italics mine)

92   ***So now I want to really throw an unexpected thought:*** please also see the following two articles on my website http://www.advancedpersonaltherapy.com on the 'Articles' Page:
   * Create a New Life: One Intention at a Time
   * How Your Thoughts Change your Body

Read some of the work by: Candace Pert, Bruce Lipton, Masaru Emoto, Deepak Chopra – a listing of these authors' major works can be found in the Bibliography

94   ***The Importance of Forgiving & the Law of Attraction:*** Caroline Myss (from whose work I have borrowed the term *cellular responsibility*), pointed out well over a decade ago in 1999 in the immensely rich audio program *The Science of Medical Intuition*, which she produced together with neurosurgeon Dr. Norman Shealy that it is also at this point *that you begin to create and manifest*. In other words, no matter how much visualization and affirmation you are doing, those of you who have been vicariously reading everything you can get your hands on about the *Law of Attraction*, you will not be able to create, *until you pull your power into the present*. Forgiving those who have trespassed you is one of the biggest steps towards that goal.

Chapter 9: Your Life Meaning

118   ***The Second Brain:*** The *Other* Brain Also Deals With Many Woes http://www.nytimes.com/2005/08/23/health/23gut.html

Chapter 10: Gratitude and the Now

132   ***Genetically much has changed due to a new environment:*** http://www.newsweek.com/2009/01/27/feel-better-live-longer.html

There are changes in other areas as well: see the works listed by Jon Kabat-Zinn and Daniel Siegel in the Bibliography.

Searching Google using terms such as *Buddhism + neuroscience* or *mindfulness + neuroscience*, will bring up numerous articles. One such excellent article (but there are many others) may be found here: http://www.psychologytoday.com/blog/neuro-atheism/201101/buddhism-and-neuroscience

136   *This has nothing to do with religion:* research at Ivy League universities points to happiness being greater and more consistent for those who practice gratefulness. Also see my article *Happiness: Has it Become a Science or it is a Question of Good Luck?* at my website http://www.advancedpersonaltherapy.com on the Articles Page.

Chapter 11: Soothing the Self Without Losing Your Way

147   *Here is how Chris Griscom puts it: "As each soul creates a reality:* Griscom, Chris. *Ecstasy is a New Frequency.* New York: Simon & Schuster, 1987, p.33.

   The connection of love to the self: Griscom, Chris. *Ecstasy is a New Frequency.* New York: Simon & Schuster, 1987, p.33.

   This self, also called the divine self: Griscom, Chris. *Ecstasy is a New Frequency.* New York: Simon & Schuster, 1987, pp. 27-28.

Chapter 13: Establishing the Inner Connection

168   *Being of this world is part of it:* even Antonio Damasio, the world-renowned neuroscientist – famous for his *Looking for Spinoza: Joy, Sorrow, and the Feeling Brain*, calls it intuition, as do researchers at the Max Planck Institute for Human Development in Berlin, which published a book by Gert Gigerenzer about this subject called *Gut Feelings: The Intelligence of the Unconscious.*

Chapter 14: Loving the Self

175   *Poor Attachment Bonds Formed in Early Childhood:* see for example:

http://www.psychology.sunysb.edu/attachment/online/inge_o
rigins.pdf

180   *Believing That Loving the Self is Selfish:* see the entire
Fromm article from which I have included several citations
on pp. 180 – 182 here: http://www.erich-
fromm.de/biophil/en/images/stories/pdf-Dateien/1939b-e.pdf

Chapter 15: Relationships: Loving Others

185   *Relationships are the place where we can grow most
quickly:* Cousineau, Phil, ed. *The Hero's Journey: Joseph
Campbell on His Life and Work.* New York:
HarperSanFrancisco, 1991. p. 122

Chapter 16: Compassion: Loving the World

203   *Careful now, I am not suggesting we simply excuse all
these people:* for more about *destructive emotions*, see the
collaboration in book format between Western positive
psychologists, neuroscientists, philosophers and Buddhist
scholars, narrated by Daniel Goleman: Goleman, Daniel, ed.
*Destructive Emotions: How Can We overcome Them? A
Scientific Dialogue with the Dalai Lama.* New York: Bantam
Books, 2003

204   *As you begin to allow compassion into your life:* for
example: http://www.compassionlab.com/related.htm (this
page includes many other links for similar areas of research
in other institutions).

Chapter 17: Intermingled Molecules: We Are All One

209   *Many of us (back in the dark ages of the mid-twentieth
century):*
Das Wesen der Materie [The Nature of Matter], speech at
Florence, Italy (1944) (from Archiv zur Geschichte der Max-
Planck-Gesellschaft, Abt. Va, Rep. 11 Planck, Nr. 1797)

213   *Fascinating studies are being carried out on:*
http://www.nytimes.com/2010/04/12/science/12psychedelics.
html?src=me&ref=homepage

BIBLIOGRAPHY

Why does a book as deceptively simple as this one require such an extensive bibliography? It doesn't. Nevertheless, these books are a portion of those that have shaped my life and in so doing have shaped my thoughts and my understanding. And it is in the shaping of these that this book could be written so simply and so directly. Psychology, neuroscience, biology, sociology, history, politics, religion, spirituality, philosophy, mythology, dreams and fairy tales, body work, metaphysics and esoteric thought, motivational books, biographies and autobiographies all form part of this mélange, as well as some journals of certain writers or thinkers and several dozen novels that have also been included because they too, were significant.

I have returned over and over again to some of these books, as one returns to old and loved friends; friends that are beloved because of what has been shared and because of the support that has been given, and what has been learned. Sometimes, however, I return to a book, no longer certain if I remember it, and then I see the highlighting, the underlining and the scribbled notes on *precisely* those passages that still resonate with me now, and that reminded me then, when I first read them, of what I really already knew. *Just as you do.* It's not terribly important if you look at this list at all. But perhaps you'll enjoy doing so.

A Course in Miracles Vol. I, II, III. Foundation for Inner Peace, 1985.
Abelar, Taisha. *The Sorcerers' Crossing: A Woman's Journey.* Penguin, 1992.
Abrams, Jeremiah, ed. *Reclaiming the Inner Child.* Jeremy P. Tarcher, 1990.
Abreu-Gomez, Ermilo. *Leyendas y consejas del antiguo Yucatán.* 1985.
Ackermann, Paul, and Murray Kappelman. *Signals: What Your Child Is Really Telling You.* The Dial Press/James Wade, 1978.
Aeppli, Ernst. *Der Traum und seine Deutung.* Knaur, 1943.
Albom, Mitch. *Tuesdays With Morrie: An Old Man, a Young Man, and Life's Greatest Lesson.* New York: Doubleday, 1997.
Alcina-Franch, José. *Mitos y literatura maya.* Alianza, 1989.
Alcott, Louisa May. *Little Women.* Nelson Doubleday, 1950.
Aldred, Cyril. *Akhenaton: Faraón de Egipto.* 1989.
Alexander, F. Matthias. *The Alexander Technique: The World-Renowned System of Mind-Body Coordination.* Edited by Edward Maisel. A Lyle Stuart Book, 1995.
Alexander, Jo, Debi Berrow, Lisa Domitrovich, Margarita Donnelly, and Cheryl McLean. *Women and Aging: An Anthology by Women.* Calyx Books, 1986.
Alexander, Thea. *2150 A.D.* Warner Books, 1976.
Allende, Isabel. *Ines del alma mía.* deBolsillo, 2007.

—. *La casa de los espíritus*. Editorial Sudamericana, 1982.

—. *Retrato en sepia*. deBolsillo, 2004.

Alper, Frank. *Exploring Atlantis I*. Quantum Productions, 1980.

—. *Exploring Atlantis II*. Quantum Productions, 1982.

—. *Exploring Atlantis III*. Arizona Metaphysical Society, 1986.

Alvarez-Peña, Alberto. *Mitología Asturiana*. 2005.

Anderson, Greg. *The 22 (Non-Negotiable) Laws of Wellness: Feel, Think, and Live Better Than You Ever Thought Possible*. HarperSanFrancisco, 1995.

Anderson, Joan Wester. *Where Angels Walk: True Stories of Heavenly Visitors*. Ballantine, 1993.

Andrews, Lynn V. *Medicine Woman*. Perennial Library, 1981.

Angier, Natalie. *Woman: An Intimate Geography*. A Peter Davison Book, 1999.

Appleton, William S. *Fathers & Daughters: For Every Woman - The Startling Truth About You and the First Man in Your Life*. New York: Berkley Books, 1986.

Archer, Sally L., ed. *Interventions For Adolescent Identity Development*. Sage Publications, 1994.

Argüelles, José. *The Mayan Factor: Path Beyond Technology*. Bear & Company, 1987.

Arnold, Paul. *El Libro Maya de los Muertos*. Editorial Diana, 1991.

Arroyo, Stephen. *Astrology, Karma & Transformation: The Inner Dimensions of the Birth Chart*. CRCS Publications, 1978.

—. *Astrology, Psychology, and the Four Elements: An Energy Approach to Astrology and Its Use in the Counseling Arts*. CRCS Publications, 1975.

—. *Relationships & Life Cycles: Modern Dimensions of Astrology*. CRCS Pubications, 1979.

Atienza, Juan G. *La mística solar de los Templarios*. Martínez Roca, 1983.

Atkinson, W.W. *Reincarnation and the Law of Karma*. Yogi Publication Society, 1936.

Bach, Richard. *Illusions: The Adventures of a Reluctant Messiah*. Laurel Books, 1981.

—. *Jonathan Livingston Seagull*. Scribner, 1970.

—. *Messiah's Handbook: Reminder for the Advanced Soul, The Lost Book From Illusions*. Hampton Roads, 2004.

—. *Running From Safety: An Adventure of the Spirit*. Delta, 1994.

—. *The Bridge Across Forever*. Dell, 1984.

—. *Uno*. Javier Vergara, 1988.

Bache, Christopher M. *Dark Night, Early Dawn: Steps to a Deep Ecology of Mind*. State University of New York Press, 2000.

Bachofen, J.J. *Myth, Religion & Mother Right: Selected Writings of J.J. Bachofen*. Bollingen Series, Princeton University Press, 1973.

Bader, Ellyn, and Peter T. Pearson. *In Quest of the Mythical Mate: A Developmental Approach to Diagnosis and Treatment in Couples Therapy*. New York: Brunner/Mazel, Inc., 1988.

Bader, Ellyn, Peter T. Pearson, and Judith D. Schwartz. *Tell Me No Lies: How To Stop Lying To Your Partner - and Yourself - In the 4 Stages of Marriage*. New York: St Martin's Griffin, 2001.

Badinter, Elisabeth. *Ich bin Du: Die neue Beziehung zwischen Man und Frau oder Die Androgyne Revolution*. Piper, 1988.

Baginski, Bodo J., and Shalila Sharamon. *Reiki Universal Life Energy.* LifeRhythm, 1985.

Baigent, Michael, and Richard Leigh. *The Dead Sea Scrolls Deception.* Summit Books, 1991.

—. *The Temple and the Lodge.* Arcade Publishing, 1989.

Baigent, Michael, Richard Leigh, and Henry Lincoln. *The Holy Blood and the Holy Grail.* Corgi Books, 1988.

—. *The Messianic Legacy.* A Dell Book, 1989.

Bailey, Alice A. *Ponder on This.* Lucis Publishing Co., 1987.

Baker, Ron. *Revelations for a Healing World: A Personal Process for Resurrecting the Soul.* Children of Light, 2001.

Balsekar, Ramesh S. *Peace and Harmony in Daily Living: Facing Life Moment to Moment, Being Anchored in Tranquility.* Yogi Impressions, 2003.

—. *Sin & Guilt: Monstrosity of Mind.* Zen Publications, 2002.

Bancroft, Anne. *Weavers of Wisdom: Women Mystics of the Twentieth Century.* Arkana, 1989.

Barasch, Marc Ian. *Healing Dreams: Exploring the Dreams That Can Transform Your Life.* Riverhead Books, 2000.

—. *The Healing Path: A Soul Approach to Illness.* Penguin Arkana, 1993.

Barber, Elizabeth Wayland. *Women's Work: The First 20,000 Years.* W.W. Norton & Co., 1994.

Baring, Anne, and Jules Cashford. *The Myth of the Goddess: Evolution of an Age.* Viking Arkana, 1991.

Barz, Helmut. *Selbstverwirklichung.* ECON, 1981.

Bass, Ellen, and Laura Davis. *The Courage To Heal.* Perennial Library, 1988.

Bataille, Georges. *La Experiencia Interior.* Taurus, 1981.

Battegay, Raymond, and Arthur Trenkel. *Der Traum aus der Sicht verschiedener psychotherapeutischer Schulen.* Hans Huber, 1987.

Baumeister, Roy F. *Evil: Inside Human Violence and Cruelty.* W.H. Freeman and Company, 1999.

Bauval, Robert, and Graham Hancock. *Keeper of Genesis: A Quest for the Hidden Legacy of Mankind.* Mandarin, 1997.

Bays, Brandon. *The Journey: A Practical Guide to Healing Your Life and Setting Yourself Free.* A Fireside Book, 1999.

Beattie, Melody. *Codependent No More & Beyond Codependency.* New York: MFJ Books, 1992.

Beauvoir, Simone de. *Ein sanfter Tod.* RoRoRo, 1968.

—. *Force of Circumstance.* Penguin Books, 1965.

—. *Memoiren eine Tochter aus gutem Hause.* RoRoRo, 1970.

—. *The Mandarins.* Collins, 1962.

Beck, Aaron T. *Cognitive Therapy and the Emotional Disorders.* Meridian, 1979.

Beck, Aaron T., and Arthur Freeman. *Cognitive Therapy of Personality Disorders.* Guilford Press, 1990.

Beck, Charlotte Joko. *El Zen de Cada Dia: Amor y Trabajo.* DEMAC, 1993.

Begg, Ean. *Las vírgenes negras: El gran misterio templario.* ROCA, 1989.

Begley, Sharon. *Train Your Mind, Change Your Brain: How a New Science Reveals Our Extraordinary Potential to Transform Ourselves.* Ballantine, 2007.

Benjamin, Jessica. *The Bonds of Love: Psychoanalysis, Feminism, and the Problem of Domination.* New York: Pantheon Books, 1988.

Bennett, Hal Zina. *Invitation to Success: An Allegory About Creativity.* Tenacity Press, 1997.

Bennett, Hal Zina, and Susan J. Sparrow. *Follow Your Bliss: Let the Power of What You Love Guide You to Personal Fulfillment in Your Work and Relationships.* Avon Books, 1990.

Bennett-Goleman, Tara. *Emotional Alchemy: How The Mind Can Heal the Heart.* Three Rivers Press, 2001.

Benoist, Luc. *The Esoteric Path: An Introduction to the Hermetic Tradition.* Crucible, 1988.

benShea, Noah. *Jacob the Baker: Gentle Wisdom for a Complicated World.* Ballantine Books, 1989.

Benson, Herbert, and William Proctor. *La Relajación: Una Terapia imprescindible para mejorar su salud.* Grijalbo, 1987.

Berceli, David. *The Revolutionary Trauma Release Process: Transcend Your Toughest Times.* Namaste Publishing, 2008.

Berenstein, Frederick H. *Lost Boys: Reflections on Psychoanalysis and Countertransference.* W.W. Norton & Co., 1995.

Berg, Philip S. *Wheels of a Soul: Reincarnation: Your Life Today - and Tomorrow.* Research Centre of Kabbalah Books, 1984.

Berne, Eric. *What Do You Do After You Say Hello?* Corgi Books, 1984.

Bettelheim, Bruno. *The Uses of Enchantment: The Meaning and Importance of Fairy Tales.* Vintage Books, 1977.

Biedermann, Hans. *Dictionary of Symbolism: Cultural Icons and the Meanings Behind Them.* Facts on File, 1992.

Bierlein, J.F. *Living Myths: How Myth Gives Meaning to Human Experience.* Ballantine Wellspring, 1999.

—. *Parallel Myths.* Ballantine Wellspring, 1994.

Birren, Faber. *The Symbolism of Color.* Citadel Press, 1988.

Blixen, Karen. *Out of Africa.* Penguin Books, 1985.

Bly, Robert, and Marion Woodman. *The Maiden King: The Reunion of Masculine and Feminine.* Henry Holt and Company. Inc, 1998.

Bolen, Jean Shinoda. *Crossing to Avalon.* New York: HarperCollins, 1995.

—. *Goddesses in Everywoman: A New Psychology of Women.* Harper Colophon Books, 1985.

—. *Gods in Everyman: A New Psychology of Men's Lives & Loves.* Perennial Library, 1989.

—. *Ring of Power: The Abandoned Child, The Authoritarian Father, and The Disempowered Feminine: A Jungian Understanding of Wagner's Ring Cycle.* New York: HarperSanFrancisco, 1993.

Bolsta, Phil. *Sixty Seconds: One Moment Changes Everything.* Atria Books, 2008.

Boorstein, Seymour. *Clinical Studies in Transpersonal Psychotherapy.* State University of New York Press, 1997.

Borel, Henri. *Wu Wei: La Via del No Actuar.* Ediciones Obelisco, 1992.

Bornstein, Marc H., ed. *Handbook of Parenting.* Vol. 1. Lawrence Erlbaum Associates, Publishers, 1995.

Borysenko, Joan. *Guilt is the Teacher, Love is the Lesson.* New York: Warner Books, 1990.

Borysenko, Joan, and Larry Rothstein. *Minding the Body, Mending the Mind.* Bantam Books, 1988.

Bouwmeester, Joos. *Jugando con la fuerza de la vida.* LibrosEnRed, 2007.

Braden, Gregg. *The Divine Matrix: Bridging Time, Space, Miracles, and Belief.* Hay House, Inc., 2007.

—. *Zwischen Himmel und Erde: Der spirituelle Weg des Mitgefühls.* Heyne, 2005.

Braghine, Colonel A. *The Shadow of Atlantis.* The Aquarian Press Limited, 1980.

Branden, Nathaniel. *The Art of Living Consciously: The Power of Awareness to Transform Everyday Life.* New York: Fireside, 1999.

—. *The Six Pillars of Self-Esteem.* New York: Bantam, 1994.

Brandon-Jones, David. *Las Líneas de la Mano y el Amor.* Editorial Pomaire, S.A., 1983.

Branson, Richard. *Losing My Virginity: How I've Survived, Had Fun, and Made a Fortune Doing Business My Way.* Times Books, 1998.

Breaux, Charles. *Viaje a la Conciencia: La Erótica Mística del Tantra, los Chakras y la psicología de Jung.* Heptada, 1990.

Brennan, Barbara Ann. *Hands of Light: A Guide to Healing Through the Human Energy Field.* Bantam Books, 1988.

Bridges, William. *Transitions: Making Sense of Life's Changes.* Addison-Wesley, 1980.

Briggs, Robert. *The American Emergency: A Search for Spiritual Renewal in an Age of Materialism.* Celestial Arts, 1989.

Brinkley, Dannion. *Saved by the Light.* HarperPaperbacks, 1995.

Brinton-Perera, Sylvia. *Descent to the Goddess: A Way of Initiation for Women.* Toronto: Inner City Books, 1981.

—. *The Scapegoat Complex: Toward a Mythology of Shadow and Guilt.* Toronto: Inner City Books, 1986.

Broadribb, Donald. *The Dream Story.* Inner City Books, 1987.

Brody, Howard. *The Placebo Response: How You Can Release the Body's Inner Pharmacy for Better Health.* Cliff Street Books, 2000.

Brook, Stephen, ed. *The Oxford Book of Dreams.* Oxford University Press, 1987.

Browne, Sylvia. *God, Creation, and Tools for Life.* Hay House, 2000.

—. *Life on the Other Side.* Dutton, 127.

—. *Soul's Perfection.* Hay House, 2000.

Brunas-Wagstaff, Jo. *Personality: A Cognitive Approach.* Routledge, 1998.

Brunner, Cornelia. *Anima As Fate.* Spring Publications, 1986.

Brunton, Paul. *A Search in Secret Egypt.* Samuel Weiser, Inc., 1988.

Bryant, Alice, and Phyllis Galde. *The Message of the Crystal Skull.* Llewellyn Publications, 1989.

Buhlman, William. *Adventures Beyond the Body.* HarperOne, 1996.

Burman, Edward. *Los Secretos de la Inquisición: Historia y legado del Santo Oficio, desde Inocencio III a Juan Pablo II.* Ediciones Martínez Roca, 1988.

Burnett, Frances Hodgson. *The Secret Garden.* Heinemann, 1962.

Buscaglia, Leo. *Amándonos Los Unos A Los Otros.* Plaza y Janes, 1985.

—. *Amor.* Plaza y Janes, 1978.

—. *Ser Persona.* Plaza y Janes, 1978.

—. *Vivir, Amar y Aprender.* Plaza y Janes, 1984.

Buzan, Tony. *Use Both Sides of Your Brain.* Dutton Paperback, 1983.

Buzan, Tony, and Barry Buzan. *The Mind Map Book.* BBC, 2003.

Caldwell, Taylor. *La Leyenda de Atlantida.* Grijalbo, 1977.

Callahan, Roger J., and Richard Trubo. *Tapping the Healer Within: Using Thought Field Therapy to Instantly Conquer Your Fears, Anxieties, and Emotional Distress.* Contemporary Books, 2001.

Camp, L. Sprague de. *Lost Continents: The Atlantis Theme in History, Science, and Literature.* Dover Publications, Inc., 1970.

Campbell, Joseph. *An Open Life: Joseph Campbell in Conversation with Michael Toms.* Edited by John M. Maher and Dennie Briggs. Perennial Library, 1990.

Campbell, Joseph, ed. *Man and Time: Papers From the Eranos Yearbooks.* Vol. 3. Bollingen Series, Princeton University Press, 1983.

Campbell, Joseph, ed. *Man and Transformation: Papers From the Eranos Yearbooks.* Vol. 5. Bollingen Series, Princeton University Press, 1980.

—. *Myths To Live By.* Bantam Books, 1988.

Campbell, Joseph, ed. *Myths, Dreams and Religion.* Spring Publications, Inc., 1988.

—. *Primitive Mythology: The Masks of God.* Penguin Arkana, 1991.

—. *Reflections on the Art of Living: A Joseph Campbell Companion.* Edited by Diane K. Osbon. HarperCollinsPublishers, 1991.

Campbell, Joseph, ed. *Spirit and Nature: Papers From the Eranos Yearbooks.* Vol. 1. Bollingen Series, Princeton University Press, 1982.

—. *The Flight of the Wild Gander: Explorations in the Mythological Dimension.* HarperPerennial, 1990.

—. *The Hero With A Thousand Faces.* Palladin Grafton Books, 1988.

—. *The Hero's Journey: Joseph Campbell on His Life and Work.* Edited by Phil Cousineau. HarperSanFrancisco, 1990.

—. *The Inner Reaches of Outer Space: Metaphor As Myth and As Religion.* Perennial Library, 1988.

—. *The Mythic Dimension: Selected Essays 1959 - 1987.* Edited by Anthony Van Couvering. HarperSanFrancisco, 1997.

—. *The Mythic Image.* Princeton University Press, 1981.

—. *Thou Art That: Transforming Religious Metaphor.* Edited by Eugene Kennedy. New World Library, 2001.

—. *Transformations of Myth Through Time: Thirteen Lectures.* Perennial Library, 1990.

Campbell, Joseph, Riane Eisler, Marija Gimbutas, and Charles Musès. *In All Her Names: Explorations of the Feminine in Divinity.* Edited by Joseph Campbell and Charles Musés. HarperSanFrancisco, 1991.

Capra, Fritjof. *The Tao of Physics: An Exploration of the Parallels Between Modern Physics and Eastern Mysticism* . Shambhala Publications, 1975.

—. *The Web of Life: A New Scientific Understanding of Living Systems.* Anchor Books, 1996.

—. *Uncommon Wisdom: Conversations With Remarkable People.* Bantam, 1989.

Carey, Ken. *Starseed: The Third Millennium.* HarperSanFrancisco, 1991.

—. *The Starseed Transmissions, Volume I.* Uni Sun Book, 1988.

Carlson, Richard. *You Can Feel Good Again.* A Dutton Book, 1993.

Carlson, Richard, and Benjamin Shield, . *Healers on Healing.* Jeremy P. Tarcher, Inc., 1989.

Carnac, Pierre. *La Historia Empieza en Bimini.* Plaza y Janes, 1977.

Carroll, Lee, and Jan Tober. *The Indigo Children: The New Kids Have Arrived.* Hay House, 1999.

Carter, Howard, and A.C. Mace. *The Discovery of the Tomb of Tutankhamen.* Dover Publications Inc., 1977.

Cartwright, Rosalind D. *Night Life: Explorations in Dreams.* Prentice-Hall, Inc., 1977.

Cartwright, Rosalind, and Lynne Lamberg. *Crisis Dreaming: Using Your Dreams to Solve Your Problems.* The Aquarian Press, 1993.

Carutenuto, Aldo. *The Spiral Way: A Woman's Healing Journey.* Inner City Books, 1986.

Casewit, Curtis W. *Grafología Práctica.* Ediciones Martinez Roca S.A., 1983.

Castaneda, Carlos. *El Segundo Anillo de Poder.* Editorial Pomaire, 1979.

—. *Relatos de Poder.* Fondo de Cultura Económica, 1980.

—. *The Art of Dreaming.* HarperCollinsPublishers, 1993.

—. *The Eagle's Gift.* Penguin, 1981.

—. *The Fire From Within.* Pocket Books, 1984.

—. *The Power of Silence.* Pocket Books, 1988.

—. *The Teachings of Don Juan: A Yaqui Way of Knowledge.* University of California Press, 1968.

—. *Una Realidad Aparte.* Fondo de Cultura Económica, 1981.

—. *Viaje a Ixtlan.* Fondo de Cultura Económica, 1981.

Castillejo, Irene Claremont de. *Knowing Woman: A Feminine Psychology.* Shamhbala, 1990.

Cayce, Edgar. *Edgar Cayce on Atlantis.* Edited by Hugh Lynn Cayce. Warner Books, 1988.

—. *Edgar Cayce's Story of Karma.* Edited by Mary Ann Woodward. Berkley Books, 1983.

Cerminara, Gina. *Erregende Zeugnisse von Karma und Wiedergeburt.* Hermann Bauer, 1981.

Chardin, Pierre Teilhard de. *Activation of Energy.* Harcourt, Brace, Jovanovich, 1970.

Chernin, Kim. *Reinventing Eve: Modern Woman in Search of Herself.* Perennial Library, 1988.

Chevalier, Jean, and Alain Gheerbrant. *The Penguin Dictionary of Symbols.* Penguin Books, 1996.

Childre, Doc, Howard Martin, and Donna Beech. *The Heartmath Solution.* HarperSanFrancisco, 1999.

Chopra, Deepak. *Ageless Body, Timeless Mind: The Quantum Alternative to Growing Old.* Harmony Books, 1993.

—. *Boundless Energy: The Complete Mind/Body Program for Overcoming Chronic Fatigue.* Harmony Books, 1995.

—. *Cómo Crear Salud; Más allá de la prevención y hacía la perfección.* Grijalbo, 1987.

—. *Creating Affluence: Wealth Consciousness in the Field of All Possibilities.* New World Library, 1993.

—. *Journey Into Healing: Awakening the Wisdom Within You.* Harmony Books, 1994.

—. *Life After Death: The Burden of Proof.* Harmony Books, 2006.

—. *Quantum Healing: Exploring the Frontiers of Mind/Body Medicine.* Bantam Books, 1989.

—. *Reinventing the Body: Resurrecting the Soul: How to Create a New Self.* Rider, 2009.

—. *The Book of Secrets: Who Am I? Where Did I Come From? Why Am I Here?* Rider, 2004.

—. *The Path to Love: Renewing the Power of Spirit in Your Life.* Random House, 1997.

—. *The Seven Spiritual Laws of Success.* New World Library, 1994.

—. *The Way of the Wizard: Twenty Spiritual Lessons for Creating the Life You Want.* Harmony Books, 1995.

—. *Unconditional Life: Discovering the Power to Fulfill Your Dreams.* Bantam Books, 1992.

Chopra, Deepak, and David Simon. *Grow Younger, Live Longer.* Harmony Books, 2001.

Christou, Evangelos. *The Logos of the Soul.* Spring Publications, Inc., 1987.

Church, Dawson. *The Genie in Your Genes: Epigenetic Medicine and the New Biology of Intention.* Elite Books, 2007.

Church, Dawson, Geralyn Gendreau, and Randy Peyser. *Healing the Heart of the World: Harnessing the Power of Intention to Change Your Life and Your Planet.* Edited by Dawson Church, Geralyn Gendreau and Randy Peyser. Elite Books, 2005.

Churton, Tobias. *Los Gnósticos: La Tradición Cristiana Oculta.* EDAF, 1988.

Cirlot, J.E. *A Dictionary of Symbols.* Philosophical Library, 1971.

Cleckley, Hervey. *The Mask of Sanity.* Emily S. Cleckley, 1988.

Clift, Jean Dalby, and Wallace B. Clift. *Symbols of Transformation in Dreams.* Crossroad, 1988.

Clinton, Bill. *My Life.* London: Hutchinson, 2004.

Coelho, Paolo. *The Alchemist.* HarperSanFrancisco, 1993.

Cohen, Alan. *Dare to Be Yourself: How to Quit Being an Extra in Other People's Movies and Become the Star of Your Own.* New York: Fawcett Columbine, 1991.

Colegrave, Sukie. *By Way of Pain: A Passage Into Self.* Park Street Press, 1988.

—. *Uniting Heaven & Earth: A Jungian and Taoist Exploration of the Masculine and Feminine in Human Consciousness.* Jeremy P. Tarcher, Inc., 1979.

Colette. *Claudine erwacht.* RoRoRo, 1958.

Coll, Cynthia Garcia, Elaine L. Bearer, and Richard M. Lerner. *Nature and Nurture: The Complex Interplay of Genetic and Environmental Influences on Human Behavior and Development.* Edited by Cynthia García Coll, Elaine L. Bearer and Richard M. Lerner. Lawrence Erlbaum Associates, Publishers, 2004.

Collins, Andrew. *Gateway to Atlantis: The Search for the Source of a Lost Civilization.* Carroll & Graf Publishers, Inc., 2000.

Collins, Bryn C. *Emotional Unavailability: Recognizing It, Understanding It, and Avoiding Its Trap.* Lincolnwood, Illinois: Contemporary Books, 1997.

Condos, Theony. *Star Myths of the Greeks and Romans: A Sourcebook.* 1997.

Conger, John P. *Jung & Reich: The Body As Shadow.* North Atlantic Books, 1988.

Conway, D.J. *The Ancient & Shining Ones: World Myth, Magic & Religion.* Llewelyn Publications, 1993.

Cooper, Robert K. *The Other 90%: How To Unlock Your Vast Untapped Potential For Leadership & Life.* Crown Business, 2001.

Corbett, Cynthia L. *Power Trips: Journeys to Sacret Sites as a Way of Transformation.* Timewindow Publications, 1988.

Cota-Robles, Patricia Diane. *Tú Decides Tu Vida: Una Llave Mágica al Mundo de la Metafísica.* Arbol Editorial, 1992.

Cott, Jonathan. *La reencarnación de Omm Seti: La búsqueda del amor eterno.* Javier Vergara, 1992.

Cotterell, Arthur. *La Gran Tumba Imperial de China.* Planeta, 1986.

Cousins, Norman. *Anatomy of an Illness: How One Man Proved Your Mind Can Cure Your Body.* New York: Bantam, 1981.

Covey, Stephen R. *The 7 Habits of Highly Effective People.* A Fireside Book, 1990.

Covitz, Joel. *Visions in the Night: Jungian and Ancient Dream Interpretation.* Inner City Books, 2000.

Cowan, Lyn. *Masochism: A Jungian View.* Dallas: Spring Publications, Inc., 1982.

Cramer, Kathryn D. *Roads To Me: Seven Pathways to Midlife Wisdom.* William Morrow and Company, Inc., 1995.

Cranston, Sylvia, and Carey Williams. *Reincarnation: A New Horizon in Science, Religion, and Society.* Julian Press, 1984.

Crispino, Anna Maria, Fabio Giovannini, and Marco Zatterin. *Das Buch vom Teufel: Geschichte, Kult, Erscheinungsformen.* Eichborn Verlag, 1987.

Csikszentmihalyi, Mihaly. *Finding Flow: The Psychology of Engagement With Everyday Life.* BasicBooks, 1997.

Cummings, E. Mark, Patrick T. Davies, and Susan B. Campbell. *Developmental Psychopathology and Family Process.* The Guilford Press, 2000.

Cunningham, Donna. *An Astrolgoical Guide to Self-Awareness.* CRCS Publications, 1978.

—. *Healing Pluto Problems.* Samuel Weiser, Inc., 1986.

Dalai, Lama, and Howard C. Cutler. *The Art of Happiness: A Handbook For Living.* Riverhead Books, 1998.

Dallett, Janet O. *When the Spirits Come Back.* Toronto: Inner City Books, 1988.

Damasio, Antonio. *Looking For Spinoza: Joy, Sorrow, and the Feeling Brain.* Harcourt, Inc., 2003.

—. *The Feeling of What Happens: Body, Emotion In the Making of Consciousness.* William Heinemann: London, 2000.

Damon, William, and Richard M. Lerner. *Handbook of Child Psychology.* Edited by William Damon and Richard M. Lerner. Vol. 1. John Wiley & Sons, Inc.

Dark, Gregory. *The Prophet of the New Millennium.* O Books, 2005.

Dass, Ram. *Compassion In Action: Setting Out on the Path of Service.* New York: Bell Tower, 1992.

Davies, Robertson. *Fifth Business.* The Macmillan Company, 1970.

Davis, Bruce. *The Magical Child Within You.* Celestial Arts, 1985.

Davis, Flora. *La Comunicación No Verbal.* Alianza, 1981.

Davison, Ronald. *Synastry: Understanding Human Relations Through Astrology.* ASI Publishers, Inc., 1977.

Day, Laura. *Practical Intuition.* Villard, 1996.

Day, Tanis. *The Whole You: Healing and Transformation Through Energy Awareness.* iUniverse, Inc., 2008.

deLaszlo, Violet S., ed. *The Basic Writings of C.G. Jung.* New York: The Modern Library, 1959.

DesMaisons, Kathleen. *Potatoes not Prozac.* Simon & Schuster, 1999.

Dethlefsen, Thorwald. *Das Erlebnis der Wiedergeburt: Heilung durch Reinkarnation.* Goldmann, 1987.

—. *Das Leben nach dem Leben: Gespräche mit Wiedergeborenen.* Goldmann, 1987.

—. *Schicksal als Chance: Das Urwissen zur Vollkommenheit des Menschen.* Goldmann, 1985.

Devi, Indra. *Yoga Para Todos.* Editorial Diana, 1989.

—. *Yoga: Por Siempre Joven, Por Siempre Sano: Los Beneficios Físicos y Espirituales del Yoga.* Javier Vergara Editor, S.A., 1988.

Diamond, John. *Life Energy: Using the Meridians to Unlock the Hidden Power of Your Emotions.* Paragon House, 1990.

Diaz-Plaja, Fernando. *The Spaniard & The Seven Deadly Sins.* Cox & Wyman, Ltd., 1968.

DiCarlo, Russell E. *Towards a New World View: Conversations at the Leading Edge.* Epic Publishing, 1996.

Dieckmann, Hans. *Träume als Sprache der Seele: Einführung in die Traumdeutung der Analytischen Psychologie C.G. Jungs.* Bonz, 1987.

Doidge, Norman. *The Brain That Changes Itself: Stories of Personal Triumph From the Frontiers of Brain Science.* New York: Viking Penguin, 2007.

Donnelly, Ignatius. *Atlantis: The Antediluvian World.* Gramercy Publishiing Co., 1949.

Donner, Florinda. *Being-In-Dreaming: An Initiation into the Sorcerer's World.* HarperSanFrancisco, 1991.

Dossey, Larry. *Recovering the Soul: A Scientific and Spiritual Search.* Bantam, 1989.

—. *Reinventing Medicine: Beyond Mind-Body to a New Era of Healing.* HarperSanFrancisco, 1999.

Dougherty, Ned. *Fast Lane to Heaven.* Hampton Roads, 2001.

Dowling, Colette. *Perfect Women: Hidden Fears of Inadequacy and the Drive to Perform.* Fontana/Collins, 1989.

Downing, Christine, ed. *Mirrors of The Self: Archetypal Images That Shape Your Life.* Los Angeles: Jeremy P. Tarcher, Inc., 1991.

Duffel, Nick, and Helena Lovendal. *Sex, Love and the Dangers of Intimacy: A Guide to Passionate Relationships When the "Honeymoon" is Over.* London: Thorsons, 2002.

Dumas, Didier. *Sons, Lovers, & Fathers: Understanding Male Sexuality.* Jason Aronson, Inc., 1997.

Dumas, Marguerite. *The Lover.* Harper Perennial, 1992.

Dupuis, Richard. *From the Mouth of God: Changing Life's Struggles to Powerful Energy.* Book Partners, 1998.

Dürckheim, Karlfried Graf. *The Way of Transformation: Daily Life as Spiritual Exercise.* A Mandala Book, 1988.

Durrell, Lawrence. *The Alexandria Quartet.* Faber & Faber, 1962.

Dyer, Wayne. *El Cielo es el Limite.* Barcelona: Grijalbo, 1981.

—. *La Fuerza de Creer: Como Cambiar Su Vida.* Mexico City: Grijalbo, 1989.

—. *Manifest Your Destiny: The Nine Spiritual Principles for Getting Everything You Want.* HarperPaperbacks, 1999.

—. *Pulling Your Own Strings: Dramatic Techniques For Dealing With Other People and Mastering Your Own Life.* Avon, 1979.

—. *Real Magic: Creating Miracles in Everyday Life.* HarperCollins, 1992.

—. *There's a Spiritual Solution to Every Problem.* HarperCollins, 2001.

—. *Your Erroneous Zones.* New York: Funk & Wagnalls, 1976.

—. *Your Sacred Self: Making the Decision To be Free.* HarperPaperbacks, 1995.

Easwaran, Eknath. *Conquest of Mind.* Nilgiri Press, 1988.

—. *Gandhi, The Man: The Story of His Transformation.* Tomales, CA: Nilgiri Press, 1997.

Eco, Umberto. *El Nombre de la Rosa.* Círculo de Lectores, 1984.

Edelman, Hope. *Motherless Daughters: The Legacy of Loss.* Doubleday, 1995.

Eden, Donna, and David Feinstein. *Energy Medicine.* Jeremy P. Tarcher, 1999.

Edinger, Edward F. *The Creation of Consciousness: Jung's Myth for Modern Man.* Toronto: Inner City Books, 1984.

Edward, Joyce, and Jean Sanville. *Fostering Healing & Growth: A Psychoanalytic Social Work Approach.* Edited by Joyce Edward and Jean Sanville. Jason Aronson, Inc., 1996.

Ehrenreich, Barbara. *Nickel and Dimed: On (Not) Getting By in America.* A Metropolitan/Owl Book, 2001.

Eisler, Riane. *Sacred Pleasure: Sex, Myth, and the Politics of the Body - New Paths to Power and Love.* HarperSanFrancisco, 1995.

—. *The Chalice & the Blade: Our History, Our Future.* Perennial Library, 1987.

Eliade, Mircea. *El Chamanismo y las técnicas del éxtasis.* Fondo de Cultura Económica, 1986.

—. *The Myth of the Eternal Return: Or, Cosmos and History.* Bollingen Series, Princeton University Press, 1991.

—. *The Sacred & The Profane: The Nature of Religion: The Significance of Religious Myth, Symbolism, and Ritual Within Life and Culture.* Harcourt Brace & Company, 1987.

Eliot, T.S. *Four Quartets.* Orlando, FL: Harcourt, Brace, Jovanovich, 1971.

Elkins, Don, Carla Rueckert, and James Allen McCarty. *The Ra Material.* Whitford Press, 1984.

Emery, Marcia. *The Intuitive Healer: Accessing Your Inner Physician.* St. Martin's Griffin, 1999.

Emoto, Masaru. *The Hidden Messages in Water.* Beyond Words Publishing, 2004.

Erickson, Marilyn T. *Behavior Disorders of Children and Adolescents: Assessment, Etiology, and Intervention.* Prentice Hall, 1998.

Erikson, Erik H., Joan M. Erikson, and Helen Q. Kivnick. *Vital Involvement in Old Age.* New York: W.W. Norton & Company, 1986.

Esquivel, Laura. *Como Agua Para Chocolate.* Editorial Planeta Mexicana, 1990.

Estés, Clariss Pinkola. *Women Who Run With the Wolves: Myths and Stories of the Wild Woman Archetype.* Ballantine Books, 1992.

Estés, Clarissa Pinkola, ed. *Tales of the Brothers Grimm.* Quality Paperback Book Club, 1999.

Evola, Julius. *Die Hermetische Tradition: Von der alchemistischen Umwandlung der Metalle und des Menschen in Gold.* Ansata-Verlag, 1989.

Eyre, Richard. *Spiritual Serendipity: Cultivating and Celebrating the Art of the Unexpected.* Simon & Schuster, 1997.

Faber, Adele, and Elaine Mazlish. *Siblings Without Rivalry.* Avon Books, 1987.

Faludi, Susan. *Backlash: The Undeclared War Against American Women.* Anchor Books, 1991.

Farrell, Deborah, and Carole Presser. *The Herder Symbol Dictionary: Symbols from Art, Archaeology, Mythology, Literature and Religion.* Chiron Publications, 1988.

Fast, Julius. *El Lenguaje del Cuerpo.* Kairós, 1980.

Feinstein, David. *Energy Psychology Interactive: Rapid Interventions for Lasting Change.* Innersource, 2004.

Feinstein, David, and Stanley Krippner. *Personal Mythology: The Psychology of Your Evolving Self.* Jeremy P. Tarcher, Inc., 1988.

—. *The Mythic Path: Discovering the Guiding Stories of Your Past - Creating a Vision For Your Future.* Jeremy P. Tarcher, 1997.

Ferguson, Marilyn. *The Aquarian Conspiracy.* J.P. Tarcher, 1987.

Fernández, Adela. *Dioses Prehispánicos de México.* Panorama, 1993.

Ferrucci, Piero. *Inevitable Grace: Breakthroughs in the Lives of Great Men and Women: Guides to Your Self-Realization.* Los Angeles: Jeremy P. Tarcher, Inc., 1990.

—. *What We May Be: The Visions and Techniques of Psychosynthesis.* Wellingborough, Northhamptonshire: Turnstone Press Limited, 1982.

Feuerstein, Georg, and David Frawley Subhash Kak. *In Search of the Cradle of Civilization: New Light on Ancient India.* Quest Books, 2001.

Finkelhorn, David. *Abuso Sexual al Menor: Causas, Consecuencias y Tratamiento Psicosexual.* Editorial Pax-Mexico, 1980.

Finkelstein, Adrian. *Your Past Lives and the Healing Process: A Psychiatrist Looks at Reincarnation and Spiritual Healing.* Coleman Publishing, 1985.

Fiore, Edith. *Usted Ya Estuvo Aqui: Revelación de Vidas Anteriores.* EDAF, 1980.

Firestone, Robert W. *The Fantasy Bond: Structure of Psychological Defenses.* Los Angeles: Glendon Association, 1987.

Firestone, Robert W., and Joyce Catlett. *Fear of Intimacy.* Washington: APA, 2004.

Firman, John, and Ann Gila. *The Primal Wound: A Transpersonal View of Trauma, Addiction, and Growth.* Albany, NY: State University of New York Press, 1997.

Flèche, Christian. *The Biogenealogy Sourcebook: Healing the Body by Resolving Traumas of the Past.* Healing Arts Press, 2008.

Fleet, James K. Van. *Hidden Power: How To Unleash the Power of Your Subconscious Mind.* Prentice Hall, 1987.

Fosha, Diana. *The Transforming Power of Affect: A Model For Accelerated Change.* New York: Basic Books, 2000.

Fosha, Diana, Daniel J. Siegel, and Marion F. Solomon. *The Healing Power of Emotion: Affective Neuroscience, Development & Clinical Practice.* Edited by Diana Fosha, Daniel J. Siegel and Marion F. Solomon. W.W. Norton & Co., 2009.

Foucault, Michel. *The History of Sexuality: An Introduction, Volume I.* Vintage Books, 1990.

Fowles, John. *The Magus.* Little, Brown & Co., 1965.

Fox, Matthew. *Original Blessing: A Primer in Creation Spirituality.* Bear & Company, 1983.

—. *The Coming of the Cosmic Christ: The Healing of Mother Earth and the Birth of a Global Renaissance.* Harper & Row, 1988.

Frankl, Viktor E. *Man's Search For Meaning: An Introduction to Logotherapy.* New York: Pocketbooks, 1963.

Franz, Marie-Louise von. *Creation Myths.* Shambhala, 1995.

—. *Individuation in Fairytales.* Spring Publications, 1982.

—. *On Dreams & Death: A Jungian Interpretation.* Shambhala, 1987.

—. *Projection and Re-collection in Jungian Psychology: Reflections of Soul.* La Salle, Illinois: Open Court, 1980.

—. *Shadow and Evil in Fairytales.* Spring Publications, Inc., 1983.

Franzoso, Elisabetta. *Stella's Mum Gets Her Groove Back.* Homes4Hope Publications, 2008.

Fraser, Sylvia. *My Father's House: A Memoir of Incest and Healing.* Ticknor and Fields, 1987.

Frazer, Sir James George. *The Golden Bough: A Study in Magic and Religion.* Collier Books, 1963.

Freke, Timothy, and Peter Gandy. *The Jesus Mysteries: Was the "Original Jesus" a Pagan God?* Harmony Books, 1999.

French, Marilyn. *Beyond Power: On Women, Men, and Morals.* Ballantine Books, 1985.

—. *Mujeres.* Argos, 1978.

—. *Our Father.* Ballantine Books, 1994.

—. *The Bleeding Heart.* Summit Books, 1980.

—. *The War Against Women.* Ballantine Books, 1992.

Freud, Sigmund. *A General Introduction to Psychoanalysis.* Washington Press, Inc., 1967.

Friday, Nancy. *Jealousy.* Bantam Books, 1987.

—. *My Secret Garden.* Pocket Books, 1973.

—. *The Power of Beauty.* HarperCollinsPublishers, 1996.

Friedan, Betty. *Life So Far: A Memoir.* New York: Touchstone, 2000.

—. *The Feminine Mystique.* Dell Publishing Co., Inc., 1964.

—. *The Fountain of Age.* Simon & Schuster, 1993.

Friedmann, Thomas. *The World is Flat: A Brief History of the Twenty-first Century.* Farrar, Straus and Giroux, 2005.

Fromm, Erich. *Psicoanálisis de la sociedad contemporánea.* Fondo de Cultura Económica, 1980.

—. *The Art of Loving.* Bantam Books, 1963.

—. *The Forgotten Language: An Introduction to the Understandiing of Dreams, Fairy Tales and Myths.* Grove Press inc., 1957.

—. *To Have Or To Be?* Bantam Books, 1988.

Furneaux, Rupert. *The World's Strangest Mysteries.* Ace Books, Inc., 1961.

Gallo, Fred P., ed. *Energy Psychology in Psychotherapy: A Comprehensive Source Book.* W.W. Norton & Company.

—. *Energy Psychology: Explorations at the Interface of Energy, Cognition, Behavior and Health.* CRC Press, 1998.

Gallo, Fred P., and Harry Vincenzi. *Energy Tapping: How to Rapidly Eliminate Anxiety, Depression, Cravings and More Using Energy Psychology.* New Harbinger Publications, 2000.

Garfield, Patricia. *Women´s Bodies, Women´s Dreams.* Ballantine Books, 1991.

Gauquelin, Michel. *Los Relojes Cosmicos.* Plaza y Janes, 1976.

Gawain, Shakti. *Creating True Prosperity.* New World Library, 1997.

—. *Creative Visualization.* Bantam, 1985.

Gaynor, Mitchell L. *Sounds of Healing: A Physician Reveals the Power of Sound, Voice, and Music.* New York: Broadway Books, 1999.

Gérardin, Lucien. *La Alquimia.* Martínez Roca, 1975.

Gibran, Kahlil. *The Prophet.* New York: Alfred A. Knopf, 1970.

Gilbert, Elizabeth. *Eat, Pray, Love.* London: Penguin, 2007.

Gimbutas, Marija. *The Civilization of the Goddess: The World of Old Europe.* HarperSanFrancisco, 1991.

—. *The Goddesses and Gods of Old Europe 6500 - 3500 BC: Myths and Cult Images.* University of California Press, 1996.

—. *The Language of the Goddess: Unearthing the Hidden Synmbols of Western Civilization.* Thames & Hudson, 1989.

—. *The Living Goddesses.* University of California Press, 2001.

Gladwell, Malcolm. *Outliers: The Story of Success.* Penguin Books, 2009.

—. *The Tipping Point: How Little Things Can Make A Big Difference.* Back Bay Books, 2002.

Glasser, William. *Choice Theory: A New Psychology of Personal Freedom.* Harper Perennial, 1998.

Glasser, William, and Carleen Glasser. *Eight Lessons for a Happier Marriage.* Harper, 2007.

Goldsmith, Joel S. *Invisible Supply: Finding the Gifts of the Spirit Within.* HarperOne, 1994.

—. *The Art of Spiritual Healing.* HarperSanFrancisco, 1992.

—. *The Infinite Way.* DeVorss Publications, 2008.

—. *The Thunder of Silence.* HarperOne, 1993.

Goleman, Daniel. *Destructive Emotions: How Can We Overcome Them? A Scientific Dialogue with the Dalai Lama.* Bantam, 2003.

—. *Emotional Intelligence.* Bantam, 1995.

Goleman, Daniel, Richard Boyatzis, and Annie McKee. *The New Leaders: Transforming the Art of Leadership Into the Science of Results.* Time Warner Paperbacks, 2003.

Grabhorn, Lynn. *Excuse Me, Your Life is Waiting: The Astonishing Power of Feelings.* Hampton Roads, 2000.

Grass, Günther. *Beim Häuten der Zwiebel.* Göttingen: Steidl Verlag, 2006.

Graves, Robert. *The White Goddess: A Historical Grammar of Poetic Myth.* Farrar, Strauss & Giroux, 1980.

Gray, John. *Men, Women and Relationships: Making Peace With the Opposite Sex.* Beyond Words Publishing, Inc., 1993.

Gray, William G. *The Tree of Evil.* York Beach, Maine: Samuel Weiser, Inc., 1984.

Green, Celia. *Lucid Dreams*. Oxford Institute of Psychophysical Research, 1968.
Green, Jeffrey Wolf. *Pluto: The Evolutionary Journey of the Soul*. Llewellyn Publications, 1986.
—. *Pluto: The Soul's Evolution Through Relationships*. Llewellyn Publications, 1997.
Greene, Graham. *The Honorary Consul*. Penguin Books, 1974.
Greene, Liz. *Relating: An Astrological Guide to Living with Others on a Small Planet*. Coventure Ltd., 1978.
—. *Relationships and How to Survive Them*. CPA, 1999.
—. *Saturn: A New Look At An Old Devil*. Samuel Weiser, Inc., 1979.
—. *The Art of Stealing Fire*. CPA, 1996.
—. *The Astrological Neptune and the Quest for Redemption*. Samuel Weiser, Inc., 1996.
—. *The Astrology of Fate*. George Allen & Unwin, 1984.
—. *The Outer Planets & Their Cycles: The Astrology of the Collective*. CRCS Publications, 1983.
Greene, Liz, and Howard Sasportas. *Dynamics of the Unconscious: Seminars in Psychological Astrology, Vol. 2*. Samuel Weiser, Inc., 1988.
—. *The Development of the Personality: Seminars in Psychological Astrology Vol. 1*. Samuel Weiser, Inc., 1988.
—. *The Inner Planets: Building Blocks of Personal Reality: Seminars in Psychological Astrology, Vol. 4*. Samuel Weiser, Inc., 1993.
—. *The Luminaries: The Psychology of the Sun and Moon in the Horoscope: Seminars in Psychological Astrology, Volume 3*. Samuel Weiser, Inc., 1992.
Greene, Liz, and Juliet Sharman Burke. *The Mythic Journey: The Meaning of Myth As A Guide for Life*. Fireside, 2000.
Greene, Liz, and Stephen Arroyo. *The Jupiter/Saturn Conference Lectures*. CRCS Publications, 1984.
Greenspan, Miriam. *Healing Through the Dark Emotions: The Wisdom of Grief, Fear, and Despair*. Boston: Shambhala, 2003.
Griscom, Chris. *Die Heilung der Gefühle: Angst is eine Lüge*. Goldmann Verlag, 1988.
—. *Ecstasy is a New Frequency: Teachings of the Light Institute*. Fireside, 1988.
—. *Feminine Fusion: The Power to Transform Strength with Sensitivity, Logic with Intuition, and Sexuality with Spirituality*. Fireside, 1991.
—. *Nizhoni: The Higher Self in Education*. The Light Institute of Galisteo Foundation, 1889.
—. *Psychogenetics: The Force of Heredity*. Light Institute Press, 2000.
—. *Soul Bodies*. The Light Institute Press, 1996.
—. *The Ageless Body*. Light Institute Press, 1992.
—. *Time is an Illusion*. Fireside, 1988.
Grof, Stanislav. *Psychology of the Future: Lessons From Modern Consciousness Research*. State University of New York Press, 2000.
—. *The Adventure of Self-Discovery: Dimensions of Consciousness and New Perspectives in Psychotherapy and Inner Exploration*. State University of New York Press, 1988.
Grof, Stanislav, and Christina Grof. *Spiritual Emergency: When Personal Transformation Becomes A Crisis*. Edited by Stanislav Grof and Christina Grof. Jeremy P. Tarcher, 1989.

—. *The Stormy Search For the Self: A Guide to Personal Growth Through Transformational Crisis.* Jeremy P. Tarcher, Inc., 1990.

Grof, Stanislav, and Hal Zina Bennett. *The Holotropic Mind: The Three Levels of Human Consciousness and How They Shape Our Lives.* HarperSanFranscisco, 1992.

Hagen, Victor von. *En Busca de los Mayas: La Historia de Stephens y Catherwood.* Diana, 1991.

Haggard, H. Rider. *Allan Quatermain.* Dover Publications, 1951.

—. *Ayesha - Sie kehrt zurück.* Wolfgang Jeschke, 1984.

—. *King Solomon's Mines.* Dover Publications, 1951.

—. *She.* Hodder and Stoughton, 1949.

—. *The Days of My Life.* London: Dodo Press, 2011.

—. *Wisdom's Daughter: The Life and Love Story of She-Who-Must-Be-Obeyed.* Ballantine Books, 1978.

Haich, Elisabeth. *Inititation.* Seed Center, 1974.

Haich, Elisabeth, and Selvarajan Yesudian. *Self Healing, Yoga & Destiny.* Aurora Press, 1966.

Haines-Sargent, Lois. *How To Handle Your Human Relations.* AFA, 1958.

Hall, James A. *Jungian Dream Interpretation: A Handbook of Theory and Practice.* Inner City Books, 1983.

—. *Patterns of Dreaming: Jungian Techniques in Theory and Practice.* Shambhala, 1991.

Halper, Jan. *Quiet Desperation: The Truth About Successful Men.* Warner Books, 1988.

Hamaker-Zondag, Karen. *Aspects and Personality.* Samuel Weiser, Inc., 1990.

—. *Elements & Crosses as the Basis of the Horoscope: Jungian Symbolism & Astrology, Vol. 1.* Samuel Weiser, Inc., 1984.

—. *The Houses and Personality Development: Jungian Symbolism & Astrology, Vol. 3.* Samuel Weiser, Inc., 1988.

—. *The Twelfth House: The Hidden Power in the Horoscope.* Samuel Weiser, Inc., 1992.

Hammarskjöld, Dag. *Markings.* Ballantine, 1989.

Hancock, Graham. *Fingerprints of the Gods.* Crown Trade Paperbacks, 1995.

—. *The Sign and the Seal: The Quest for the Lost Ark of the Covenant.* Crown Publishers, 1992.

Hancock, Graham, and Robert Bauval. *The Message of the Sphinx: A Quest for the Hidden Legacy of Mankind.* 1996.

Hancock, Graham, and Santha Faiia. *Heaven's Mirror: Quest For the Lost Civilization.* Three Rivers Press, 1998.

Hand-Clow, Barbara. *Chiron: Rainbow Bridge Between the Inner & Outer Planets.* Llewellyn Publications, 1988.

—. *Eye of the Centaur: A Visionary Guide into Past Lives.* Llewellyn Publications, 1987.

—. *Heart of the Cristos: Starseeding from the Pleiades.* Bear & Company, 1989.

—. *Liquid Light of Sex: Understanding Your Key Life Passages.* Bear and Company, 1991.

—. *The Pleiadian Agenda: A New Cosmology for the Age of Light.* Bear & Company, Inc., 1995.

Hanish, O. Zar-Adusht. *El Poder de la Respiración: Sistema Mazdaznan de Autorrealización.* Editorial Posada, 1990.

Hannah, Barbara. *Encounters With the Soul: Active Imagination as Developed by C.G. Jung.* Sigo Press, 1981.

Hansen, Mark Victor, and Jack Canfield. *Dare To Win.* Berkley Books, 1994.

Hanson, Rick, and Richard Mendius. *Buddha's Brain: The Practical Neuroscience of Happiness, Love & Wisdom.* New Harbinger Publications, 2009.

Harding, M. Esther. *Psychic Energy: Its Sources and Its Transformation.* Bollingen Series, Princeton University Press, 1973.

—. *The I and the Not I: A Study in the Development of Consciousness.* Princeton, NJ: Princeton/Bollingen, 1973.

—. *The Way of All Women: A Psychological Interpretation.* Rider, 1983.

—. *Woman's Mysteries: Ancient and Modern, A Psychological Interpretation of the Feminine Principle as Portrayed in Myth, Story and Dreams.* Rider, 1982.

Hare, Robert D. *Without Conscience: The Disturbing World of the Psychopaths Among Us.* The Guilford Press, 1993.

Harnisch, Günther. *Träume lösen Lebenskrisen: Anleitung zur Traumarbeit mit Kindern.* Herderbücherei, 1985.

Harris, Amy, and Thomas Harris. *Staying OK.* Pan Books, 1985.

Harris, Maria. *Dance of the Spirit: The Seven Steps of Women's Spirituality.* Bantam Books, 1989.

Harris, Thomas A. *Yo Estoy Bien - Tú Estás Bien.* Barcelona: Grijalbo, 1973.

Hartmann, Thom. *The Prophet's Way: Touching the Power of Life.* Mythical Books, 1997.

Haskins, Susan. *Mary Magdalen: Myth and Metaphor.* Harcourt Brace & Co., 1993.

Hawkins, David R. *Power Vs. Force: The Hidden Determinants of Human Behavior.* Hay House, 2002.

—. *The Eye of the I: From Which Nothing is Hidden.* Veritas, 2001.

Hay, Louise. *You Can Heal Your Life.* Hay House, 1987.

Heindel, Max. *The Rosi-Crucian Cosmo-Conception or Mystic Christianity.* Wood & Jones, 1971.

Heintschel, Aglaja. *Zeugen für das Jenseits.* Swedenborg Verlag, 1995.

Hendler, Sheldon Saul. *The Oxygen Breakthrough: 30 Days to an Illness-Free Life.* Pocket Books, 1989.

Henry, Patty. *The Emotionally Unavailable Man: A Blueprint for Healing.* Highland City, FL: Rainbow Books, Inc., 2004.

Heraso-Aragón, María Isabel. *Viajeros en Tránsito: Una perspectiva diferente de la muerte.* Fundación Internacional del Dolor, 2002.

Herrera, Germán. *La Puerta: Una Entrada a Otra Realidad.* Arbol Editorial, 1990.

Herrera, Hayden. *Frida: Una Biografía de Frida Kahlo.* México, D.F.: Editorial Diana, 1988.

Hesse, Hermann. *Narcissus and Goldmund.* Bantam Books, 1971.

—. *Siddhartha.* The Noonday Press, 1969.

—. *The Journey to the East.* The Noonday Press, 1969.

Hickey, Isabel M. *Minerva or Pluto: The Choice is Yours.* 1977.

Hicks, Esther, and Jerry Hicks. *Abraham Spreaks - A New Beginning I: Handbook for Joyous Survival.* Abraham-Hicks Publications, 1996.
—. *Abraham Spreaks - A New Beginning II.* Abraham-Hicks Publications, 1995.
—. *Ask and It Is Given: Learning to Manifest Your Desires.* Hay House, 2004.
Hill, Napoleon. *Think and Grow Rich.* Barnes & Noble, 2008.
Hillman, James. *Anima: An Anatomy of a Personified Notion.* Spring Publications, 1985.
Hillman, James, ed. *Facing the Gods.* Spring Publications, Inc., 1988.
—. *The Dream and the Underworld.* Harper and Row, 1979.
—. *The Soul's Code: In Search of Character and Calling.* New York: Random House, 1996.
Hirigoyen, Marie-France. *Stalking the Soul: Emotional Abuse and the Erosion of Identity.* New York: Helen Marx Books, 2004.
Hirsch, Edwin W. *The Power to Love.* The Citadel Press, 1948.
Hite, Shere. *El Informe Hite sobre la sexualidad masculina.* Plaza y Janes, 1981.
—. *The Hite Report: A Nationwide Study of Female Sexuality.* Dell, 1976.
Hoff, Lee Ann. *People in Crisis: Understanding and Helping.* Addison-Wesley Publishing Company, Inc., 1989.
Hogan, R. Craig. *Your Eternal Self.* Greater Reality Publications, 2008.
Holbe, Rainer. *Wir von Atlantis: Protokolle aus fernen Zeiten.* Knaur, 1988.
Holland, Gail Bernice. *A Call For Connection: Solutions For Creating a Whole New Culture.* New World Library, 1998.
Hollis, James. *The Eden Project: In Search of the Magical Other - A Jungian Perspective on Relationship.* Toronto: Inner City Books, 1998.
Hopcke, Robert H. *Men's Dreams, Men's Healing: A Psychotherapist Explores A New View of Masculinity Through Jungian Dreamwork.* Shambhala, 1990.
—. *There Are No Accidents: Synchronicity and the Stories of Our Lives.* Riverhead Books, 1976.
Horney, Karen. *Neurosis and Human Growth: The Struggle Toward Self-Realization.* New York: W.W. Norton & Company, 1991.
—. *Our Inner Conflicts: A Constructive Theory of Neurosis.* New York: W.W. Norton & Company, 1972.
—. *Psicología Femenina.* Alianza, 1980.
—. *Self-Analysis.* New York: W.W. Norton & Company, 1970.
Houston, Jean. *A Mythic Life: Learning to Live Our Greater Story.* New York: HarperSanFrancisco, 1996.
—. *A Passion For the Possible: A Guide to Realizing Your True Potential.* HarperSanFrancisco, 1998.
—. *The Possible Human: A Course in Enhacing Your Physical, Mental and Creative Abilities.* Jeremy P. Tarcher, 1982.
—. *The Search for the Beloved: Journeys in Mythology and Sacred Psychology.* Jeremy P. Tarcher, Inc., 1987.
Howard, Michael. *The Occult Conspiracy: Secret Societies - Their Influence and Power in World History.* Destiny Books, 1989.
Howell, Alice O. *Jungian Synchronicity in Astrological Signs and Ages.* Quest Books, 1990.

—. *The Dove in the Stone: Finding the Sacred in the Commonplace.* Quest Books, 1988.

Hubbard, Barbara Marx. *Conscious Evolution: Awakening the Power of Our Social Potential.* New World Library, 1998.

Hume, Robert Ernest. *The Thirteen Principal Upanishads Translated from the Sanskrit.* Oxford University Press, 1954.

Hunt, Harry T. *Multiplicity of Dreams: Memory, Imagination and Consciousness.* Yale University Press, 1989.

Huskey, Alice. *Stolen Childhood: What You Need to Know About Sexual Abuse.* InterVarsity Press, 1990.

Hutchison, Michael. *Mega Brain Power: Transform Your Life With Mind Machines and Brain Nutrients.* 1994, Hyperion.

—. *Mega Brain: New Tools and Techniques For Brain Growth and Mind Expansion.* Ballantine Books, 1991.

Isha. *Why Walk When You Can Fly?* New World Library, 2008.

Ishbel. *The Secret Teachings of the Temple of Isis.* Llewellyn, 1989.

Iyengar, Sheena. *The Art of Choosing.* Twelve, 2010.

Izutsu, Toshihiko. *El Kôan Zen.* Editorial Eyras, 1978.

Jackson, Eve. *Jupiter: An Astrologer's Guide.* The Aquarian Press, 1986.

Jackson, Rosie. *Mütter, die ihre Kinder verlassen - alles Rabenmütter?* Europaverlag, 1995.

Jacobi, Jolande. *The Way of Individuation: The Indispensable Key to Understanding Jungian Psychology.* New York: Meridian, 1983.

Jaffé, Aniela. *The Myth of Meaning in the Work of C.G. Jung.* Zurich: Daimon, 1984.

James, Oliver. *Affluenza.* Vermillion, 2007.

—. *They F*** You Up: How To Survive Family Life.* London: Bloomsbury, 2002.

Jennifer M. Jenkins, Keith Oatley, Nancy L. Stein, ed. *Human Emotion: A Reader.* Blackwell Publishers, 1998.

Johnson, Robert A. *He: Understanding Masculine Psychology.* Perennial Library, 1989.

—. *Inner Work: Using Dreams & Active Imagination For Personal Growth.* San Francisco: Harper& Row, 1986.

—. *Owning Your Own Shadow: Understanding the Dark Side of the Psyche.* HarperSanFrancisco, 1991.

—. *She: Understanding Feminine Psychology.* Perennial Library, 1989.

—. *We: Understanding the Psychology of Romantic Love.* Harper & Row, 1983.

Johnson, Spencer. *Who Moved My Cheese?* P.G. Putnam's Sons, 1998.

Jong, Erica. *Fear of Flying.* New American Library, 1975.

—. *How To Save your Own Life.* New American Library, 1977.

Joy, W. Brugh. *Joy's Way: A Map for the Transformational Journey.* Jeremy P. Tarcher Inc., 1979.

Judith, Anodea. *Wheels of Life: A User's Guide to the Chakra System.* Llewellyn Publications, 1990.

Jung, Carl Gustav. *Aion: Researches Into the Phenomenology of the Self.* Bollingen Series / Princeton, 1978.

—. *Civilization in Transition.* Routledge & Kegan Paul, 1981.

—. *Dreams.* Bollingen Series, Princeton University Press, 1974.

—. *Los Complejos y el Inconsciente.* Alianza, 1980.

—. *Memories, Dreams, Reflections.* New York: Vintage Book, 1963.
—. *Modern Man in Search of a Soul.* London: Ark Paperbacks, 1984.
—. *Mysterium Coniunctionis.* Bollingen Series / Princeton, 1989.
—. *Psychological Types.* Routledge & Kegan Paul, 1981.
—. *Symbols of Transformation.* Bollingen Series / Princeton, 1976.
—. *Synchronicity: An Acausal Connecting Principle.* Routledge & Kegan Paul, 1981.
—. *The Structure and Dynamics of the Psyche.* Routledge & Kegan Paul, 1977.
—. *The Undiscovered Self.* Routledge & Kegan Paul, 1982.
Jung, Carl Gustav, and R. Wilhelm. *El Secreto de la Flor de Oro.* Paidos Studio, 1981.
Jung, Carl Gustav, Marie-Louise von Franz, and John Freeman. *Man and His Symbols.* Pan Books, 1964.
Jung, Emma. *Animus and Anima.* Spring Publications, 1985.
Jussek, Eugene G. *Die Begegnung mit dem Weisen in uns: Gespräche mit Yan Su Lu.* Goldmann, 1986.
Kabat-Zinn, Jon. *Full Catastrophe Living: Using the Wisdom of Your Body and Mind to Face Stress, Pain, and Illness.* Delta Trade Paperbacks, 1990.
—. *Wherever You Go There You Are: Mindfulness Meditation in Everyday Life.* Hyperion, 1994.
Kahlo, Frida. *The Diary of Frida Kahlo: An Intimate Self-Portrait.* Harry N. Abrams, Inc., Publishers, 1995.
Kaplan, Helen Singer. *The Sexual Desire Disorders: Dysfunctional Regulation of Sexual Motivation.* Brunner/Mazel, Publishers, 1995.
Kapleau, Philip. *The Wheel of Life and Death: A Practical and Spiritual Guide.* 1989, Doubleday.
Karmadharaya. *Quiromancia.* Editorial De Vecchi, S.A., 1979.
Kast, Verena. *The Dynamics of Symbols: Fundamentals of Jungian Psychotherapy.* Fromm International Publishing Corporation, 1992.
Kaufman, Barry Neil. *Happiness Is A Choice.* Fawcett Columbine, 1994.
—. *To Love Is To Be Happy With.* Fawcett Books, 1997.
Keleman, Stanley. *Körperlicher Dialog in der therapeutischen Beziehung.* Kösel, 1990.
—. *Verkörperte Gefühle: Der anatomische Ursprung unserer Erfahrungen und Einstellungen.* Kösel, 1992.
—. *Your Mind Speaks Its Body.* Center Press, 1981.
Kelly, Robin. *The Human Antenna: Reading the Language of the Universe in the Songs of Our Cells.* Energy Psychology Press, 2008.
Keneally, Thomas. *Schindler's List.* Touchstone, 1993.
Kennedy-Moore, Eileen, and Jeanne C. Watson. *Expressing Emotion: Myths, Realities and Therapeutic Strategies.* The Guilford Press, 1999.
Kerényi, Karl. *Goddesses of Sun and Moon.* Dallas: Spring Publications, 1987.
Kessler, David. *Visions, Trips, and Crowded Rooms: Who and What You See Before you Die.* Hay House, 2010.
Khalsa, Dharma Singh, and Cameron Stauth. *Brain Longevity: The Breakthrough Medical Program that Improves Your Mind and Memory.* Warner Books, 1997.
King, Francis. *Tantra als Selbsterfahrung: Einführung in den indischen Weg zum Wachstum der Persönlichkeit.* Wilhelm Heyne Verlag, 1986.

King, Laurel. *Women of Power: 10 Visionaries Share Their Extraordinary Stories of Healing & Secrets of Success.* Celestial Arts, 1989.

Kingma, Daphne Rose. *The Future of Love: The Power of the Soul in Intimate Relationships.* Doubleday, 1998.

Klein, Naomi. *The Shock Doctrine: The Rise of Disaster Capitalism.* Penguin Books, 2007.

Knapp, Mark L. *La Comunicación No Verbal: El Cuerpo y el Entorno.* Paidós Comunicación, 1982.

Knight, Gareth. *The Rose Cross and the Goddess: The Quest for the Eternal Feminine Principal.* Destiny Books, 1985.

Koechlin-de-Bizemont, Dorothée. *Karma-Astrologie: Das Horoskop als Spiegel vergangener Leben.* Knaur, 1985.

Kolbenschlag, Madonna. *Kiss Sleeping Beauty Good-Bye.* Perennial Library, 1988.

Koltuv, Barbara Black. *The Book of Lilith.* York Beach, Maine: Nicolas-Hays, 1987.

Kopp, Sheldon. *Raise Your Right Hand Against Fear, Extend the Other in Compassion.* Ballantine Books, 1988.

Koven, Jean-Claude. *Going Deeper: How To Make Sense of Your Life When Your Life Makes No Sense.* Prism House Press, 2004.

Krippner, Stanley, ed. *Dreamtime & Dreamwork: Decoding the Language of the Night.* Jeremy P. Tarcher, Inc., 1990.

Krishna, Gopi. *Kundalini: The Evolutionary Energy in Man with psychological commentary by James Hillman.* Shambhala, 1985.

Krishnamurti, J., and David Bohm. *The Ending of Time.* Harper & Row, 1985.

Krishnaswami, O.R. *Open Your Heart to God Through Bhakti Yoga.* Integral Yoga Centre, 2006.

Kroger, Jane. *Identity Development: Adolescence Through Adulthood.* Sage Publications, Inc., 2000.

Kübler-Ross, Elisabeth. *Death: The Final Stage of Growth.* A Touchstone Book, 1986.

—. *On Death and Dying: What the Dying Have To Teach Doctors, Nurses, Clergy and Their Own Families.* Collier Books, 1970.

—. *Working It Through: An Elisabeth Kübler-Ross Workshop on Life, Death and Transition.* Collier Books, 1982.

Kübler-Ross, Elizabeth, and David Kessler. *Life Lessons: Two Experts on Death and Dying Teach Us About the Mysteries of Life and Living.* Scribner, 2000.

Küng, Hans. *The Catholic Church.* A Modern Library Chronicles Book, 2001.

LaBerge, Stephen. *Lucid Dreaming: The Power of Being Awake & Aware in Your Dreams.* Ballantine Books, 1985.

Laing, R.D. *The Divided Self: An Existential Study in Sanity and Madness.* Penguin Books, 1990.

Lake, Catherine Ann. *Linking Up: How the People in Your Life are Roadsigns to Self-Discovery.* The Donning Company, 1988.

Lammers, Willem. *Worte wirken Wunder: Selbstcoaching mit Logosynthese.* ias Verlag, 2008.

Landa, Friar Diego de. *Yucatan Before and After the Conquest.* San Fernando, 1991.

Landsberg, Max. *The Tao of Coaching.* HarperCollinsBusiness, 1997.

—. *The Tao of Motivation.* HarperCollinsBusiness, 2000.

—. *The Tools of Leadership.* HarperCollinsBusiness, 2000.

Lapham, Lewis H. *Money and Class In America: Notes and Observation on the Civil Religion.* Ballantine Books, 1988.

Larsen, Earnie. *From Anger to Forgiveness: A Practical Guide to Breaking the Negative Power of Anger and Achieving Reconciliation.* Hazelden Books, 1992.

Laszlo, Ervin, ed. *The Consciousness Revolution: A Translantic Dialogue: Two Days With Stanislav Grof, Ervin Laszlo and Peter Russell.* Element, 1999.

Laurie, Donald L. *The Real Work of Leaders.* Perseus Publishing, 2000.

Leeming, David Adams. *The World of Myth.* Oxford University Press, 1990.

Leeming, David, and Margaret Leeming. *A Dictionary of Creation Myths.* Oxford University Press, 1994.

Leiblum, Sandra, and Raymond C. Rosen. *Principles and Practice of Sex Therapy.* Edited by Sandra Leiblum and Raymond C. Rosen. The Guilford Press, 2000.

Leipprand, Eva. *Dornröschen und Eva: Zwei Seiten der Frau.* Walter-Verlag, 1989.

Lelord, François. *El Viaje de Hector: o el secreto de la felicidad.* Salamandra, 2003.

L'Engle, Madeleine. *A Wrinkle in Time.* Yearling, 1973.

Lenz, Frederick. *Lifetimes: True Accounts of Reincarnation.* Fawcett Crest, 1986.

Lenz, Friedel. *Bildsprache der Märchen.* Urachhaus, 1976.

Leonard, George, and Michael Murphy. *The Life We Are Given.* Jeremy P. Tarcher, 1995.

Leonard, Linda Schierse. *Meeting the Madwoman: An Inner Challenge for Feminine Spirit.* Bantam Books, 1993.

—. *On the Way To the Wedding: Transforming the Love Relationship.* Shambhala, 1987.

—. *The Wounded Woman: Healing the Father-Daughter Relationship.* Shambhala, 1983.

Levine, Barbara Hoberman. *Your Body Believes Every Word You Say: The Language of the Body/Mind Connection.* Aslan Publishing, 1991.

Levoy, Gregg. *Callings: Finding and Following an Authentic Life.* Three Rivers Press, 1998.

Lewis, C.S. *A Grief Observed.* Bantam Books, 1988.

—. *Mere Christianity.* HarperCollins, 1977.

—. *Miracles: How God Intervenes in Nature and Human Affairs.* Collier Books, 1978.

—. *The Narnia Chronicles.* Macmillan Publishing Co., 1950.

Lind-Kyle, Patt. *Heal Your Mind, Rewire Your Brain: Applying the Exciting New Science of Brain Synchrony for Creativity, Peace and Presence.* Energy Psychology Press, 2009.

Lindner, Robert. *The Fifty-Minute Hour: A Collection of True Psychoanalytic Tales.* A Delta Diamond, 1986.

Lipton, Bruce H. *The Biology of Belief: Unleashing the Power of Consciousness, Matter & Miracles.* Mountain of Love/Elite Books, 2005.

Lipton, Bruce H., and Steve Bhaerman. *Spontaneous Evolution: Our Positive Future (And a Way To Get There From Here)*. Hay House, Inc., 2009.

Locke, Steven, and Douglas Colligan. *El Médico Interior: La nueva medicina que revela la incidencia de la mente en nuestra salud y en el tratamiento de las enfermedades*. Editorial Sudamericana, 1991.

Lofthus, Myrna. *A Spiritual Approach to Astrology*. CRCS Publications, 1983.

Lowen, Alexander. *Bioenergetics: The Revolutionary Therapy That Uses the Language of the Body to Heal the Problems of the Mind*. Penguin, 1984.

—. *Love and Orgasm*. Collier Books, 1975.

—. *The Language of the Body: Physical Dynamics of Character Structure*. Collier, 1971.

Lubell, Winifred Milius. *The Metamorphosis of Baubo: Myths of Woman's Sexual Energy*. Vanderbilt University Press, 1994.

Lubicz, Isha Schwaller de. *The Opening of the Way: A Practical Guide to the Wisdom Teachings of Ancient Egypt*. Inner Traditions International, 1981.

Mack, Carol K., and Dinah Mack. *A Field Guide to Demons: Fairies, Fallen Angels, and other Subversive Spirits*. An Owl Book, 1998.

MacLaine, Shirley. *Dancing in the Light*. Bantam Books, 1986.

—. *Going Within: A Guide for Inner Transformation*. Bantam Books, 1989.

—. *It's All In the Playing*. Bantam Books, 1987.

—. *The Camino: A Journey of the Spirit*. Pocket Books, 2000.

—. *Zwischenleben*. Goldmann, 1985.

MacMullen, Ramsay. *Christianity & Paganism in the Fourth to Eighth Centuries*. Yale University Press, 1997.

Mahoney, Maria F. *The Meaning in Dreams and Dreaming: The Jungian Viewpoint*. Carol Publishing Group, 1991.

Malby, André. *Agape: Los jueves del señor G...* Enrique Marín, 1994.

—. *Una Horas en Marzo: Dichos y hechos del señor G...* Enrique Marin, 1997.

Maltz, Maxwell. *Psycho-Cybernetics*. Pocket Books, 1969.

Mandel, Bob. *Two Hearts Are Better Than One: A Handbook on Creating & Maintaining a Lasting & Loving Relationship*. Celestial Arts, 1986.

Mandela, Nelson. *Long Walk to Freedom, Vol. 2, 1962 - 1994*. London: Abacus, 2003.

Mandino, Og. *El Secreto más Grande del Mundo*. Editorial Diana, 1990.

Mann, Thomas. *Buddenbrooks: Verfall einer Familie*. S. Fischer Verlag, 1960.

—. *Der Zauberberg*. S. Fischer, 1952.

Mariechild, Diane. *Mother Wit: A Guide to Healing & Psychic Development*. The Crossing Press, 1988.

Marks, Tracy. *The Astrology of Self-Discovery*. CRCS Publications, 1985.

—. *Your Secret Self: Illuminating the Mysteries of the Telfth House*. CRCS Publications, 1989.

Márquez, Gabriel Garcia. *Cien Años de Soledad*. Editorial Sudamericana, 1970.

—. *El Amor en los tiempos del cólera*. Bruguera, 1985.

Márquez, M. Gómez. *La Atlántida de Piri Reis*. Martinez Roca, 1984.

Martin, Gerald. *Gabriel Garcia Marquez*. London: Bloomsbury, 2008.

Mascetti, Manuela Dunn. *The Song of Eve: An Illustrated Journey Into the Myths, Symbols, and Rituals of the Goddess.* A Fireside Book, 1990.

Maslow, Abraham H. *El Hombre Autorrealizado: Hacia una Psicología del Ser.* Kairos, 1987.

Masters, Robert. *Neurospeak: Transform Your Body While You Read!* Quest Books, 1994.

Matthews, Margli, Signe Schaefer, and Betty Staley. *Ariadne's Awakening: Taking Up the Threads of Consciousness.* The Mount, Whiteshill, Stroud, Gloucestershire: Hawthorn Press, 1986.

Mattoon, Mary Ann. *Understanding Dreams.* Spring Publications, Inc., 1984.

Maugham, W. Somerset. *A Writer's Notebook.* Penguin Books, 1967.

—. *Collected Short Stories Volume 3.* Penguin, 1967.

—. *Of Human Bondage.* Penguin, 1963.

—. *The Complete Short Stories of W. Somerset Maugham I: Rain & Other Stories.* Washington Square Press, 1968.

—. *The Razor's Edge.* Penguin Books, 1968.

—. *The Summing Up.* Penguin Books, 1971.

—. *Up At the Villa.* Penguin Books, 1967.

May, Rollo. *Love and Will.* Delta, 1989.

—. *The Courage to Create.* Bantam Books, 1985.

Mayer, Bernard. *Entombed: My True Story: How Forty-five Jews Lived Underground and Survived the Holocaust.* Ojus, FL: Aleric Press, 1994.

McTaggart, Lynne. *The Field: The Quest for the Secret Force of the Universe.* HarperCollinsPublishers, 2001.

—. *The Intention Experiment: Using Your Thoughts to Change Your Life and the World.* Free Press, 2007.

Medina, John. *Brain Rule: 12 Principles for Survivng and Thriving at Work, Home, and School.* Pear Press, 2008.

Mendelssohn, Kurt. *The Riddle of the Pyramids.* Thames and Hudson, 1989.

Merz, Blanche. *Points of Cosmic Energy.* Saffron Waldon, 1985.

Meurois-Givaudan, A. y D. *Viaje a Shambhala: Peregrinaje hacia si mismo.* Ediciones Luciérnaga, 1990.

Meyer, Marvin W., ed. *The Ancient Mysteries: A Sourcebook.* HarperSanFrancisco, 1987.

—. *The Secret Teachings of Jesus: Four Gnostic Gospels.* Vintage Books, 1986.

Meyer, Robert G. *Case Studies in Abnormal Behavior.* Allyn & Bacon, 1999.

Michener, James A. *Iberia.* Random House, 1968.

—. *The Source.* Fawcett Crest, 1967.

Middelton-Moz, Jane. *Children of Trauma: Rediscovering Your Discarded Self.* Health Communications, Inc., 1989.

Mill, John Stuart. *On Liberty.* The Library of Liberal Arts, 1956.

Miller, Alice. *For Your Own Good: Hidden Cruelty in Child-Rearing and the Roots of Violence.* Farrar, Straus, Giroux, 1989.

—. *The Untouched Key: Tracing Childhood Trauma in Creativity and Destructiveness.* Doubleday, 1990.

—. *Thou Shalt Not Be Aware: Society's Betrayal of the Child.* Meridian Book, 1986.

Miller, Carolyn. *Creating Miracles: Understanding the Experience of Divine Intervention.* H.J. Kramer Inc., 1995.

Miller, Geri. *Incorporating Spirituality in Counseling and Psychotherapy.* John Wlley & Sons, Inc., 2003.

Miller, Henry. *Big Sur und die Orangen des Hieronymus Bosch.* RoRoRo, 1966.

—. *Cartas a Anäis Nin.* Bruguera, 1981.

—. *Der Koloß von Maroussi: Eine Reise nach Griechenland.* RoRoRo, 1965.

—. *Land der Erinnerung (Remember to Remember).* RoRoRo, 1967.

—. *Nexus.* RoRoRo, 1970.

—. *Plexus.* RoRoRo, 1970.

—. *The Air-Conditioned Nightmare.* New Directions, 1945.

—. *The Books in My Life.* New York: New Directions Publishing, 1969.

—. *The Cosmological Eye.* Editions Poetry London, 1945.

—. *The Red Notebook.* Jargon, 1971.

—. *Tropic of Capricorn.* Grove Press, Inc., 1961.

Miller, William R., ed. *Integrating Spirituality Into Treatment.* American Psychological Association, 1999.

Millman, Dan. *No Ordinary Moments.* H.J. Kramer, Inc., 1972.

—. *The Life You Were Born to Live: A Guide to Finding Your Life Purpose.* H.J. Kramer, Inc., 1993.

Millon, Theodore, Morten Birket-Smith, Erik Simonsen, and Roger D. Davis. *Psychopathy: Antisocial, Criminal, and Violent Behavior.* Edited by Theodore Millon, Morten Birket-Smith Erik Simonsen and Roger D. Davis. The Guilford Press, 1998.

Milz, Helmut. *Der wiederentdeckte Körper: Vom schöperischen Umgang mit sich selbst.* dtv, 1994.

Mindell, Arnold. *Dreambody: The Body's Role in Revealing the Self.* Routledge & Kegan Paul, 1984.

Mitchell, James E. *Points of View: Stories of Psychopathology.* Brunner-Routledge, 2001.

Mitchell, John. *Nueva visión sobre la Atlántida.* Martinez Roca, 1987.

Modi, Shakuntala. *Remarkable Healings: A Psychiatrist Discovers Unsuspected Roots of Mental and Physical Illness.* Hampton Roads, 1997.

Moffatt, Gregory K. *Wounded Innocents and Fallen Angels: Child Abuse and Child Aggression.* Praeger, 2003.

Monick, Eugene. *Phallos: Sacred Image of the Masculine.* Toronto: Inner City Books, 1987.

Monroe, Robert A. *Far Journeys.* Doubleday, 1985.

—. *Ultimate Journey.* Doubleday, 1994.

Montgomery, Ruth. *Companions Along the Way.* Fawcett Crest, 1986.

—. *Threshold to Tomorrow.* Ballantine, 1984.

Moody, Jr., Raymond. *The Light Beyond.* Bantam Books, 1989.

Moody, Raymond A. *Life After Life.* Stackpole Books, 1976.

—. *Reencuentros: Contactos Con Los Seres Queridos Tras Su Muerte.* EDAF, 1994.

—. *Reflections on Life After Life.* Stackpole books, 1977.

—. *The Last Laugh: A New Philosophy of Near-Death Experiences, Apparitions, and the Paranormal.* Hampton Roads, 1999.

Moon, Sheila. *Dreams of a Woman: An Analyst's Inner Journey.* Sigo Press, 1983.

Moore, Robert, and Douglas Gillette. *King, Warrior, Magician, Lover: Rediscovering the Archetype of the Mature Masculine.* HarperSanFrancisco, 1991.

Moore, Thomas. *A Life at Work: The Joy of Discovering What You Were Born To Do.* Broadway Books, 2008.

—. *Care of the Soul: A Guide For Cultivating Depth and Sacredness in Everyday Life.* New York: HarperCollins, 1992.

—. *Dark Nights of the Soul: A Guide to Finding Your Way Through Life's Ordeals.* New York: Gotham Books, 2004.

—. *Original Self: Living With Paradox and Originality.* HarperCollinsPublishers, 2000.

—. *Soul Mates: Honoring the Mysteries of Love and Relationship.* New York: HarperCollins, 1994.

Morgan, Elaine. *The Descent of Woman.* Stein & Day, 1985.

Morgan, Marlo. *Mutant Message Down Under.* HarperCollinsPublishers, 1994.

Morse, Melvin, and Paul Perry. *Closer to the Light: Learning From the Near-Death Experiences of Children.* Ballantine, 1991.

Mortenson, Greg, and David Oliver Relin. *Three Cups of Tea: One Man's Mission to Promote Peace ... One School at a Time.* London: Penguin Books, 2007.

Moss, Richard. *The I That is We: Awakening to Higher Energies Through Unconditional Love.* Celestial Arts, 1981.

Moss, Robert. *Dreaming True: How to Dream Your Future and Change Your Life For the Better.* Pocket Books, 2000.

Moyers, Bill. *Healing and the Mind.* New York: Doubleday, 1993.

Muktananda, Swami. *El Misterio de la Mente.* Fundación SYDA, 1981.

—. *Kundalini: The Secret of Life.* Syda Foundation, 1990.

Murdock, Maureen. *The Heroine's Journey.* Shambhala, 1990.

Myss, Caroline. *Anatomy of the Spirit: The Seven Stages of Power and Healing.* Harmony Books, 1996.

—. *Defy Gravity: Healing Beyond the Bounds of Reason.* Hay House, 2009.

—. *Sacred Contracts: Awakening Your Divine Potential.* Harmony Books, 2001.

—. *Why People Don't Heal and How They Can.* Three Rivers Press, 1997.

Myss, Caroline, and C. Norman Shealy. *The Creation of Health: The Emotional, Psychological and Spiritual Responses that Promote Health and Healing.* Bantam Books, 1993.

Naparestek, Belleruth. *Your Sixth Sense.* HarperSanFrancisco, 1997.

Nathanson, Donald L. *Shame and Pride: Affect, Sex, and the Birth of the Self.* New York: W.W. Norton & Company, 1992.

Neidhöfer, Loil. *Intuitive Körperarbeit.* Transform Verlag, 1993.

Nelson, Ruby. *The Door of Everything.* deVorss, 1972.

Neruda, Pablo. *Veinte Poemas de Amor y una Cancion Desesperada.* Barcelona: Seix Barral - Biblioteca Breve, 1985.

Nesbitt, Edith. *Five Children and It.*

—. *The Phoenix and the Carpet.*

Netherton, Morris, and Nancy Shiffrin. *Bericht vom Leben vor dem Leben: Reinkarnationstherapie: Ein neuer Weg in die Tiefe der Seele.* Ullstein, 1987.

Neumann, Erich. *Amor and Psyche: The Psychic Development of the Feminine - A Commentary on the Tale by Apuleius.* Princeton: Princeton University Press, 1973.

—. *Depth Psychology and a New Ethic.* Shambhala, 1990.

—. *The Child.* Shambhala, 1990.

—. *The Great Mother: An Analysis of the Archetype.* Bollingen Series - Princeton University Press, 1974.

—. *The Origins and History of Consciousness.* Bollingen Series, 1973.

Neville, Katherine. *The Eight.* Ballantine Books, 1988.

Newton, Michael. *Destiny of Souls: New Case Studies of Life Between Lives.* Llewellyn Publications, 2001.

—. *Journey of Souls: Case Studies of Life Between Lives.* Llewellyn Publications, 1996.

Nicholson, Shirley, ed. *The Goddess Re-Awakening: The Feminine Principle Today.* Quest books, 1989.

Nickell, Molli, ed. *Life Before, During & After.* Spirit Speaks, Inc., 1988.

Nietzsche, Friedrich. *Also sprach Zarathustra.* Kröner, 1941.

—. *El Anticristo.* Alianza, 1981.

—. *El nacimiento de la tragedia.* Alianza, 1980.

Nin, Anäis. *The Diary of Anäis Nin: Volume 1: 1931 - 1934.* Harcourt, Brace, and World, Inc., 1966.

—. *The Diary of Anäis Nin: Volume 2: 1934 - 1939.* Edited by Gunther Stuhlman. Harcourt, Brace & World, 1967.

—. *The Diary of Anäis Nin: Volume 5: 1947 - 1955.* Edited by Gunther Stuhlmann. Harcourt Brace Jovanovich, 1974.

—. *The Diary of Anäis Nin: Volume 6: 1955 - 1966.* Edited by Gunther Stuhlman. Harcourt Brace Jovanovich, 1976.

Nola, Alfonso M. di. *Historia del Diablo.* EDAF, 1992.

Nolle, Richard. *Chiron: The New Planet in Your Horoscope, The Key to Your Quest.* AFA, 1983.

Noorbergen, Rene. *Nostradamus.* Pinnacle Books, 1982.

Novak, Philip. *The World's Wisdom: Sacred Texts of the World's Religions.* Castle Books, 1994.

NurrieStearns, Rick, Mary NurrieStearns, and Melissa West. *Soulful Living: The Process of Personal Transformation.* Edited by Rick NurrieStearns, Mary NurrieStearns and Melissa West. Health Communications, Inc., 1999.

Nydahl, Lama Ole. *Vom Reichtum des Geistes: Buddhistische Inspirationen.* Knaur, 2006.

Obama, Barack. *Dreams From My Father.* New York: Three Rivers Press, 1995.

O'Flaherty, Wendy Doniger. *Dreams, Illusion and Other Realities.* The University of Chicago Press, 1984.

Orban, Peter. *Pluto: Über den Dämon im Inneren der eigenen Seele.* RoRoRo, 1989.

Oriah, Mountain Dreamer. *The Invitation.* Element, 2005.

Orloff, Judith. *Dr. Judith Orloff's Guide to Intuitive Healing.* Times Books, 2000.

—. *Second Sight.* Warner Books, 1996.

Ornish, Dean. *The Spectrum.* Ballantine Books, 2007.

Orr, Leonard. *El Sentido Común de la Inmortalidad Física.* Ediciones CS.

Orr, Leonard, and Sondra Ray. *Rebirthing in the New Age.* Celestial Arts, 1983.

Orynski, Wanda, ed. *Hegel: Highlights, An Annotated Selection.* Wisdom Library, 1960.

Osman, Ahmed. *Extranjero en el Valle de los Reyes.* Planeta, 1988.

—. *Moisés, faraón de Egipto.* Planeta, 1992.

Ouspensky, P.D. *The Fourth Way.* Vintage Books, 1971.

Pagels, Elaine. *Adam, Eve, and the Serpent.* Vintage Books, 1989.

—. *The Gnostic Gospels.* Penguin Books, 1982.

—. *The Origin of Satan.* Vintage Books, 1996.

Paul, Haydn. *Revolutionary Spirit: Exploring the Astrological Uranus.* Element Books, 1989.

—. *Visionary Dreamer: Exploring the Astrological Neptune.* Element Books, 1989.

Pearl, Eric. *The Reconnection: Heal Others, Heal Yourself.* Hay House Inc., 2001.

Pearson, Carol. *The Hero Within: Six Archetypes We Live By.* Harper & Row, 1986.

Peat, F. David. *Synchronicity: The Bridge Between Matter and Mind.* Bantam, 1988.

Peck, M. Scott. *Further Along the Road Less Traveled: The Unending Journey Toward Spiritual Growth.* Simon & Schuster, 1993.

—. *People of the Lie: The Hope For Healing Human Evil.* Touchstone, 1983.

—. *The Road Less Traveled: A New Psychology of Love, Traditional Values and Spiritual Growth.* Touchstone, 1978.

Peissel, Michel. *El Mundo Perdido de los Mayas: Exploraciones y Aventuras en Quintana Roo.* Editorial Juventud, 1981.

Peradejordi, Julio. *El libro de Toth: Orígen, simbolismo e interpretación de los Arcanos del tarot.* Ediciones Obelisco, 1981.

Pert, Candace. *Molecules of Emotion: Why You Feel the Way You Feel.* Pocket Books, 1999.

Petrinovich, Toni Sar'h. *The Call: Awakening the Angelic Human.* Xlibris, 2002.

Phares, Vicky. *Understanding Abnormal Child Psychology.* John Wiley & Sons, Inc.

Phillips, Maggie. *Finding the Energy to Heal: How EMDR, Hypnosis, TFT, Imagery, and Body-Focused Therapy Can Help Restore Mindbody Health.* W.W. Norton & Company, 2000.

Phylos, the Thibetan. *A Dweller on Two Planets or The Dividing of the Way.* Harper & Row, 1974.

Pierrakos, Eva. *The Pathwork of Self-Transformation.* Bantam Books, 1990.

Pipher, Mary. *Reviving Ophelia: Saving the Selves of Adolescent Girls.* G.P. Putnam's Sons, 1994.

Poitier, Sidney. *The Measure of a Man: A Spiritual Autobiography.* New York: HarperSanFrancisco, 2000.

Polis, Ben. *Only a Mother Could Love Him: My Life With and Triumph Over ADD.* Ballantine Books, 2001.

Poncé, Charles. *Working the Soul: Reflections on Jungian Psychology.* North Atlantic Books, 1988.

Praagh, James van. *Healing Grief: Reclaiming Life After Any Loss.* Dutton, 2000.

—. *Reaching to Heaven: A Spiritual Journey Through Life and Death.* Dutton, 1999.

—. *Talking to Heaven: A Medium's Message of Life After Death.* Dutton, 1997.

Prather, Hugh. *Notes To Myself: My Struggle to Become a Person.* Bantam, 1990.

Prather, Hugh, and Gayle Prather. *Notes to Each Other.* Bantam Books, 1990.

Prozan, Charlotte, ed. *Construction and Reconstruction of Memory: Dilemmas of Childhood Sexual Abuse.* Jason Aronson Inc, 1997.

Qualls-Corbett, Nancy. *The Sacred Prostitute: Eternal Aspect of the Feminine.* Toronto: Inner City Books, 1988.

Quinn, Daniel. *Ishmael: An Adventure of the Mind and Spirit.* A Bantam / Turner Book, 1993.

Radice, Betty, ed. *The Bhagavad Gita.* Penguin Books, 1988.

Raffay, Anita von. *Abschied vom Helden: Das Ende einer Faszination.* Walter-Verlag, 1989.

Ramos, Jorge. *Atravesando Fronteras: Un Periodista en Busca de Su Lugar en el Mundo.* New York: Rayo, 2002.

Rampa, Lopsang. *Feeding the Flame.* Corgi Books, 1971.

—. *Living with the Lama.* Corgi Books, 1973.

—. *The Thirteenth Candle.* Corgi Books, 1973.

—. *Twilight.* Corgi Books, 1975.

—. *Wisdom of the Ancients.* Corgi Books, 1974.

Rand, Ayn. *Atlas Shrugged.* New American Library, 1970.

—. *The Fountainhead.* New American Library, 1971.

Ratey, John J., and Catherine Johnson. *Shadow Syndromes: The Mild Forms of Major Mental Disorders That Sabotage Us.* Bantam, 1998.

Ray, Barbara. *The 'Reiki' Factor.* Radiance Associates, 1988.

Ray, Sondra. *Celebration of Breath.* Celestial Arts, 1986.

—. *I Deserve Love.* Celestial Arts, 1976.

—. *Loving Relationships.* Celestial Arts, 1980.

—. *The Only Diet There Is.* Celestial Arts, 1981.

Ray, Sondra, and Bob Mandel. *Birth & Relationships: How Your Birth Affects Your Relationships.* Celestial Arts, 1987.

Redfield, James. *The Celestine Prophecy: An Adventure.* Warner Books, 1993.

—. *The Tenth Insight: Holding the Vision.* Warner Books, 1996.

Reinhart, Melanie. *Chiron and the Healing Journey: An Astrological and Psychological Perspective.* Arkana, 1989.

Rich, Adrienne. *Of Woman Born: Motherhood As Experience and Institution.* W.W. Norton & Company, 1976.

Rijckenborgh, J. van, and Catharose de Petri. *Die Grosse Umwälzung.* Eckstein, 1980.

Rilke, Rainer Maria. *Cartas a un joven poeta.* Alianza Tres, 1979.

Rinpoche, Sogyal. *The Tibetan Book of Living and Dying.* HarperSanFrancisco, 1994.

Robbins, Anthony. *Awaken the Giant Within.* A Fireside Book, 1992.

—. *Notes From A Friend.* A Fireside Book, 1995.

—. *Unlimited Power.* Fawcett Columbine, 1987.

Roberts, Jane. *Die Natur der Psyche: Ihr menschlicher Ausdruck in Kreativität, Liebe, und Sexualität*. Goldmann, 1987.
—. *Oversoul Seven and the Museum of Time*. Prentice Hall, 1986.
—. *Seth Speaks: The Eternal Validity of the Soul*. Prentice Hall, 1972.
—. *Seth: Dreams and Projection of Consciousness*. Stillpoint Publishing, 1987.
—. *The Afterdeath Journal of an American Philosopher: The World View of William James*. Prentice Hall, 1978.
—. *The Education of Oversoul Seven*. Prentice Hall, 1983.
—. *The Further Education of Oversoul Seven*. Prentice Hall, 1986.
Roddick, Anita. *Business As Usual: The Journey of Anita Roddick and The Body Shop*. London: Thorsons, 2000.
Rogers, Carl R. *A Way of Being*. Houghton Mifflin Company, 1980.
Rolf, Eric. *La Medicina del Alma*. Colleccion Terapion, 1997.
Romer, John. *Los últimos secretos del Valle de los Reyes: Una singular aventure arqueológica*. 1983.
Rosen, Raymond C., and Sandra R. Leiblum. *Case Studies in Sex Therapy*. Edited by Raymond C. Rosen and Sandra R. Leiblum. The Guilford Press, 1995.
Ross, Julia. *The Mood Cure: The 4-Step Program to Rebalance Your Emotional Chemistry and Rediscover Your Natural Sense of Well-Being*. Viking, 2002.
Roth, Cecil. *La Inquisición española*. Ediciones Martínez Roca, 1989.
Rothberg, Donald, and Sean Kelly. *Ken Wilber in Dialogue: Conversations With Leading Transpersonal Thinkers*. Edited by Donald Rothberg and Sean Kelly. Quest Books, 1998.
Rothschild, Joel. *Signals: An Inspiring Story of Life After Life*. New World Library, 2000.
Royal, Lyssa. *Millennium: Tools for the Coming Changes*. Royal Priest Research Press, 1997.
Rubenfeld, Ilana. *The Listening Hand: Self-Healing Through the Rubenfeld Synergy Method of Talk and Touch*. Bantam Books, 2000.
Rubin, Lillian. *The Transcendent Child: Tales of Triumph Over the Past*. Basic Books, 1996.
—. *Worlds of Pain: Life in the Working-Class Family*. Basic Books, Inc., 1976.
Rubin, Peggy. *To Be and How To Be: Transforming Your Life Through Sacred Theatre*. Quest Books, 2010.
Rubner, Jeanne. *Was Frauen und Männer so im Kopf haben*. Deutscher Taschenbuch Verlag, 1996.
Rucker, Rudy. *The Fourth Dimension and How To Get There*. Penguin Books, 1988.
Rudhyar, Dane. *Astrology and the Modern Psyche*. CRCS Publications, 1976.
—. *Person Centered Astrology*. Aurora Press, 1980.
—. *The Astrological Houses: The Spectrum of Individual Experience*. Doubleday, 1972.
—. *Un Mandala Astrológico: El Ciclo de las Transformaciones y sus 360 fases simbólicas*. Luis Cárcamo, 1984.
Ruperti, Alexander. *Cycles of Becoming: The Planetary Pattern of Growth*. CRCS Publications, 1978.

—. *La rueda de la experiencia individual.* Luis Cárcamo, 1986.

Russell, Bertrand. *La Conquista de la Felicidad.* Selecciones Austral, 1978.

Russell, Peter. *The TM Technique: An Introduction to Transcendental Meditation and the Teachings of Maharishi Mahesh Yogi.* Arkana, 1978.

Russo, Richard A., ed. *Dreams Are Wiser Than Men.* North Atlantic Books, 1967.

Rýzl, Milan. *Der Tod und was danach kommt: Das Weiterleben aus der Sicht der Parapsychologie.* Goldmann, 1981.

Sacks, Oliver. *The Man Who Mistook His Wife For a Hat.* New York: Perennial Library, 1987.

Saint-Exupéry, Antoine de. *The Little Prince.* Harcourt, 1971.

Salomé, Lou Andreas. *Mirada Retrospectiva.* Madrid: Alianza Tres, 1981.

Sanford, John A. *The Invisible Partners: How the Male and Female in Each of Us Affects our Relationships.* Paulist Press, 1980.

Sanford, John A., and George Lough. *What Men Are Like: The Psychology of Men.* Paulist Press, 1988.

Sanford, Linda Tschirhart, and Mary Ellen Donovan. *Women & Self-Esteem: Understanding and Improving the Way We Think and Feel About Ourselves.* Penguin Books, 1985.

Sasportas, Howard. *Las Doce Casas.* Ediciones Urano, S.A., 1987.

—. *The Gods of Change: Pain, Crisis and the Transits of Uranus, Neptune and Pluto.* Arkana, 1989.

Scheffler, Lilian. *Magia y brujería en México.* Panorama, 1992.

Schellenbaum, Peter. *Abschied von der Selbstverstörung: Befreiung der Lebensenergie.* dtv, 1990.

—. *Nimm deine Couch und geh! Heilung mit Spontanritualen.* Kösel, 1992.

Schmid, Mavis. *Living Proof: Surviving Five Primary Cancers.* London: Rudling House, 2009.

Schnarch, David. *Constructing the Sexual Crucible: An Integration of Sexual and Marital Therapy.* W.W. Norton & Company, 1991.

—. *Passionate Marriage: Keeping Love & Intimacy Alive in Committed Relationships.* An Owl Book, 1997.

Schreiber, Flora Rheta. *Sybil.* New York: Warner Paperback Library, 1974.

Schulman, Martin. *Karmic Astrology: Joy and the Part of Fortune, Volume III.* Samuel Weiser, Inc., 1988.

—. *Karmic Astrology: Retrogrades and Reincarnation, Volume II.* Samuel Weiser, Inc., 1989.

—. *Karmic Astrology: The Karma of the Now, Volume IV.* Samuel Weiser, Inc., 1989.

—. *Karmic Astrology: The Moon's Nodes and Reincarnation, Volume I.* Samuel Weiser, Inc., 1990.

Schulz, Mona Lisa. *Awakening Intuition: Using Your Mind-Body Network For Insight and Healing.* Three Rivers Press, 1998.

Schwartz, David J. *The Magic of Thnking Big.* A Fireside Book, 1987.

Schwartz, Gary E., and William L. Simon. *The Afterlife Experiments: Breakthrough Scientific Evidence of Life After Death.* Pocket Books, 2002.

Schwartz, Gary E.R., and Linda G.S. Russek. *The Living Energy Universe: A Fundamental Discovery That Transforms Science & Medicine.* Hampton Roads, 1999.

Schwartz, Robert. *Your Soul's Plan: Discovering the Real Meaning of the Life You Planned Before You Were Born.* Whispering Winds Press, 2007.

Scolastico, Ron. *Doorway to the Soul.* Pocket Books, 1997.

Scott, Cyril. *Der Eingeweihte: Eindrücke einer grossen Seele Band 1.* Knaur, 1985.

—. *Der Eingeweihte: Eindrücke einer grossen Seele Band 2.* Knaur, 1986.

Scouézec, Gwen Le. *Cartomancia y Quiromancia.* Ediciones Martinez Roca, 1974.

Scovel-Shinn, Florence. *El Juego de la Vida y cómo jugarlo.* Tomo Dos, 1992.

—. *The Writings of Florence Scovel Shinn.* DeVorss, 1996.

Secunda, Victoria. *Women and Their Fathers: The Sexual and Romantic Impact of the First Man in Your Life.* New York: Delacorte Press, 1992.

Sède, Gérard de. *El Tesoro Cátaro.* Plaza y Janes, 1976.

Segal, Robert A. *Joseph Campbell: An Introduction.* A Mentor Book, 1990.

Sepúlveda, María Teresa. *Magia, brujería y supersticiones en México.* Editorial Everest S.A., 1983.

Shapiro, Francine, and Margot Silk Forrest. *EMDR: Eye Movement Desensitization & Reprocessing: The Breakthrough "Eye Movement" Therapy For Overcoming Anxiety, Stress, and Trauma.* Basic Books, 1997.

Sharma, Robin. *The Leader Who Had No Title: A Modern Fable on Real Success in Business and in Life.* Simon & Schuster, 2010.

Sharp, Kimberly Clark. *After the Light: What I Discovered on the Other Side of Life That Can Change Your World.* William Morrow, 1995.

Sheehy, Gail. *New Passages: Mapping Your Life Across Time.* Random House, 1995.

—. *Passages.* Bantam Books, 1976.

—. *Pathfinders: Overcoming the Crises of Adult Life and Finding Your Own Path to Well-Being.* Bantam Books, 1985.

—. *Understanding Men's Passages: Discovering the New Map of Men's Lives.* Random House, 1998.

Sheldrake, Rupert. *A New Science of Life: The Hypothesis of Morphic Resonance.* Park Street Press, 1995.

Siegel, Alan B. *Dreams That Can Change Your Life: Navigating Life's Passages Through Turning Point Dreams.* Berkley Books, 1996.

Siegel, Bernie S. *Love, Medicine & Miracles: Lessons Learned About Self-Healing From a Surgeon's Experience With Exceptional Patients.* Harper Perennial, 1990.

Siegel, Daniel J. *Mindsight: The New Science of Personal Transformation.* Bantam Books, 2010.

—. *The Mindful Therapist.* W.W. Norton & Company, 2010.

Siegel, Daniel J., and Mary Hartzell. *Parenting from the Inside Out: How A Deeper Slef-Understanding Can Help You Raise Children Who Thrive.* Jeremy P. Tarcher, 2004.

Signell, Karen A. *Wisdom of the Heart: Working With Women's Dreams.* Bantam Books, 1990.

Silverman, Marcus. *La pirámide sumergida en el Triángulo de las Bermudas.* Martinez Roca, 1984.

Silverstein, Olga, and Beth Rashbaum. *The Courage to Raise Good Men.* Viking, 1994.

Sinetar, Marsha. *To Build the Life You Want, Create the Work You Love: The Spiritual Dimension of Entrepreneuring.* St. Martin's Griffin, 1995.

Singer, June. *Androgyny: The Opposites Within.* Sigo Press, 1989.

—. *Boundaries of the Soul: The Practice of Jung's Psychology.* Anchor Books, 1973.

—. *Love's Energies.* Sigo Press, 1990.

Sitchin, Zecharia. *El Libro Perdido de Enki.* Ediciones Obelisco, 2003.

—. *The 12th Planet.* Avon Books, 1978.

—. *The Lost Realms.* Avon Books, 1990.

Sjöö, Monica, and Barbara Mor. *The Great Cosmic Mother: Rediscovering the Religon of the Earth.* Harper & Row, 1987.

Skogemann, Pia. *Weiblichkeit und Selbstverwirklichung: Die Individuation der Frau heute.* Kösel, 1988.

Sokoloff, Arthur. *Life Without Stress: The Far Eastern Antidote to Tension and Anxiety.* Broadway Books, 1997.

Solotaroff, Paul. *Group: Six People in Search of a Life.* Berkley Books, 2000.

Spence, Lewis. *Ancient Egyptian Myths and Legends.* Dover Publications, Inc., 1990.

Spiegelman, J. Marvin. *The Quest: Further Adventures in the Unconscious.* Phoenix, Arizona: Falcon Press, 1984.

Spreads, Carola. *Ways to Better Breathing.* Healing Arts Press, 1992.

Sri, Aurobindo. *Renacimiento y Karma: El problema de la reencarnación.* Plaza y Janes, 1989.

Steiger, Brad & Francie. *Discover Your Past Lives.* Whitford Press, 1987.

Stein, Diane. *Stroking the Python: Women's Psychic Lives, Awakening to the Power Within.* Llewellyn Publications, 1988.

Stein, Murray, ed. *Jungian Analysis.* Shambhala, 1985.

Steinem, Gloria. *Revolution From Within: A Book of Self-Esteem.* Little, Brown, and Company, 1992.

Steiner, Rudolf. *Reincarnation and Immortality.* Harper & Row, 1980.

Sternberg, Esther. *The Balance Within: The Science Connecting Health and Emotions.* W.H. Freeman & Co., 2001.

Stibal, Vianna. *Theta Healing.* Rolling Thunder Publishing, 2007.

Stone, Merlin. *When God Was A Woman.* Harcourt, Brace, Jovanovich Publishers, 1976.

Stone, W. Clement. *El Sistema Infalible Para Triunfar.* Grijalbo, 1982.

Storr, Anthony. *Solitude: A Return To the Self.* Ballantine Books, 1988.

—. *The Art of Psychotherapy.* Routledge, 1980.

Strauch, Ralph. *The Reality Illusion: How You Make the World You Experience.* Station Hill Press, 1989.

Streep, Peg. *Sanctuaries of the Goddess: The Sacred Landscapes and Objects.* Little, Brown and Company, 1994.

Styron, William. *Sophie's Choice.* Random House, 1979.

Sullivan, Erin. *Saturn in Transit: Boundaries of Mind, Body and Soul.* Arkana, 1991.

—. *Venus and Jupiter.* CPA, 1996.

Sutphen, Dick. *Earthly Purpose: The Incredible True Story of a Group Reincarnation.* Pocket Books, 1990.

—. *Lighting the Light Within.* Valley of the Sun Publishing, 1987.

Sutphen, Dick, and Tara Sutphen. *Soul Agreements.* Hampton Roads, 2005.

Suzuki, D.T. *Introducción al Budismo Zen.* Editorial Mensajero, 1972.

Szabó, Zoltán. *Astrologie der Wandlung: Der Weg zur Gralsburg im Horoskop.* Hugendubel, 1985.

Szekely, Edmond Bordeaux, ed. *The Gospel of the Essenes.* Saffron Walden, 1988.

Tagore, Rabindranath T. *El Jardinero.* Madrid: Ediciones Felmar, 1981.

Taleb, Nassim Nicholas. *The Black Swan: The Impact of the Highly Improbable.* Penguin Books, 2007.

Tannen, Deborah. *You Just Don't Understand: Women and Men in Conversation.* Ballantine Books, 1990.

Tarnas, Richard. *The Passion of the Western Mind: Understanding the Ideas That Have Shaped Our World View.* Pimlico, 1996.

Taylor, Jeremy. *Dream Work: Techniques for Discovering the Creative Power in Dreams.* Paulist Press, 1983.

—. *Where People Fly and Water Runs Uphill: Using Dreams to Tap the Wisdom of the Unconscious.* Warner Books, 1993.

Tenberken, Sabriye. *My Path Leads To Tibet: The Inspiring Story of How One Young Blind Woman Brought Hope to the Blind Children of Tibet.* New York: Arcade Publishing, 2003.

Terr, Leone. *Unchained Memories: True Stories of Traumatic Memories, Lost and Found.* Basic Books, 1994.

Terzani, Tiziano. *Das Ende is mein Anfang: Ein Vater, ein Sohn und die grosse Reise des Lebens.* München: Spiegel Buchverlag, 2007.

Thornton, Peggy. *Synastry: A Comprehensive Guide to the Astrology of Relationships.* The Aquarian Press, 1983.

Tick, Edward. *The Practice of Dream Healing: Bringing Ancient Greek Mysteries into Modern Medicine.* Quest Books, 2001.

Tiller, William A. *Science and Human Transformation: Subtle Energies, Intentionality and Consciousness.* Pavior, 1997.

Timms, Moira. *Zeiger der Apokalypse: Hermageddon und neues Zeitalter.* Knaur, 1979.

Tolle, Eckhart. *A New Earth: Awakening to Your Life's Purpose.* A Plume Book, 2006.

—. *The Power of Now: A Guide to Spiritual Enlightenment.* New World Library, 1999.

Tompkins, Peter. *Secretos de la Gran Piramide.* Diana, 1990.

Toynbee, Arnold, and Arthur Koestler. *La Vida Después de la Muerte.* Edhasa, 1980.

Tracy, Brian. *Maximum Achievement.* Simon & Schuster, 1993.

Travers, P.L. *Mary Poppins.* Harcourt Brace Jovanovich, 1962.

—. *Mary Poppins Comes Back.* Harcourt Brace Jovanovich, 1963.

Tres, Iniciados. *El Kybalion: Estudio sobre la Filosofía Hermética del Antiguo Egipto y Grecia.* EDAF, 1983.

Tresidder, Jack. *Dictionary of Symbols: An Illustrated Guide to Traditional Images, Icons, and Emblems.* Chronicle Books, 1997.

Trungpa, Chögyam, and Herbert V. Guenther. *El Amanecer del Tantra.* Kairós, 1982.

Tuby, Molly, ed. *In the Wake of Jung.* London, Coventure, Ltd., 1986.

Twyman, James F. *Emissary of Love: The Psychic Children Speak to the World.* Hampton Roads, 2002.

Ullman, Montague, and Claire Limmer. *The Variety of Dream Experience.* Edited by Monatague Ullman and Claire Limmer. Continuum, 1988.

Ullman, Montague, and Nan Zimmerman. *Working With Dreams: Self-Understanding, Problem-Solving, and Enriched Creativity Through Dream Appreciation.* Jeremy P. Tarcher, 1979.

Utset, L. *Los grandes iniciados: ENOC.* Libro Exprés, 1982.

Vanzant, Iyanla. *In the Meantime.* Fireside, 1999.

Varenne, Jean. *El Tantrismo o la sexualidad sagrada.* Kairós, 1985.

Vaughan, Alan. *Incredible Coincidence: The Baffling World of Synchronicity.* Ballantine, 1979.

Velikovsky, Immanuel. *Welten im Zusammenstoss: Als die Sonne still stand.* Europa Verlag, 1959.

Verny, Thomas, and John Kelly. *The Secret Life of the Unborn Child: How you can prepare your unborn baby for a happy, healthy life.* Delta, 1981.

Waitley, Denis. *Empires of the Mind.* William Morrow & Co., Inc., 1995.

—. *Seeds of Greatness.* Pocket Books, 1984.

Walker, Barbara G. *The Crone: Woman of Age, Wisdom, and Power.* Perennial Library, 1985.

—. *The Woman's Dictionary of Symbols & Sacred Objects.* Harper & Row, 1988.

—. *The Woman's Encyclopedia of Myths and Secrets.* HarperSanFrancisco, 1983.

Walker, Sydney. *A Dose of Sanity.* John Wiley & Sons, 1996.

Wallerstein, Judith, and Sandra Blakeslee. *Second Chances: Men, Women, and Children a Decade After Divorce.* Ticknor & Fields, 1990.

Walls, Jeanette. *The Glass Castle: A Memoir.* New York: Scribner, 2005.

Walsch, Neale Donald. *Conversations with God: An Uncommon Dialogue Book 1.* G.P. Putnam's Sons, 1996.

—. *Conversations with God: An Uncommon Dialogue Book 2.* Hampton Roads, 1997.

—. *Conversations with God: An Uncommon Dialogue Book 3.* Hampton Roads, 1998.

—. *Home With God In a Life That Never Ends.* Hodder Mobius, 2007.

—. *The New Revelations: A Conversation with God.* Hodder Mobius, 2003.

—. *When Everything Changes Change Everything: In a Time of Turmoil, a Pathway to Peace.* Hodder & Stoughton, 2009.

Walsh, Roger. *Essential Spirituality: The 7 Central Practices to Awaken Heart and Mind.* John Wiley & Sons, 1999.

Waltari, Mika. *Sinuhe, the Egyptian.* Putnam, 1953.

Wambach, Helen. *Vida Antes de la Vida.* EDAF, 1979.

Watkins, Mary. *Waking Dreams.* Spring Publications, Inc., 1986.

Watts, Alan. *El futuro del éxtasis y otras meditaciones.* Kairós, 1981.

—. *El libro del Tabú.* Kairós, 1979.

—. *Om: La sílaba sagrada.* Kairós, 1981.

Wawro, James. *Ask Your Inner Voice: Conscious Communication With the Truth Within.* Ozark Mountain Publishing, 2010.

Weed, Joseph J. *Wisdom of the Mystic Masters.* Parker Publishing Co., Inc., 1987.

Wehr, Gerhard. *Carl Gustav Jung: Leben, Werk, Wirkung.* Zürich: Diogenes, 1988.

—. *Heilige Hochzeit: Symbol und Erfahrung menschlicher Reifung.* Kösel, 1986.

Weinberg, George, and Dianne Rowe. *The Projection Principle*. St. Martin's Press, 1988.

Weiss, Brian L. *Many Lives, Many Masters*. Fireside, 1988.

—. *Mirrors of Time: Using Regression for Physical, Emotional and Spiritual Healing*. Hay House, 2002.

—. *Same Soul, Many Bodies*. Free Press, 2004.

Weiss, Jean Claude, and Verena Bachmann. *Pluto: Das Erotische und Dämonische*. Edition Astrodata, 1989.

Wenar, Charles. *Developmental Psychopathology*. McGraw-Hill, Inc., 1994.

West, John Anthony. *Serpent in the Sky: The High Wisdom of Ancient Egypt*. Quest Books, 1993.

White, John, ed. *La Experiencia Mística y los Estados de Conciencia*. Editorial Kairos, 1980.

Whitmont, Edward C. *Return of the Goddess*. Crossroad, 1988.

Whitton, Joel L., and Joe Fisher. *Life Between Life*. Warner Books, 1988.

Wickes, Frances G. *The Inner World of Childhood: A Study in Analytical Psychology*. London: Coventure Ltd., 1977.

—. *The Inner World of Choice*. London: Coventure Ltd., 1983.

—. *The Inner World of Man*. Boston: Sigo Press, 1988.

Wiggin, Kate Douglas, and Nora A. Smith. *The Arabian Nights: Their Best-Known Tales*. Edited by Kate Douglas Wiggin and Nora A. Smith. Barnes & Noble, Inc., 1993.

Wilber, Ken. *A Brief History of Everything*. Shambhala, 1996.

—. *Grace and Grit: Spirituality and Healing in the Life and Death of Treya Killam Wilber*. Boston: Shambhala, 2000.

—. *Integral Psychology: Consciousness, Spirit, Psychology, Therapy*. Shambhala, 2000.

—. *One Taste: The Journals of Ken Wilber*. Shambhala, 1999.

—. *The Essential Ken Wilber: An Introductory Reader*. Shambhala, 1998.

—. *The Eye of Spirit: An Integral Vision for a World Gone Slightly mad*. Shambhala, 1997.

—. *Up From Eden: A Transpersonal View of Human Evolution*. Shambhala, 1981.

Wilber, Ken, Terry Patten, Adam Leonard, and Marco Morelli. *Integral Life Practice: A 21st-Century Blueprint for Physical Health, Emotional Balance, Mental Clarity and Spiritual Awakening*. Integral Books, 2008.

Wilde, Stuart. *Life Was Never Meant to be a Struggle*. White Dove International, Inc., 1987.

—. *The Force*. White Dove International, Inc., 1989.

—. *The Quickening*. White Dove International, Inc., 1988.

Wilhelm, Richard. *I Ching or Book of Changes*. Princeton University Press, 1967.

Williams, Mark, John Teasdale, Zindal Segal, and Jon Kabat-Zinn. *The Mindful Way Through Depression: Freeing Yourself From Chronic Unhappiness*. The Guilford Press, 2007.

Williams, Paul. *Remember Your Essence*. Harmony Books, 1987.

Williams, Strephon. *Durch Traumarbeit zum eigenen Selbst: Kreative Nutzung der Träume*. Ansata Verlag, 1984.

Williston, Glenn, and Judith Johnstone. *Discovering Your Past Lives: Spiritual Growth through a Knowledge of Past Lifetimes*. The Aquarian Press, 1988.

Wilson, Colin. *Lo Oculto: La facultad X del hombre.* Noguer, 1974.

—. *Mysteries: An Investigation into the Occult, the Paranormal and the Supernatural.* Grafton Books, 1986.

Wilson, R. H. *El Cuerpo Astral y su Proyección en Vida y Muerte.* Ediciones Doble-R, 1985.

Wind, Wabun. *Woman of the Dawn.* Berkley Books, 1991.

Wise, Elia. *Letter to Earth: Who We Are Becoming ... What We Need to Know.* Harmony Books, 2000.

Wolf, Naomi. *Fire With Fire: The New Female Power and How It Will Change the 21st Century.* Random House, 1993.

—. *The Beauty Myth: How Images of Beauty are used Against Women.* Anchor Books, 1991.

Wolff, Sula. *Children Under Stress.* Penguin Books, 1983.

Wolman, Richard N. *Thinking With Your Soul: Spiritual Intelligence and Why It Matters.* Harmony Books, 2001.

Wonder, Jacqueline, and Priscilla Donovan. *Whole Brain Thinking: Working From Both Sides of the Brain to Achieve Peak Job Performance.* Ballantine Books, 1984.

Woodman, Marion. *Addiction to Perfection: The Still Unravished Bride.* Toronto: Inner City Books, 1982.

—. *The Pregnant Virgin: A Process of Psychological Transformation.* Toronto: Inner City Books, 1985.

—. *The Ravaged Bridegroom: Masculinity in Women.* Toronto: Inner City Books, 1990.

Woodman, Marion, Kate Danson, Mary Hamilton, and Rita Greer Allen. *Leaving My Father's House: A Journey to Conscious Femininity.* Shambhala, 1992.

Woods, Jackie, and Russell Woods. *Spiritual Energy Cycles.* Adawehi Press, 1998.

Woolger, Roger J. *Other Lives, Other Selves: A Jungian Psychotherapist Discovers Past Lives.* Bantam Books, 1988.

Wootton, Tom. *Bipolar In Order: Looking at Depression, Mania, Hallucination and Delusion From the Other Side.* Bipolar Advantage, Publishers, 2009.

Yalom, Irvin D. *Momma and the Meaning of Life: Tales of Psychotherapy.* Basic Books, 1999.

—. *The Gift of Therapy: An Open Letter to a New Generation of Therapists and Their Patients.* HarperCollinsPublishers, 2002.

—. *The Theory and Practice of Group Therapy.* Basic Books, 1995.

Yalom, Irvin D., and Randolph S. Charlton. *Treating Sexual Disorders.* Edited by Irvin D. Yalom and Randolph S. Charlton. Jossey-Bass Publishers, 1997.

Yogananda, Paramahansa. *Autobiography of a Yogi.* Los Angeles: Self-Realization Fellowship Publishers, 1979.

—. *Metaphysical Meditations.* Self Realization Fellowship, 1989.

Young-Eisendrath, Polly. *You're Not What I Expected: Breaking the "He Said - She Said" Cycle.* Touchstone, 1993.

Young-Eisendrath, Polly, and Florence Wiedemann. *Female Authority: Empowering Women Through Psychotherapy.* The Guilford Press, 1987.

Zander, Rosamunde Stone, and Benjamin Zander. *The Art of Possibility: Transforming Professional and Personal Life.* Harvard Business School Press, 2000.

Ziglar, Zig. *See You At the Top.* Pelican Publishing Company, 1983.

—. *Steps to the Top.* Pelican Publishing Company, 1992.

Zimbardo, Philip. *The Lucifer Effect: How Good People Turn Evil.* Rider, 2007.

Zimberoff, Diane. *Breaking Free From the Victim Trap: Reclaiming Your Personal Power.* Issaquah, WA: Wellness Press, 1997.

Zukav, Gary. *The Seat of the Soul.* New York: Simon & Schuster, 1985.

Zweig, Connie, ed. *To Be A Woman: The Birth of the Conscious Feminine.* Jeremy P. Tarcher, Inc., 1990.

Zweig, Connie, and Steve Wolf. *Romancing the Shadow: A Guide to Soul Work for a Vital, Authentic Life.* New York: Ballantine Wellspring, 1997.

Zweig, Stefan. *Los ojos del hermano eterno.* Acantilado, 2004.

INDEX

11374368R0018

Made in the USA
Lexington, KY
29 September 2011